D0893282

My Country 'Tis of Thee

Also by David Harris

Dreams Die Hard:
Three Men's Journey through the Sixties

Goliath

I Shoulda Been Home Yesterday:
20 Months in Jail for Not Killing Anybody

Our War: What We Did in Vietnam and What It Did to Us

Shooting the Moon:
The True Story of an American Manhunt Unlike Any Other, Ever

The Crisis: The President, the Prophet,
and the Shah—1979 and the Coming of Militant Islam

The Genius: How Bill Walsh Reinvented Football
and Created an NFL Dynasty

The Last Scam: A Novel

The Last Stand: The War Between Wall Street and Main Street
over California's Ancient Redwoods

The League: The Rise and Decline of the NFL

My Country 'Tis of Thee

Reporting, Sallies, and Other Confessions

David Harris

Heyday, Berkeley, California

The essays and articles in this book originally appeared in the following publications, sometimes under slightly different titles: the *New York Times*, the *New York Times Magazine*, *Rolling Stone*, *Penthouse*, *Our War: What We Did in Vietnam and What It Did to Us* (Random House, 1996), *An Actual Man: Michael Murphy and the Human Potential Movement* (Minuteman Press, 2010), and *The Once and Future Forest: California's Iconic Redwoods* (Heyday, 2019).

Library of Congress Cataloging-in-Publication Data

Names: Harris, David, 1946- author.
Title: My country 'tis of thee : reporting, sallies, and other confessions / David Harris.
Description: Berkeley : Heyday, 2020.
Identifiers: LCCN 2020022143 (print) | LCCN 2020022144 (ebook) | ISBN 9781597145152 (cloth) | ISBN 9781597145213 (ebook)
Classification: LCC PN4874.H2285 A25 2020 (print) | LCC PN4874.H2285 (ebook) | DDC 071.3--dc23
LC record available at https://lccn.loc.gov/2020022143
LC ebook record available at https://lccn.loc.gov/2020022144

Cover Photo: Jason Henry
Cover Design/Typesetting: Ashley Ingram

Published by Heyday
P.O. Box 9145, Berkeley, CA 94709
(510) 549-3564
heydaybooks.com

Printed in East Peoria, Illinois, by Versa Press, Inc.

10 9 8 7 6 5 4 3 2 1

FSC
www.fsc.org
MIX
Paper from
responsible sources
FSC® C005010

Contents

Acknowledgments

This collection spans much of my career, and I was boosted by the help of hundreds of people along the way. I am grateful to all of them. I offer particular thanks to Steve Wasserman, my friend, editor, and now publisher at Heyday, and to his colleague Marthine Satris, who made this volume happen.

Preface

I have earned my living reporting and writing stories for forty-seven of my seventy-three years.

I started my professional career in March 1973, after the signing of peace agreements that withdrew American combat troops from Vietnam. I had been organizing civil disobedience against the war for almost a decade at that point, including the twenty months I spent incarcerated in federal prison. I was not only a convicted felon but I had dropped out of college (having left Stanford University six years earlier, just fifteen units short of my bachelor's degree), I was divorced and sharing joint custody of my then three-year-old son, and I was close to broke. I knew I could write, having already authored a peace movement memoir published while I was in prison, but I had never taken a journalism course or worked for a newspaper, and I had only the vaguest idea about the workings of the wordsmithing business I was about to enter.

I started by sending an unsolicited letter to Jann Wenner, the founder, publisher, and editor in chief of *Rolling Stone*. His magazine had run a story about my release from prison two years earlier, and I thought he might recognize my name. Wenner wrote back and told me to bring him a magazine story and he'd see if I was up to the task. A month later, I returned with "Ask a Marine," which was not only published but eventually selected for the anthology *The Best of Rolling Stone*, a volume published in 1993 for the twenty-fifth anniversary of the magazine. After Wenner read my article, he offered me a contract as a contributing editor, a job that paid fifty cents a word plus expenses. I signed on without hesitation and have been at it ever since.

It was a fortuitous time to have entered journalism. With the Watergate scandal inching closer and closer to presidential impeachment, the staid gray lady that journalism had been during the sixties was undergoing a transformation as the mantra "Speak Truth to Power"—heretofore the marching orders of the peace movement I had been part of for a decade—was now becoming the mantra of the fourth estate as it pursued the corruption, dishonesty, and hypocrisy infecting the American body politic at its highest levels. The investigations at the core of this new journalistic flourishing became the principal instrument for bringing transparency, values, and accountability into the heart of democracy. I didn't need to think twice about adopting that purpose for my own, and it defined my professional life for almost five decades.

The collection of writing in this volume samples the arc of my work, which altogether generated some eleven books and four dozen articles, from its roots in the war and the counterculture that had dominated my coming-of-age; through the stature and professionalism at the *New York Times Magazine*, where I landed for a decade and won my spurs as a true professional; and eventually to the vagabond life of a freelance wordsmith, still speaking Truth to Power as best I was able. Each of these pieces carries a backstory about their making as well. The article titled "Behind America's Marijuana High" was, for instance, the greatest risk I ever took to secure a story, and even though it was run on the cover of the *New York Times Magazine*, I swore afterward never to repeat such risk again. "Understanding Mondale" (published in this volume as "Will the Real Walter Mondale Stand Up?") was the apex of my journalistic stature, reporting on the leading candidate for the Democratic presidential nomination for the *New York Times*, again on the cover, and after it came out, I received a telegram from the *Times*'s executive editor, the legendary Abe Rosenthal, calling it a "purely fine piece," such high praise being accounted a considerable achievement in the internal byways of the *Times*. Writing "The Agony of the Kurds" was another risk, but it was also the result of the best expedition I ever mounted on a publisher's nickel: in tracing the plight and flight of Kurdish refugees as they fled to the West to save themselves, I spent five weeks following them around Syria, Iraq, Turkey, Azerbaijan, Lithuania, and Germany, travels that included my sneaking into Saddam Hussein's Iraq in a rowboat across the Tigris River.

And so I went over the decades, hopping from one story to the next, convincing one editor after another to back my play, always motivated by the belief that the more America honestly examined itself, the better a people we would be.

That golden age of journalism I was blessed to participate in is over now, overrun by the informational landfill that is the internet, but my faith in that lost era's tenets remains. Hopefully this look back over those decades will help in its own small way to seed another golden age in which Truth outranks all comers. Certainly today's America is in desperate need of such committed and heartfelt self-examination, as well as another generation of wordsmiths to induce it.

David Harris
Mill Valley, California
September 2019

I Picked Prison

GROWING UP IN FRESNO, California, I believed in "my country, right or wrong," just like everyone I knew. I could not have anticipated that when I came of age I would realize that my country was wrong and that I would have to do something about it. When I did, everything changed for me.

I went from Fresno High School Boy of the Year 1963, Stanford Class of 1967, to Prisoner 4697-159, C Block, maximum security, La Tuna Federal Correctional Institution, near El Paso.

I was among the quarter-million to half-million men who violated the draft law that required us to register for military service and face deployment to Vietnam. About 25,000 of us were indicted for our disobedience, with almost 9,000 convicted and 3,250 jailed. I am proud to have been one of the men who, from behind bars, helped pull our country out of its moral quagmire.

I was just twenty when I first stepped outside the law. After months of late-night dorm-room conversations and soul searching, I decided doing so was my duty as a citizen. It was 1966 and draft calls were escalating every month as the American army in Southeast Asia built up to half a million men, dozens of whom were coming home in coffins every week. I had just been elected Stanford's student body president on a "radical" platform calling for an end to the university's cooperation with the war, and I had already refused to accept a student deferment that would have allowed me to avoid the draft. But I knew that even such a challenging protest was an insufficient response to the moral arithmetic of sending an army thousands of miles from home to kill more than two million people for no good reason.

At stake was not just the nation's soul but mine as well. So I took the draft card I was required by law to have on my person at all times and returned it to the government with a letter declaring I would no longer cooperate. Carrying that card had been my last contribution to the war effort. If the law was wrong, then the only option was to become an outlaw.

Some would call me a draft dodger, but I dodged nothing. There was no evasion of any sort, no attempt to hide from the consequences. I courted arrest, speaking truth to power, and power responded with an order for me to report for military service. While delaying that order with a succession of bureaucratic maneuvers, I helped found the Resistance, an organization devoted to generating civil disobedience against conscription. Three or four of us lived out of my car and crashed on couches, going from campus to campus, gathering crowds and making speeches, looking for people willing to stand up against the wrong that had hijacked our nation.

On October 16, 1967, the Resistance staged its first National Draft Card Return, during which hundreds of cards were sent back to the government at rallies in eighteen cities. We staged more rallies and teach-ins. Hundreds more draft cards were returned, at two more national returns as well as individually or in small groups. We provided draft counseling for anyone, whether he wanted to resist or not.

At draft centers, we distributed leaflets encouraging inductees to turn around and go home. At embarkations, we urged troops to refuse to go before it was too late. We gave legal and logistical support to soldiers who resisted their orders. We destroyed draft records. We arranged religious sanctuary for deserters ready to make a public stand, surrounding them to impede their arrest. We smuggled other deserters into Canada. We even dug bomb craters in front of a city hall and posted signs saying that if you lived in Vietnam, that's what your front lawn would look like.

Then we stood trial, one after another. Most of us were ordered to report for induction, then charged with disobeying that order, though there were soon so many violators that it was impossible to prosecute more than a fraction of us.

I was among that fraction. On January 17, 1968, I refused to "submit to a lawful order of induction." I had my day in court that May. As was the case in almost every draft trial, my judge refused to allow me to present any testimony about the wrong I had set out to right, saying the war was not at issue. Nonetheless, my jury stayed out for more than eight hours before finally convicting me. I was sentenced to three years. I appealed my conviction but abandoned that appeal in July 1969 and began my sentence.

My fellow resisters and I brought our spirit of resistance to the prison system, organizing around prisoner issues of health care, food, and visits. I was a ringleader in my first prison strike while still in San Francisco County Jail, awaiting transfer. After being sent on to a federal prison camp in Safford, Arizona, I was in three more strikes, after which I was shipped to La Tuna. My first two months there, I was locked in a punishment cellblock known as "the hole" with three other ringleaders from Safford. When I was finally moved upstairs, I learned that our army had expanded the war into Cambodia several weeks earlier.

My home was five feet by nine feet. I was frisked when I was sent to work in the morning, when I returned from work in the afternoon, and when I both left for and returned from evening recreation.

Doing time well required what I now recognize as a Buddhist state of mind, being present where you are and not thinking of yourself in places where you couldn't be. The latter is slow torture for a prisoner. Doing time well also required being your own person despite the guards' efforts to make you otherwise. "They've got your body," we used to say, "but they can only get your mind if you give it to them." The result of this determination, in my case, was a running series of disciplinary violations (for the likes of refusing to make my bed) and return trips to the punishment cellblock.

Nonetheless, the parole board released me on March 15, 1971. The war was still going on. Not long after I first reported to my parole officer, a group of Vietnam veterans protested the war in Washington and threw the medals they'd been awarded onto the steps of the Capitol.

By then, draft calls were now steadily shrinking as air power replaced ground troops, and military conscription would soon be gutted altogether. My parole ended the following summer. I stopped organizing eight months later, when peace agreements were finally signed.

Several years after that, I was invited to testify at a Senate hearing considering pardons for our draft crimes. I told the senators I had no use for their forgiveness, but I would accept their apology.

I'm still waiting to hear back from them on that.

I am now seventy-one and the war that defined my coming-of-age is deep in my rearview mirror, but the question it raised—"What do I do when my country is wrong?"—lives on.

For those looking for an answer today, here are some lessons I learned:

We are all responsible for what our country does. Doing nothing is picking a side.

We are never powerless. Under the worst of circumstances, we control our own behavior.

We are never isolated. We all have a constituency of friends and family who watch us. That is where politics begins.

Reality is made by what we do, not what we talk about. Values that are not embodied in behavior do not exist.

People can change, if we provide them the opportunity to do so. Movements thrive by engaging all comers, not by calling people names, breaking windows, or making threats.

Whatever the risks, we cannot lose by standing up for what is right. That's what allows us to be the people we want to be.

[*New York Times*, June 23, 2017]

Ask a Marine

RON KOVIC WAS BORN ON the Fourth of July, 1946, and spent much of his youth laying cap pistol ambushes for the Long Island Railway trains that clanked in and out of Massapequa. In those days, the Fourth of July still meant something in the state of New York. Every year, the American Legion marched and Ron's birthday shone through it all as a blessing, if not a small miracle, in the family. Being born like that was not something the Kovics took lightly. Ron's father had left the family farm to work for A&P, and Ron's Uncle Jim fought all over Korea with the United States Marine Corps. The two of them sat in the kitchen behind beers and talked. Uncle Jim said he had seen good men splattered for the birthday his nephew had been given as a gift from God. Ron's dad nodded his head.

After overhearing a few of these family discussions, Ron had his heart set. He ran his body until it was a young bunch of ropes. He was Massapequa High's finest wrestler and the American Legion cannon's biggest fan. The sign by the road said MARINE CORPS BUILDS MEN: BODY, MIND AND SPIRIT, and Ron knew it was true. No one in the neighborhood was surprised when Ron Kovic finished high school and joined up. He was meant for the marines. They were just in his stars.

When Ron signed his life over to the corps, he went to Parris Island with all the others just like himself. His dream commenced with the drill instructor lining all eighty-two recruits up on the parade deck. Their heads were shaved and they wore their first khaki in wrinkles and lumps. The DI introduced himself and told them they were a bunch of maggots. He would address them as "the herd" and they would respond with "aye, aye, sir." They would say *aye, aye, sir* when they opened their mouths and *aye, aye, sir* before they closed them. If they did everything he said and did it quicker than he could say it, then he would transform them from lowly maggots into something the Marine Corps could use. That was the DI's first promise. His second promise was to beat their asses if they did not. Ron listened hard. The walls of his stomach grew hair and he settled into his life. He was going to be a marine. For goddamn sure, he was going to be a marine.

The first thing the Marine Corps taught Ron Kovic was how to take a quick shit. It seemed strange and Ron had always been a slow one to crap, but he learned like a beaver. He had to. The DI refused to have it any other way.

Ron and his squad were standing at attention, just like they always stood, and Ron felt a shit coming. The private stood erect and shouted.

"Sir! Private Kovic requests permission to make a sitting head call, sir."

The DI sucked his face in. "Come here, maggot."

Ron ran to the front of the squad bay and locked all his bones in place.

"Sir!" Ron shouted. "Private Kovic requests permission to make a sitting head call, sir."

"What for?"

"Sir, the private has to, sir."

"Five hundred bends and thrusts, maggot," the DI answered. Then he said, "Do it," and Ron ran out into the corridor and did five hundred of the prescribed exercise.

"Five hundred bends and thrusts, aye, aye, sir. One, two . . . aye, aye, sir . . . three, four . . ." When he finished, Ron ran back and asked again.

"Does the private think he's ready?"

"Aye, aye, sir. The private is ready, sir."

"All right, private, you have one minute." The DI's voice bounced along the squad bay like a live grenade and Ron sprinted to the toilet bowl.

Thirty seconds later, Private Kovic heard the DI scream from the room next door.

"Countdown!" he screamed.

"Countdown," all eighty-two privates repeated. "Thirty . . . twenty-nine . . . twenty-eight . . ."

At twenty-four, Private Kovic had his ass wiped, and his pants up and buckled by seventeen. He looked around to make sure he had everything and sprinted back. At the count of ten, the squad began to clap with each tick. Being late was worth five hundred more bends and thrusts, aye, aye, sir. It also meant the next time his bowels moved, the DI wouldn't give permission. Then, sooner or later, Private Kovic would have to ask the sergeant if he could change uniforms and that was a motherfucker.

Ron learned quick enough to keep his pants clean. It is something he's always been grateful for, even today.

Private Kovic was even better at push-ups. They became his specialty. He was held up to the squad as the "push-up body," the supreme push-up principle. He did push-ups in his rack at night after the lights were out. It squeaked and everybody who heard it thought Ron was crazy. Maybe he was. If so, it was not quite crazy enough to satisfy his DI. Ron never did become the best push-up marine at Parris Island. Three times he came in second at the island championships. After his third try, when Ron collapsed on his 283rd, the DI assembled the squad and called Ron to the front.

"Private Kovic!" he bellowed. "I want the private to know that second is as good as last. I am sick of seeing the private's scabby face. The private has failed his platoon and come in second. I am sick of the private's bald head. The private is a maggot, a lady maggot and a poor excuse for a marine. Two hundred bends and thrusts. Do it."

"Aye, aye, sir. One, two . . ."

Nothing seemed to slow Ron down. He wanted to be a marine too bad. He shot expert with his rifle and learned to repeat the chain of command. Recruits were required to, every night before lights out.

"Chain of command!" the DI screamed.

"Chain of command," they answered and began, "The President of the United States is Lyndon Baines Johnson . . . the Secretary of Defense is Robert S. . . ." The chain dangled down to "My junior drill instructor is . . ." and stopped. The eighty-two shaved heads said it like a prayer to put themselves to sleep at night.

The prayer worked. Ron Kovic became Private Kovic officially and marched in the graduation parade. The Marine Corps gave him the same dress blue uniform he'd seen on the posters. When he wore it, Ron Kovic was a proud son of a bitch and wanted everybody to see.

After boot camp, Private Kovic was sent to Camp Lejeune and then on to Radio School at Norfolk Marine Barracks. When he was done in Norfolk, the private was a private first class and assigned to the Second Field Artillery. It chafed Ron a little. He wanted to charge up a hill but mostly he cleaned radios. It was getting hard on him, being ready and not asked, but then he heard about Vietnam. Right away he wanted to go. That was where the marines were fighting and that's what a marine is supposed to do.

PFC Kovic requested immediate transfer to WESPAC, Vietnam. When the form asked why, he wrote, "To serve my country." It's so much later now that it's hard to believe, but back then Ron and everybody in the battalion office had no doubts. PFC Kovic received orders in ten days and flew to Camp Pendleton, then on to Okinawa, to Da Nang, and into his dreams.

At Pendleton, everything had been serious. They were there to get trimmed into final fighting shape, and the marines slogged their hardest for three weeks. The last day he had been taught the last lesson. The sergeant called it "survival." The lesson started with a rabbit. The rabbit was fluffy and white and shook its feet when the sergeant held it by the ears. "If you want to come back," the sergeant said, "you better learn this one real good." With that, he pulled his trench knife and gutted the bunny, then flopped the carcass in his hands and skinned it. Finally, the sergeant threw the guts into the crowd. The pieces dropped in pitter-patters all over their helmets.

By the time Ron Kovic reached Okinawa, the approaching reality of Vietnam was rising in short hairs all over his arms. He was ready. It was his job to make the world safe for Sparky the Barber and Scadato's delicatessen and he wanted to do it better than anybody else. He was Massapequa's boy going to war and he planned to be Audie Murphy and John Wayne all rolled into 150 pounds. In an Okinawa bar, the waiting hero got a glimpse into his future crusted on the boots of the marines sitting in the silent corners. It was yellow mud, and someone told Ron they were "in country." They'd been "down south." Their uniforms were faded and they all had a gaze, just a stare off past the walls. Ron did not stare at them for long. He wanted to do it for himself before he watched it on somebody else.

The next day, Private First Class Kovic got the chance he had waited eighteen years for.

From Da Nang, Kovic was sent in a C-190 to Chu Lai and into the admin office of the Third Battalion, Seventh Marines.

"How many days you got left?" the clerk asked.

"I just got here today," Ron said

"He just got here today," the clerk repeated to the sergeant behind him. "He just got here today." They both laughed and Ron had no idea why.

PFC Kovic was too busy to waste time figuring it out. He was soon out with the 3/7, hustling along with the captain's radio on his back. It was the old model PRC-10 and it carried like a stack of fucking bricks. It was also a target. When they went out after the VC, the antenna stood like a flag over the elephant grass. The VC sighted in on it and popped. As hard as the gooks tried, Ron never got hit. Instead, Kovic looked for the action and moved as quickly as he'd been taught. He got the feel for it on his first patrol.

The action happened down by a river. Some VC suspects had been sighted and chased into mud caves along the bank. They would not come out, so the marines set to killing them where they sat. As Ron and the captain approached, he could hear the gas canisters sizzling and the sounds of M-16s. When they were finished, the marines pulled the bodies into a fishing net. The net was tied to the back of an amtrac and dragged through the mud to the village. The caravan passed Ron and he saw the bodies were covered with slop and frozen in weird shapes.

The captain was standing a few steps away. He had two silver bars on his helmet, blue eyes, and a face that never quite got the fear out of it.

"How'd you like it?" he asked.

"I liked it, sir," Ron answered. "I really liked it."

The captain shook his head and walked off for the landing zone.

RON KOVIC REALLY DID LIKE IT. Just like he knew he would back in Massapequa. He liked it so much he went right for its middle. After three months, PFC Kovic had been promoted to lance corporal and he volunteered for what was called "Recon." It was April and Sgt. Jimmy Howard and a reconnaissance platoon from Delta Company had been surrounded on Hill 488 west of Chu Lai. Only eight grunts got back, so the reconnaissance platoon had to be "rebuilt." The sergeant asked for volunteers and Ron was the first to step forward. He'd already heard about Recon.

Recon were studs. They were jungle thugs and said they ate Cong for lunch. Every mean thing Ron had ever heard, he'd heard about Recon, and Ron was ready for it.

Kovic fit right in at Bravo Company, second platoon. He was the radio operator and artillery FO. Ron and seventeen others got up on Monday morning before light and painted themselves to look like tree stumps. The chaplain said a prayer in front of the choppers and they were gone. Off to a set of lines on a map, hovering twenty feet over the long grass, and jumping out one by one. As long as somebody back in the office didn't fuck up and drop them into a VC base camp, they were all right. As soon as they were on the ground, the second platoon started moving and kept it that way for five days, stalking along under the canopy and across streams. The leeches dropped out of trees and hung on their marine bodies but they didn't stop. Their job was to look. If they saw large enemy outfits, they broke radio silence and called in. That was Ron's job:

"Crepe Myrtle," he'd say, "this is Crepe Myrtle three, over."

"Crepe Myrtle three, this is Crepe Myrtle," the radio answered. "Over."

"Fire mission. Coordinates 353/271, azimuth 270 degrees. Target: VC in open. Shell VT. Fuse quick. Over."

"Roger, Crepe Myrtle three," the radio said.

Then the shells walked in, blowing hunks of flesh and jungle left and right. Ron talked into the box, moved the explosions in and out and down and up until the lieutenant was satisfied. As soon as he was, the second platoon got their asses in gear. At this point the platoon was "compromised." That meant someone knew they were there—a fair assumption to make—and Recon was trained to take one response. They headed for a prearranged landing zone and told the radio. At the spot marked exit, they hacked the brush down and went out in the H-34s. The H-34 was a smaller chopper and it took four to extract the whole platoon. Ron went on twenty-two of these patrols, five days out and dead-bone, sore-assed tired when they got back. His last mission was his closest.

While the platoon was squatted, waiting in the LZ, someone lobbed a ChiCom grenade into the clearing and opened up with an automatic weapon from the treeline. The marines returned fire blind. The air was full of lead but nobody in the second platoon was hit. The lieutenant, the medic, and Ron were always the last ones to leave. When they jumped in and the chopper lifted, Ron could hear the pops follow them up. The door gunner was chopping back with his M-60 and so was everybody else. Ron emptied his clip into the jungle and lay back. Nobody had been hit. He was in Recon for eight months and not a hit in his outfit. He laughed, ripped the leech off his face, and flung it past the gunner and out the door. "Wooowhee!" Corporal Kovic shouted to himself. "I'm a Recon motherfucker. Too fast for a bullet to catch, too good a marine to die."

When he got home, the Marine Corps gave Ron Kovic a Commendation medal with a combat V and a promotion to E-4.

Ron had a good taste in his mouth right up to the time he left. He was tied in a tight knot with the second platoon and he loved them the same way he loved his gun. It was hairy, silent work they did together and it made them close. Only one last memory had an edge on it.

Ron was sitting on his sea bag in the middle of base camp waiting for the jeep ride to his plane. He was right by the sign that said DUNN'S RAIDERS. That was his outfit, Dunn's Raiders, like the sign said: WE CAME TO KILL. NEVER HAVE SO FEW DONE SO FOUL TO SO MANY. There was a skull and crossbones on its bottom edge.

The heat was burrowing into his back when someone called him. "Hey, Kovic," they said. "Come here and see what we got."

Ron walked over to one of the tents with three marines inside. The grunt in the middle had a jar in his hands. Inside the jar there were two fingers and an ear. "Look at this," he said. "Nice, huh? I'm gonna mail 'em back to the States. Wheatstraw says he knows how to get them through."

Ron got stiff, cringed inside, and a strap tightened around his gut. The fingers hung halfway up in the fluid and the ear was floating on the top. Since he was about to leave, no one held his reaction against him. It was to be expected.

Charging up the runway, to the plane back to the States, Ron forgot about the jar and sailed home to Massapequa to show the neighborhood his yellow boots.

THE C-130 TOOK HIM TO a different world, miles away. And it got old quick. Ron missed Recon. His memories burned at him. Kovic was stationed with a Hawk Missile Battalion while his buddies were getting cut up back in the jungle. That was no good. It ate at him and ate at him until he couldn't stand it any longer.

A copy of the *New York Daily News* was Ron's last straw. The front page was covered with four longhairs burning a flag in Central Park. That pissed Ron off so bad he sat on his foot locker and cried for the first time since he'd become a marine. Then E-4 Kovic went down to the admin office and requested a transfer back to Vietnam. Transfer was denied four days later. Going back had come to be thought of as insane, and the sergeant stared when Kovic came in fourteen more times to repeat his request. By then he was considered crazy enough to return.

His new orders made Ron Kovic a full sergeant with three stripes on his arm. He was sent to Pendleton and staging battalion right away. Sgt. Kovic wanted to serve his country and he meant it. It was the right thing to do. He knew it was, as sure as he had been born. He trained a platoon and marched them all onto the plane. They sang the Marine Corps hymn going up the gangway and some cried. It was late in 1966 and Ron Kovic was twenty years old. He sat by himself in the chapel at Travis Air Force Base the night before he left and prayed. He had a feeling something was waiting for him back in Nam and he trusted God to keep him clear. In truth, his future had him worried. His orders wouldn't let him join his old outfit. He was going to the Third Marine Division in the DMZ instead. From what he had heard, the DMZ was a different kind of place from the one he remembered.

It sure enough looked that way on the plane he took to Đông Hà. No one talked. The only sounds were the marines loading their ammo magazines. When speaking broke out, the dirty ones said there was lots of "arty" up there, and Ron had never been under arty before. Not that it took long to find out what arty meant. He looked out the window and the Đông Hà airfield was full of craters. People there said the shit was coming in every day, a hundred at a time.

And that is the way things were in the DMZ that winter. The shellings came like the mail. When the arty wasn't falling, the Third Marines were up against the North Vietnamese Army in the wet slop, and the NVA was good. Make no mistake, it was something every marine kept in mind.

Ron's base was at the mouth of the Cửa Việt River, past Geo Lin. The Third Marines' job was sweeping an area called Charlie four. Khe Sanh was across the river, and a place they called the Rockpile on past that. The country was all sand and stumpy pine trees and the marines worked mostly off amtracs: steel boxes with a cave inside big enough to carry a squad. The camp was dug into bunkers, eight sandbags high. At night, Ron led a scout team outside the perimeter and laid ambushes one thousand meters from the wire.

They sat in the rain and watched for the NVA. During the day, the scouts slept. At least they tried to. They had to ask arty's permission first. When it was arty's turn to talk, nobody slept.

As soon as the marines heard the crack with the whistle on the end of it, every son of a bitch with any sense ran for the bunkers. The rounds came in right on top, each one sounding like it had a ticket for the hairs on your ass. Noses bled and ears ached. A lot of the Third Marines got to keeping rosaries close by, to use in the shelters. It was nothing but scary. The worst Ron ever saw was when they took 150 hits, right after lunch.

As soon as the arty lifted, Ron grabbed a medic bag and ran out on the compound. He saw his own tent first and it was just shrapnel holes held together with canvas threads. Past that there was a crowd where Sgt. Bodigga's supply tent had once been. Sgt. Bodigga never left the camp. He handled paper in his tent and had a rug on his floor. Whatever you wanted, Sgt. Bodigga could get it if you just gave him a day. Ron pushed through the ring of marines and found a hole. No tent. Just a hole. In the bottom was something that looked like five or six bodies. They were all powder-burned and torn up. Ron reached in to find IDs and could only find Bodigga's wallet. After looking again, Sgt. Kovic realized that Bodigga was all there was in the hole . . . all those pieces were just Bodigga. Ron stacked Sgt. Bodigga on a stretcher and cried. Over his shoulder, in the motor pool, someone was screaming.

"McCarthy!" they screamed. "They got McCarthy. Those motherfuckers. Those rotten motherfuckers. They got McCarthy."

McCarthy was from Boston and he had blue eyes. When he was laid out with the rest of the dead, stripped naked in front of the command bunker with his loose parts piled next to him, McCarthy's eyes were open and looked straight up into the rain.

Ron saw him there and wanted to kill somebody. He wanted to kill somebody and use them to paste McCarthy and Bodigga back together.

It did not turn out that simple. As soon as Ron Kovic got to wanting that, something happened to make him feel just the opposite. It was a night patrol.

A lieutenant took Ron's detail out to search for sappers across the river. There was a village on the far bank and the colonel was worried someone from there would put a mine to the marine boats. A hundred meters from the village, the patrol saw the light of a small fire. It was inside a hootch and it was not supposed to be there. The village had been ordered to keep lights out. The platoon spread out along a paddy dike and watched. Word was passed to hold fire, and the lieutenant set off an illumination flare. Just as the flare lit, someone to Ron's left fucked up and let go. That shot set the whole line on fire for thirty seconds at full automatic. When they finished, Ron and Leroy were sent up to check the hootch.

Inside the broken bamboo, there was an old man with the top of his head shot away. Two kids were on either side of him. One's foot just dangled. The other had taken a round in the stomach that came out his ass. The hootch's floor was covered with blood.

When the platoon crossed the paddy and saw it, the marines melted into lumps. Some dropped their weapons and only Leroy talked.

"Jesus Christ," he whined. "What'd we do? We've killed an old man and some kids."

The lieutenant yelled to form up, but Leroy kept moaning and no one else moved. The villagers started to come out of their huts and scream at the marines. It took the lieutenant five minutes to round the patrol into shape. After they called a chopper for the kid who was still breathing, the platoon went back inside the marine wire. Sgt. Kovic lay in his bunker all night and wanted to give it up. He wanted the referee to blow the whistle and call time out until he had a chance to think it over.

But wars do not work that way. Ron reported to the colonel in the morning and asked to be taken off patrols. The colonel said no. Instead the platoon got a week in camp, and Sgt. Kovic was ordered to get his shit together and act like a marine.

THE PLATOON DID NOT GO back to action until January 20th. When they did, it was in the afternoon. January 20th started late but turned into as big a day as there will ever be in the life of Sgt. Ron Kovic. Word was that the NVA had the South Vietnamese Popular Forces pinned down by the village. Ron volunteered his men to take the point and lead the company's sweep. Another company was moving north from the riverbank through the village graveyard. The platoon spread out and headed toward the treeline one hundred meters off. Ron was on the right with just one man farther over than himself. Everyone was out in the open when January 20th exploded. Ron could not forget it now if he wanted to.

"The people on the amtracs got hit first," is the way he remembers it. "I heard the pop . . . pop . . . pop as the mortars left their tubes and the crashing as they hit around the tracks. Then rounds started cracking around us. I couldn't tell if they were coming from the village or the treeline, so I fired both places. I was completely out in the open.

"All we could do was go to the ground and return fire. After a little bit, I heard a loud crack right next to me and my whole leg went numb. A .30-caliber bullet had gone in the front of my foot and come out the heel. It took a piece out the size of a silver dollar. My foot was all smashed. I stayed standing as long as I could but then it began to feel like it was on fire. I went to a prone position and kept using my rifle until it jammed from the sand.

"When I couldn't get a round into the chamber, I decided to stand and see where the rest of my platoon was. I slammed the rifle down and pushed myself up with it. Just as I got my arms straight, I heard a huge crack next to my ear. It was like getting hit with an express train. My whole body started vibrating. Another .30-caliber bullet had hit my right shoulder, passed through my lung, and severed my spinal cord into two pieces. My whole body seemed to have left me. I felt like I was somewhere up in the air.

"I closed my eyes for just a second, then I started to breathe. My lung was collapsed so I just took little breaths. Slow little sucks. All I could think was that I didn't want to die. I couldn't think of nothin' else. I waited to die. I mean I just waited for it all to black out, for all the things that are supposed to happen when you die. I couldn't believe what was going on. Where was my body? I must've been hit with a mortar. That was it, a mortar. It had ground up everything below my chest.

"Then I moved my hands behind me and I felt legs. I felt legs but they didn't feel back. They were my legs. There was something wrong but I couldn't explain it. My body was there but I couldn't feel it. Then I got real excited. It was still there. I wasn't going to bleed to death. My body was still there.

"The next thing I knew, Leroy was over me. He was bandaging my shoulder.

"'I can't feel my body,' I said.

"'It's all right, Sarge,' he said. 'You're gonna be all right. Pretty soon you'll be back in the States with all the broads.'

"When he got the bandage on, he split toward the treeline with rounds cracking all around him.

"After Leroy, I heard Palmer calling me from off to my left. 'Hey, Sarge,' he said. 'We got to get the hell out of here.'

"'I can't move my legs!' I screamed.

"'Come on, Sarge!' Palmer kept yelling. 'Let's go. Let's get outta here.'

"'I can't feel my body,' I said. Then I heard a crack and Palmer screamed. 'Are you hit?' I yelled.

"Palmer yelled back, 'They shot my finger off. They shot my goddamn finger off.' After that I guess he left. I didn't hear him no more.

"I lay there for what seemed like hours. Once, somebody ran up in back of me. 'Hey,' he said. 'Hey, Sarge, you all right?' Then I heard another crack and he seemed to fall on the back of me. I couldn't feel it but I heard. Someone from my left yelled, 'He's dead, Sarge. They shot him through the heart.' He was a marine from the company who'd run all the way up. I yelled for everybody to stop coming. I don't know if they heard, but I yelled. I was being used as bait. Other than that, I felt nothing. I just wanted to live. I tried to calm myself. I felt cheated. I felt cheated to die. Twenty fucking years old and they were taking my life away from me.

"Then a black man came running up. He grabbed me and threw me over his shoulder. He started dragging me back. He was a big black man. Big black arms. Big black hands. All I can remember is staring up at the sky and the sky sort of spinning and jumping. I could just feel the top of my body. I felt the sun in my face and him picking me up and throwing me down. All the time he was yelling, 'You motherfuckers. Fuckers. Fuckers. Goddamn motherfuckers.' And me screaming the same thing. 'Motherfuckers. Motherfuckers.'

"Finally he threw me one last time in a hole and a corpsman jumped in on my chest. He'd been running all over and he was out of his head. I told him I felt I'd made it so far and that was the roughest part. I told him I was gonna live."

By the next morning, Sgt. Kovic had been given the last rites of the Catholic Church and gone on the operating table. He was in the Intensive Care ward at Marble Mountain in Da Nang. He had been brought there by choppers with tubes in his lungs and IVs all over his body. There was a Korean soldier (who had hit a booby trap) in the bed to his left. When the Korean wasn't babbling in sing-song, he waved his two remaining fingers over his head until he died. Then a black pilot took the Korean's place.

Ron watched the pilot die too. The corpsmen surrounded the bed and one began to beat on the pilot's chest with his fists. They brought a machine over and attached it to his heart but it didn't seem to do much better. The corpsman went back to his hands and pounded as hard as he knew how. After a half hour, the medic gave up. Ron could see his white jacket and hear him laughing like the Bob Hope show. The corpsman had to laugh. He pounded on chests all day long. The last thing Ron saw of the black pilot was the sheet they covered him with and the sound of the body cart, squeaking across the linoleum.

After that, Ron was sure he would die if he stayed at Marble Mountain. Living meant doing everything right, so Sgt. Kovic listed his dos and don'ts on a Red Cross pad. The nurse turned him over every four hours and Ron never complained. He was going to be the perfect patient who recovers miraculously. The morphine helped. He got his syringe every 120 minutes. When he was waiting for his shot, Ron Kovic noticed that he could no longer feel his dick. All day long, he explored his floppy body and checked to see if it had come back while he was asleep. It never did.

When the doctors asked Ron how he felt he said he felt great. Good enough to leave Intensive Care anyway. In desperation, Sgt. Kovic finally stuck his thermometer in an ice bucket and the reading was low enough to go to Japan. With Da Nang behind him, Ron knew he was going to live. He did not know how that living was going to be, but right then he didn't care.

Before the plane left Marble Mountain, a general came down the ward, distributing Purple Hearts, bed by bed. The general's shoes were shined and he had a private with him. The private carried a Polaroid camera and took pictures the men could send home to their families. The general handed Ron a medal, the private took a picture, and Ron put the ribbon under his pillow.

Then the general went to the bed next door. There was a nineteen-year-old marine in it. The top of his skull had been blown loose. The nineteen-year-old's brain was wrapped in wet towels. He babbled like a two-year-old and pissed in his sheets. Ron waited to see if the general's private would leave a picture.

He did. The private told the nurse to send it on to the marine's mom and dad.

Ron Kovic lay three days in Yokosuka Naval Hospital with his catheter and his striker frame and then he demanded a wheelchair. "I'm ready," he said. The doctors thought it was early but Ron insisted. They brought the chair and lifted Ron into it. He was still being Marble Mountain's best patient and made no noise. For half an hour he tried the chair. At the end of it, Sgt. Kovic puked all over himself and passed out. When he recovered, Ron decided to wait on the chair until he reached the States.

In the meantime, he concentrated. Ron kept a little chart of his progress each day. He swore to the doctors he was going to walk out. "If it's the last thing I do," is the way he said it. "Right out the fucking door." The doctors said that was impossible, but Ron wouldn't listen. He had to have something to want and that was it.

When not wanting, Sgt. Kovic watched. There was pain all around him but Ron knew it would pass. He figured out that most of the other lumps under the covers would heal. The pain would become a memory and then they would leave, tall and strong again and whole. But he would not. His wound could not. The hole in his shoulder would close up and so would his foot, but that was all. The life in Sgt. Kovic's head would never touch his feet again.

One day, when he was lying back watching, the general brought a tour through the hospital. Bart Starr of the Green Bay Packers visited Ron's ward. He stood at the end of the bed.

"How's the war going?" the quarterback asked.

"Shitty," Ron said. "Pretty shitty."

After a while, the war had almost disappeared. The radio said everybody would be home soon, but hospitals were just about the only thing Ron remembered. There was a short one in Anchorage, another in Virginia, one in New York State, and then another that looked out on New Jersey. The last one was the Kingsbridge VA. It was summer by then and Ron stayed at the Kingsbridge hospital eleven months the first time and then again for six more.

Sgt. Kovic now belonged to the Veterans Administration. The marines discharged him with a bronze star and wished him well. The VA's job was to retrain certain kinds of ex-soldiers, and Sgt. Kovic was 100 percent retired. The first thing the VA tried to teach him was how to shit slowly and once every three days.

They gave him enemas, every third day. Other than that he had to shit in his bed and lay on it. The enemas started at five in the morning. Tommy the Enema Man came by with his tube and dangled it under their noses. When everyone was awake, they each got a striker frame. Tommy and his helper rolled them all, twenty-four para- and quadriplegics, half the ward, into what was called the blue room. When it was full, the two white coats pumped all the stomachs up with soapy water. All twenty-four lay in there with their withered bodies and listened to their bowels hit the buckets like cow flop. When it was done, Tommy wiped each of their asses and rolled them into the shower.

Ron called it the car wash. The attendant ran a thin white strip of pHisoHex down the middle of Ron's body and then hosed it off. When they were shorthanded, the attendant sometimes had to leave in the middle of the scrub. The second time Ron got washed, he lay in the Kingsbridge shower for an hour waiting for the attendant to come back. All Ron did was try not to scream like he wanted to. He learned to lie on the tile and watch his body that would not move and had started to shrivel.

Every third day Ron wanted to scream, but he never did. After a couple of months, the screams did not even cross his mind. Ron lay there and felt he had been used up and thrown away and no one was treating him like the marine he had been.

THE MORE HE LOOKED AROUND the ward, the more Ron felt like a discard. C-3 was the sign over the door and it was one big mirror. He saw his friends and there he was. Propped up and flopped over, they weren't much to look at. Ron noticed Mark more than anybody else. Mark was a nineteen-year-old head. He'd been a six-foot marine once. But then his truck hit a mine on the way to Khe Sanh and Mark went out the window. He was paralyzed from the neck down. Mark got around by pushing his chin on an electric button that made the wheels on his chair spin. It was Mark who taught Ron how to fight the rats.

The rats were smallish, brown, and came out at night. Just past 2 a.m., one crawled up on Mark's chest. He screamed. Then he screamed again. No one came. He screamed for three hours until an aide arrived and told Mark he must be drunk. From then on, Mark got Ron to lob his dinner rolls behind the radiator. That kept the rats eating all night and off their chests while Mark and Ron talked. Mark had been a high school football player and asked Ron to look at the team picture and pick him out. Mark was proud and didn't take to being a loose sack of flesh very easily. He fought it as hard as he could.

He taught the rest of them to fight it too. Mark led the revolt in C-3. It started when the hospital staff canceled the paraplegics' party privileges. The VA said too many people were getting drunk. Mark was pissed as soon as he heard.

"I'm going to that fucking office," he said and everybody agreed into a line behind him: all the paras and all the quads, rolling themselves however they were able and heading for the part of Kingsbridge that had carpets. There were some things they wanted to say. It was harder the closer they got to the front. The rugs were miring up around the wheels of Ron's chair like a Chrysler in the mud. A fat man in a blue suit came out into the hall and let them know where they sat.

"The president is doing everything he can to help you boys," he said. "All of us are doing everything we can."

"Do you think you could get the president to come in and change my sheets?" one of the chairs asked.

The fat man did not laugh. Ron asked him when was the last time he'd been on C-3. The fat man in the blue suit could not remember but he was sure it was recently.

The men from C-3 listened for a while and then went back up the hall to sleep. Mark could not. He lay up all night and listened to his plastic piss bag slop over onto the floor and he hated it. He kept hating it until the day he would talk his friend in Chicago into sticking a needle through his vein. Mark would die with his eyes full of heroin and his body full of empty space. But that was much later, after Ron left the VA for the first time.

WHEN RON REACHED THE DOORS, he left just the way he had promised back in Japan. He walked. It was not like he'd pictured it, but it sure wasn't in a chair. He trained every day with braces until he could move on crutches and drag his strapped-up legs along. He scraped out the door to his mom and dad and he felt proud. Every time he got up on his crutches he felt that way. To Ron Kovic, he saw himself as tall and pretty, even if his spine did have a new bend to it. Ron walked like that all over the backyard in Massapequa. The doctors said he did it too much. He finally broke his femur when he was out on a walk and had to return to Kingsbridge.

This time there was an operation. When he got off the table, his right leg had a plate in it and was shorter than the other. The leg turned in, too, and would not fit in his braces anymore. Ron screamed at the doctors.

"You ruined it," he said. "Now I can't walk anymore. I'll never get to stand up."

"It's all right," the doctors said. "You couldn't really walk anyway."

The second time Ron left Kingsbridge he was pissed. He remembers it today and he still gets angry. His jaw freezes up and he talks louder than he means to. "It was like I'd swallowed a lie," he explains, "and then they rubbed my face in it. America made me. They made me and I gave them everything I could give and then I wasn't good enough to treat like a man. I didn't want to be a good patient anymore. I was proud and they wouldn't even let on I was still alive. I was something for a closet and a budget cut. I didn't feel lucky anymore. I was gonna live and I knew how I was gonna live. I was living with a body that was already dead. That had to be worth something, but it wasn't. All it could get me was a seat out by the pigeons and the old men from World War II."

After a while, Ron could not sit on his anger anymore. He moved to Los Angeles and called the office of Vietnam Veterans Against the War. While he dialed, he thought about Mark and a guy named Willie.

Willie was just a head too. To listen to Willie you had to put a cork in his throat and your ears next to his lips. As Ron was leaving Kingsbridge, Willie stopped him at his bed. Ron put the cork in and listened.

"Don't let them do it to anybody else," Willie said.

When the phone answered, Ron said he wanted to join and do anything he could to stop the war.

Ron meant it. He manned tables and spoke at high schools. He told them how he'd been the Massapequa flash and the push-up body. He told them how he had sung about the "Halls of Montezuma" and the "Shores of Tripoli" and how it was a lie. He told whoever would listen and half those who would not.

Ron felt better than he had felt in a long time. He liked the folks, like he was one of them. He did not feel like a freak and he wondered why it had taken so long for him to find out. His new life gave Ron a chance to meet his country again. One such meeting on Wilshire Boulevard drove the last of the bald eagle from Ron

Kovic's mind. It happened in front of the headquarters for Richard Nixon's reelection.

The picket started at 11 a.m., and by noon there was quite a crowd and almost as many cops. And these were not any run-of-the-mill, bust-a-drunk-on-a-street-corner cops. It was the LAPD, and anybody west of Barstow knows the LAPD does not take no for an answer.

The ones Ron met were young, undercover, and tried very hard. They moved in the crowd and took notes. Ron was up the block with a line of people who had wheeled over the cross street and blocked traffic. The blue line of police moved their way and they scattered back to the sidewalk. As soon as the cops returned to the cross street, the people on Wilshire did the same thing and the police scurried back. It did not take long for the LAPD to tire of the game. The captain gave an order to disperse and the people decided to take it. The blue men had their clubs out and their goggles on: two very bad signs. The decision was made to go to MacArthur Park. Ron wheeled the word up to the cops.

"We're leaving," he said. "We're going to obey the order to disperse."

With that, the line of signs made its own slow way back down the boulevard. Ron stayed at the back, making sure everybody got out all right. It was then that he met the LAPD up so close there was no way to mistake what he saw. The two long-haired ones came up from his back. The first grabbed Ron's chair. The second said, "You're under arrest," and started banging the handcuffs on Ron's wrists.

"What are you doing?" Ron said. "We're leaving."

The back of the crowd saw what was happening and ran to help. That set off a whistle and the blue line charged into a big circle with Ron inside. He was dumped out of his chair and onto the street. All Ron could think to do was shout.

"I'm a Vietnam veteran!" he yelled. "I fought in the DMZ. I'm paralyzed. Don't you know what you're doing?"

The LAPD did not shout back. The red-haired one pulled Ron's hands behind his back and locked them. Then the blue circle made a wedge and headed across the street with Ron in tow. A cop had each shoulder, and Ron's head bobbed up and down off the asphalt. The people who tried to help said they saw the police beat Ron's body with their sticks, but Ron could not feel it. He felt the curb when his forehead hit it and then all of a sudden he felt lifted up and into a squad car. They propped him up in the front seat. He immediately flopped over into the dashboard and panted.

"I have no stomach muscles," he said. "With my hands in back of me, I can't sit up. I can't hardly breathe either." Ron had to talk in a grunt.

The cop shoved him up straight. "Sit up," he said.

Ron flopped back over. "I'm a veteran," he wheezed. "Don't you see what you're doing to me? I'm paralyzed."

"Sit up," the cop said and rammed Ron against the Ford's seat. Ron flopped back. "I said sit up, you commie son of a bitch." The LAPD bounced Ron back and forth all the way to the station. At the booking desk, the cop asked the turnkey where to put the crippled one.

"Take him up on the roof and throw him off," the turnkey said.

They didn't. But it wasn't because they didn't want to. When Ron left five days later, the turnkey looked at him from behind his jowls.

"They shoulda let you die over there," he said. "You shoulda died and never come back."

RON STILL HAD SOME PEOPLE he wanted to see. All the vets did. Which is why they went to the Republican convention in Miami. The veterans went in caravans and called it the Last Patrol. They were going to expose once and for all the lie of the way they had fought. They rolled into Miami and met lines of buses, tear gas, and helmets. They came to see Richard Nixon but only a few got the chance. Ron was one of that few.

It happened on the night the president came up from Key Biscayne to accept his nomination. Ron had tickets that got him into the lobby. A reporter pushed him through the first door, and his own wheeled sprint brought him up to the back of the delegates.

Then the security guard stepped up.

"You'll have to leave," he said.

"I've got a right to be here," Ron said. "I fought in Vietnam for it."

Nobody wanted to touch him with the TV cameras on, so the guards just tried to block him from sight. Ron shouted around them to the delegates. They had signs that said FOUR MORE YEARS and didn't really want to hear about it.

"You want to see your war?" Ron yelled. "Here it is. I'm your war in a package. I'm here. I'm real."

The nearby Republicans pretended not to notice. Ron felt stymied. He was blocked off and wanted to be closer. Fortunately, the word from Muller reached Ron through another vet. "Come on back," the vet said. "Muller's got passes for you, a place down front on the side."

Ron went back around and to the right and found Bob Muller and Bill Wyman. Lieutenant Bob Muller had been leading a South Vietnamese unit when the ARVNs called olly-olly-oxen-free and split. That left the young lieutenant all alone with a bullet through his chest and spine both. Bill Wyman's legs had been blown off at the knees by a mine. Ron Kovic, Bob Muller, and Bill Wyman lined up wheel to wheel and waited for the president. He was on next. After Richard Nixon stepped into the footlights and the clapping died down, the three vets took deep breaths. With the first pause they shouted, "Stop the bombing! Stop the war!"

That made the Republicans behind the chairs stare, but Richard Nixon didn't miss a step. The next time he paused, they did the same thing. Now the crowd around them was surly and embarrassed. The delegates began to chant "Four more years" to drown the three chairs out. They screamed and clapped and one fat man with a red face spit on Ron's neck. Finally, the Secret Service came and made a ring around the vets' small noise. Moving in a circle, they carried the three chairs backward and formed a wall to screen out the cameras. Ron and Bob and Bill were taken to the rear entrance and put out. The security guard chained the door behind them and they were left in the parking lot. When no one came out to bust them, the three headed for the day's rally site. Miami was full of gas and they made their way on the side streets.

Flamingo Park was empty when the three chairs wheeled into it. The cops had run everyone off. If that happened, the vets had planned to meet out at the municipal dump. Ron and Bob and Bill found everyone else waiting. It was midnight and the men of Chu Lai and Đồng Hà and the A Sâu Valley sat in the garbage and tried to figure out who was still in jail. The dump smelled of old fish and pepper gas and all of them felt like they had been there before.

IF YOU WANT TO FIND Ron Kovic just go to the VVAW office in L.A.: follow the Arlington off-ramp from the Santa Monica Freeway and head for Pico Boulevard. The letters are painted on their storefront. I went in and found him. He looked up from writing a leaflet and I asked him how he felt.

"In the last five years," he said, "I've felt tremendous pain and bitterness both. I felt a closeness to no one but myself and my chair. I felt an anger I could never describe. I also felt a humility and a compassion I could never explain. It was a tremendous sense of loss and a tremendous sense of gain. I felt I had lost a great portion of my body but I'd gained a good deal of my soul. It was like I had to trade the one for the other."

Then I asked what he was going to do now that the war was over.

He laughed the way he does: letting it run out to the ends of his lips and vibrate there.

"The war's not over," he said. "The war is between those who catch hell and those who give it out. Just 'cause it's not on TV don't mean they stopped giving it out. Ask somebody who's fought one. They'll tell you a war don't end just because somebody says so. A war isn't over until you don't have to live with it anymore."

For a lot of us that will be a long old time. Like Ron Kovic. Sometimes when he sits up at night, he can hear the war rumbling down in his legs. It makes a sound like the Long Island Railway flashing through Massapequa and heading west.

[*Rolling Stone*, July 19, 1973]

Our War

*L*IKE A LOT OF US, I TOOK THE WAR personally in those days. And I still do. I lived molded to the war's shape for so long that, indeed, my person has retained the war's bend in ways both petty and profound. I was a boy when it began and a man when it finally came to an end. It echoes in me to this day: when pacing nervously, I walk a nine-foot oval, as though I were still confined in my cell in maximum security; when I attend a black-tie affair, there is still part of me that looks around the room and flinches, convinced that if these people had any idea who I really am, I would be sent packing; when the Pledge of Allegiance is recited, I still take a deep breath and ask myself if I really want to repeat it along with everybody else.

I REMEMBER THE WAR as someone it obsessed and imprisoned. And, while it no longer preys on my mind, it is still a subject about which I find it difficult to summon disinterest or distance. I have never known the war at arm's length. I remember it on my skin and in my bones; I remember it as a weight in the pit of my stomach and I remember it as a pain in my chest, late at night and alone.

Much has passed under my personal bridge since the war ended, and, as I have weathered further episodes of loss and helplessness, my heart has opened enough to reexamine long-standing wounds. Now fifty years old, I have come to yearn for something far more than remembrance.

What I seek is a Reckoning.

I first experienced the posture I have in mind in an intensive-care ward some three years ago, when Lacey, my wife of nineteen years, hopelessly comatose, was removed from artificial life supports. Then I held her as she died, a casualty of a desperate failed struggle with breast cancer. I knew her better than anyone, and I could tell from the calm in her heart as she passed that while she'd waited in unconsciousness, attached to a breathing machine, she had somehow taken responsibility for her life and prepared herself to leave it. I had read fictional and religious descriptions of such reckonings, in which lives are revisited in a summary accounting, and Lacey's last moments seemed to confirm them.

Reckoning has been a word full of meaning for me ever since. Coming to terms with ourselves is what we do when we reckon, and reckon with our war is what we must do: stand outside our fears, revisit what we did so many years ago, and clear our souls of this perpetual shadow.

OUR RECKONING IS NOT TO be engaged in lightly or with less than the whole of our selves. At the very least, I expect that taking a good look at the war will be a painful and demanding process. Hard things need to be said, often in hard ways. And, as raw as my memory of the war is, I still do not come easily to that task. I am not a hard man. Quite the contrary. I am usually eager to get along, am reluctant to express personal disapproval, and tend to swallow my complaints in the normal course of life. I like to please and put people at ease. But there are subjects about which there is no easiness, and this war is one of them. I cannot avoid its ugliness, nor do I think such avoidance useful.

So also with my anger. Some of it, too, is unavoidable, even necessary. Few have ever seen my temper, and while I make a point of speaking my mind, I mostly shy from enlarging confrontations, and in this instance I worry that my surviving outrage will sound bitter years after the fact. But I am outraged still. And I mean to say things that bother me deeply and that I know will disturb others, as unfortunate as that disturbance may be.

And I hope others will do likewise until we finally run out of things to say.

Last Thanksgiving I was back in Fresno, California, where I grew up, at my mom's house. I told her that I was writing, once again, about the war. She said she hoped that the country could put all that stuff that happened over Vietnam behind us now, that we needed to move on. I told her that was not exactly what I had in mind.

We need to face up to it first. For me, this is not just about us and not just about now. It is an engagement in the sacred human ritual of studying our own tracks, an attempt at the consecration of those who have gone before through the contemplation of how and why their lives were spent. If healing what the war left behind is possible, I look for such healing in this therapy of honest self-examination and informed acceptance. I also find such a process the most fundamental form of respect. It obliges us to value one another's passing and refuse to spend our lives without an accounting. So now, so much later, it is finally time to account.

THAT, OF COURSE, IS NO small piece of work. Our experience in Vietnam is a lot for any of us to take on, especially after having spent much of the last two decades avoiding it as best we could. We should not kid ourselves, however. Holding to our denial will never allow us to escape the war. That avoidance means only that, rather than owning our experience, we will continue to be owned by it.

An extreme example of being owned by our experience is described by the psychiatric diagnosis post-traumatic stress disorder, PTSD, the Vietnam generation's contribution to the study of mental health. The first patients diagnosed with PTSD were trying to grapple with leftovers from Southeast Asian combat. Their battlefield experience had been much too intense to be assimilated on the spot, so it was deferred and deferred until it began to recur spontaneously, usually at the instigation of familiar scenes or sounds: the whip of helicopter blades, backfires that crack like rounds from an AK-47, Caterpillar tracks that rumble and clank like an armored personnel carrier advancing over the red dirt, hard as concrete during those last weeks before the monsoons began. With that trigger, the patient would return to a firefight outside Chu Lai or a bunker near Marble Mountain or a paddy in the Delta or a ridge near the Rockpile, trapped in an endless repetition of the emotions surrounding the original unresolved trauma.

I never quite understood the power of the phenomenon until I was diagnosed with it myself. My PTSD emerged following Lacey's death. Some eight months after I sat with her body, laid out in a Buddhist wake in the front room of our house, I was overwhelmed by a fog of unfocused anxiety that just descended and never left. To extricate myself I spent the next year sorting out all I had gone through over the three years of illness and treatments before her death, allowing myself to feel all the fear and pain that I had held at bay in the interest of supporting her battle. Slowly, my experience became my own again as terror ebbed out of all my internal nooks and crannies; loss, grief, and panic surfaced where I could become acquainted with them face-to-face; what had happened to me in real time now happened over and over again on replay, letting me accustom myself to all that had gone on, this time at a speed I could live with.

And so it may be for all of us: our body politic clogged with undigested experience, strung up on the very same dilemmas we never dealt with twenty-five years ago, when the killing was still going on. Our disorder is plain to see: having made lying an accepted government function, our government is now overrun with liars; having made our public posture heartless as a matter of policy, we are now unable to bring our heart to public affairs; having made killing a measure of our national efforts, we watch helplessly as killing has become one of our principal cultural currencies; having failed to look our transgressions straight in the face, we have not been straight with one another since; having refused to live up to our values, we are now increasingly without values; having made language into hype, we now have nothing believable to say. I may just be shell-shocked, but that sounds a lot like PTSD to me.

In truth, that disorder is our nation's running thirty-year metaphor. And our emblem is those poor boys who grew old real quick, came home, and still live with that war every day.

When Lacey and I first set up housekeeping, we lived around the corner from a Veterans Administration hospital that specialized in outpatient psychiatric services. I often crossed paths with the patients at the neighborhood grocery store, where both they and I would stop to buy cigarettes. Occasionally one would bum a smoke off me instead. I got to know Leroy that way. He was at the store a lot. He had been a Spec 4 with the First Air Cavalry. He liked $1.50-a-quart burgundy and smoked Camels. We got so we would banter whenever we encountered each other, every day more or less the same way.

"What's up, Leroy, my man?"

"Same old same old."

"Sing me a few bars," I said.

"Jes' like always," Leroy answered. "'They's somewhere out there in the trees and we's stuck out here in the middle with no motherfuckin' place to hide.'"

I suspect every American who remembers the war knows just how Leroy felt.

BACK WHEN THE WAR WAS still going on, lots of people I knew went to great lengths to find a political theory to explain the discrepancy between who America thought it was and who it acted like. And in that search, -isms eventually proliferated, turning the issue to ideology rather than behavior, and making the discussion a lot more complicated and a lot less clear. I kept pace for a while—I was once a Stanford honors student in Social Thought and Institutions—but eventually I lost all tolerance for such theories. I have retained only one in the years since.

We Get What We Do, nothing more. Especially when lives are on the line. We do not get what we mean to do: intention is meaningless. Nor do we get what we tell ourselves we do: appearance counts little and rhetoric even less. We get only the getting, never what we have identified to be got. All means are ends in motion, as ends are means in a static state. Acts that fail to embody their object also fail to realize it. I call this the Do Theory. The war taught it to me.

And, while I am unwilling to give the Do Theory the universal subscription of an ideology, I have consulted it in making decisions throughout my life, to largely positive effect. I have also found it has value in sorting the past. Translated into that tense, of course, the theory reads, We Got What We Did, both a cogent explanation and yet another compelling reason to seek out what happened so many years ago deep in the tall grass and reckon with it once and for all.

And, if the Do Theory is accurate, doing so will prove its own reward.

AS I RECKON, I HAVE TO remind myself that making scapegoats is not the way to proceed. There are indeed those among us more deserving of blame than the rest, and they must be held individually accountable, but the healing we need requires us to look to ourselves before we single anyone out. When we account for this war, we must begin by accounting for it all together. It was, after all, *our* war.

When a nation acts, all its citizens are joined insolubly in responsibility for the consequence of their national behavior, bound to that mutuality for as long as they remember their history, bound generation after generation, carrying its weight as part of their ancestral inheritance. And so it is with us and our war: as far as the fact of it is concerned, as far as all the implications of it having happened at all, as far as carrying the weight of those years and all that carnage, at the bottom line of our enterprise, each of us was the other and vice versa, a single moral organism that must now come to terms together with what we all have done in all of our names. The war's dominant conjugation was first-person plural. We cannot lay it off on any one, any ten, any twenty, or any thirty thousand of us. We cannot exempt our individual selves, whatever we actually did while the war raged. When the question is asked,

Who did this? we must all raise our hands.

And in that communion, we eventually redeem ourselves and all those who must follow us and carry their own share of that national shame. And when we have finally declared ourselves, declared ourselves without withholding, with hearts open as though to our loved ones, our anguish will become simply memory and we will heal and grow strong. We were all truly in this together.

STOPPING THE WAR ONCE meant everything to me.

I left Stanford University after spending my senior year as student body president, ticketed to graduate with honors, winner of the Poetry Prize, and I gave up all thoughts of career and graduate school and lived out of my 1961 Rambler, traveling up and down the Pacific coast, searching for others who meant to throw their bodies on the cogs of the machine. I delivered at least a thousand speeches while America cut its swath through Southeast Asia. I spoke in auditoriums and on street corners, and in every speech I ever gave I said the war was a crime against everything America was meant to be and I urged any young man called to the draft to join me and refuse to go. Each such specific call to disobedience was technically a felony violation of the Selective Service Act, worth a maximum of five years in prison. After I accumulated some five thousand years' worth of such potential violations, I stopped counting. Nor did I bother to calculate what I had coming for all the occasions when I called on soldiers to join us and refuse their orders as well. As long as the war was the law, I wanted to be an outlaw.

That, of course, meant I was watched by the FBI and military intelligence, interrogated at length, and arrested four times in ten years for acts of civil disobedience—all misdemeanors except for one felony violation of the Selective Service Act, charging me with refusing to go to the war when my name was called. For the felony, I spent twenty months of my life "in the custody of the Attorney General of the United States," most of it shuttling between a maximum-security cellblock in a federal correctional institution on the Texas–New Mexico border and the punishment cellblock on the floor below. When they let me go, I had a parole officer to whom I reported for another sixteen months while continuing to organize against the war. I didn't stop organizing until the 1973 Paris Peace Accords formalized American withdrawal from direct combat. I participated in my final demonstration against the war in 1975, just three months before Saigon became Ho Chi Minh City. By then, the war had consumed a decade of my life.

In the darkest days, when just handfuls of us, young and scruffy, seemed to be bearing the brunt of bringing the most powerful nation in the world to its senses, I always believed that when we finally stopped the war, when the troops came home, when the bombing ceased, somehow Americans would come to a settling of accounts with ourselves, both taking responsibility for the irresponsible and doling out responsibility to those deserving it in larger measures than the rest. And in the process we would fashion a communal assessment of what we did and what doing so meant about us, who we really were, and who we really needed to be. I was young in those days and supposed that history would demand such an assessment and that we would automatically accede.

I am not young anymore, and I'm glad I didn't hold my breath waiting for that reckoning to arrive.

The closest we have come to it over the intervening decades is an informal consensus among the American body politic that the war was a "mistake." As a social construct, "mistake" was certainly a significant step out of the dispute that had surrounded our war almost since it started: "mistake" allowed the war to be mentioned in polite company with a reasonable chance of avoiding offense. Everybody agreed. The war was certainly a "mistake." Some thought it was a mistake because we never completely leveled Hanoi, some because our strategy amounted to a crime punishable under the Nuremberg precedent, and most, of course, for reasons somewhere in between.

For all of us, "mistake" provided an emotional anonymity and, as such, a refuge from the pain of what we did.

Mistakes happen. They are somehow like the weather, part of life: it is a mistake to buy the wrong size dress, a mistake to leave loose lug nuts on the wheel of an automobile, a mistake to stick your finger in boiling water, a mistake not to check the pockets of your pants before you put them in the washer, a mistake to go camping in August without mosquito repellent, a mistake to wear brown shoes with a black suit, a mistake to invest public funds in exotic financial ventures, a mistake to leave home without making sure the stove is turned off. Mistakes are what the quality control division pulls off the assembly line; mistakes are what the retailer sells out the back door as seconds; mistakes are what the cook doesn't want to let out of the kitchen and the customer will send back if he does. Mistakes earn an ass-chewing from the boss. Mistakes are apologized for or ignored, usually with little consequence. Everybody makes them.

While it may be an accurate conclusion, calling the war a mistake is the functional equivalent of calling water wet or dirt dirty. And it is now long since time that we moved on to an understanding considerably more profound.

Let us not lose sight of what actually happened.

In this particular "mistake," at least three million people died, only fifty-eight thousand of whom were Americans. These three million people died crushed in the mud, riddled with shrapnel, hurled out of helicopters, impaled on sharpened bamboo, obliterated in carpets of explosives dropped from bombers flying so high they could only be heard and never seen; they died reduced to chunks by one or more land mines, finished off by a round through the temple or a bayonet in the throat, consumed by sizzling phosphorus, burned alive with jellied gasoline, strung up by their thumbs, starved in cages, executed after watching their babies die, trapped on the barbed wire calling for their mothers. They died while trying to kill, they died while trying to kill no one, they died heroes, they died villains, they died at random, they died most often when someone who had no idea who they were killed them under the orders of someone who had even less idea than that. Some of the dead were sent home to their families, some were reduced to such indistinguishable pulp that they could not be recovered. All three million died in pain, often so intense that death was a relief. They all left someone behind. They all became markers visited by those who needed to remember and not forget. The loss was enormous, and "mistake" is no way to account for it. A course of behavior that kills three million people for no good reason cannot be passed off as something for which the generic response is Excuse Me.

WE CAN BEGIN OUR RECKONING by giving the war a different name.

Contrary to the childhood doggerel, names can make a huge difference. They are central to how we identify and perceive. Thus, I have come to prefer the name for the war the Vietnamese use. They call it the American War.

The first time I heard that formulation spoken aloud was with Vinh, a pedicab driver in Ho Chi Minh City. Vinh had been a draftee in the air force of the Republic of Vietnam and spent a brief internment in a reeducation camp after the war ended. Now he practiced his pedicab trade from a corner just down the block from the Saigon cathedral. "The American War" sounded unusual when it came out of his mouth, but it was immediately comfortable to my ear. I did not need to have it explained.

"Of course," I said, "the American War."

"Vietnam War same same?" he asked.

"Same same," I answered. I guess I had known as much for a long time.

So many Vietnamese died and so much of Vietnam was devastated, but the heart of it all was not really about Vietnam or the Vietnamese. They were just in the intersection when our convertible rolled up.

This war was about us. We made it happen. It was ours.

And, even at this late date, any genuine reckoning on our part must include assuming the full responsibilities of that ownership. Nothing less will do.

AMERICANS DON'T LIKE TO LOSE, don't like losers, and had never lost a war before. But we lost this one. There are lots of explanations, but the simple truth is that we ran into a group of people who brought considerably more seriousness to this fight than we did: they lived underground, they huddled in the jungle, they moved by foot and bicycle, they fought on a little rice and a little ammunition. They absorbed enormous punishment, bore great sacrifice, endured untold hardship, and fought us and all our war machines to a dead stop. If they survived, they fought until the whole thing was done, some for as long as a decade. They did not back off, and they held the field until we finally lost our stomach for the fight and went home.

And not only did we lose, but we were poor losers. When we finally left, we left like a whipped dog, pissing on one last bush as we fled down the street.

During the second week of May 1975, the final American military action of the war was announced. I was at the Oakland Coliseum that evening, watching a National Basketball Association playoff game between the Chicago Bulls and the hometown Golden State Warriors. Saigon had fallen days earlier, and the sight of Americans fleeing off the embassy roof was still fresh in everyone's mind. During a break in the action, the Coliseum public-address system announced that the United States Marines, in response to the detention of the civilian cargo ship *Mayaguez* by Cambodia's new Khmer Rouge government, had invaded an island off the Cambodian coast, fought a running gun battle with several Khmer Rouge units, freed the ship's crew, and evacuated. This final note was Gerald Ford's principal contribution to the history of our journey down the tunnel with no light at the end. In what would be recognized as the typical Ford fashion, the *Mayaguez* incident had a bumbling signature: the Khmer Rouge had released the ship's crew before the raid was under way. Thirty-eight marines died pointlessly in the ensuing action.

At the Oakland Coliseum that night, the initial announcement was accompanied by the illumination of a huge American flag on the far wall. The crowd, some fifteen thousand, already hyped by the game, leapt to their feet and celebrated this final outburst of American testosterone with a wave of wild applause spurred on by the flashing scoreboard.

I kept my seat and hunched my shoulders against the noise, the rippling flag, the blinking lights. Few of the people cheering looked as though they had paid much of any price during the ten years that had preceded this final chest thumping, and the war was still a tender enough subject with me that I noticed such things. It had all been vicarious for them, all television and scorecards. I wondered if they would cheer so loudly if those thirty-eight wasted grunts had been dragged out on the court below, where they could get a good look at them, all mud and blood and time run out.

I had expected better, of course, but, like it or not, this was us. We went into the war blind to ourselves, and we left the same way.

THE SUMMER BEFORE LAST, I was driving south along US 101 with my friend John, the Pacific on one side of the road and the best forests in California on the other. We were dirty and overgrown after a four-day backpack trip along the Smith River. My kids—one twenty-five years old, the other twelve—were in my van's rear seat, asleep. John and I had organized together in the old days. Oregon and Washington were his turf, and I came in every couple of months to help out during the last year before I entered the custody of the attorney general. John's a county public defense attorney now and a better Buddhist than I. That day, almost three decades later, we were talking about the war neither of us could forget.

"I'll tell you where we lost our way," John said looking out at the ocean, then turning to face me and touching his hand to his chest. "We lost it in our hearts."

I agreed. It was indeed all about heart.

When we needed ours, we could not find it and could not care enough to stop ourselves, could not value all we were about to lose, and, unable to value it, we could not save it when the time came.

I remember. We lost so much more than any of us ever imagined we would. We lost the legend of ourselves, we lost our heroism and our nobility, we lost all perspective. We lost the string-bean kid third row left in the third-grade photo, we lost the toes off a thousand feet, we lost the place we once called home. We also lost the allegiance of each of us to the other, the communion at the core of our national self. We lost our right to pretend we were much different from the people we had once so routinely dismissed as venal tinhorns and vicious thugs. We lost our innocence, our standing, our reputation, our faith in who we were, our dignity, the easy feeling when we looked at ourselves in the mirror. We lost the kid from down the block, the kid from across town, the kid from up the valley, the kid from over the creek, the kid from down by the bay, from up the state, from along the river, from downtown, from uptown, from the other side of the tracks, and from the very end of the road.

We lost in the long run, in the short run, and in every run in between. We lost coming and going, on this side and that. We lost the fantasies I once chased home after watching Roy Rogers down at the Tower Theatre and the illusions we all nurtured in the bowels of the chain of command. We lost much blood and more than a few tears. We lost legs from Dayton, spleens from Rochester, lungs from Boise, and kneecaps from Duluth. We lost billions and billions of dollars.

And we lost more sleep than we can remember, more joy than we can forget. We lost faith in our government, faith in each other, faith that anything was what it seemed. We lost our bearings, we lost our discipline, we lost our expectations of ourselves. We lost hope, we lost sight, we lost touch, we lost our good sense, our good name, and most every other good we had. We lost the knack for looking each other in the eye. We lost our clean conscience, and we lost track of who we were and who we weren't. We lost our capacity to tell real from unreal and true from false. We lost control and we never got it back.

WE ALSO LOST TRACK OF the difference between right and wrong.

This is not easy for anyone to admit, but it is an especially uneasy enterprise for us. We are, after all, Americans. It never occurred to us that this war would transform us into a case history in moral dyslexia. Most of us figured we were bred right, born right, raised right, and did not have to worry about that kind of thing anymore. I once did, and everybody I knew was the same way. We were Sunday school graduates, *Captain Kangaroo* alumni, the Duke's people, keepers of the White Hat and the eternal flame. We told ourselves that America always righted wrongs and never wronged rights.

As it turned out, we got little of it right and almost all of it wrong, and our war was the proof.

It was the wrong fight, at the wrong time, in the wrong place, against the wrong people, for the wrong reasons, with the wrong strategy, the wrong tactics, and the wrong weapons. It was the wrong approach, to the wrong situation, betraying the wrong motives, from the wrong perspective, with the wrong attitude, to the wrong end, using the wrong means, effecting the wrong result. It was both the wrong twist and the wrong turn, arriving inexorably, of course, at just the wrong moment. It was the wrong choice, the wrong answer to the wrong question, altogether the wrong way to take care of business. And it wronged just about everybody it touched: it wronged the wrong and it wronged the rest of us as well.

And now, twenty years after we finally left the war behind, all that has not changed. What remains is for us to finally engage in the public arithmetic and admit we had no right to have been there and no right to have done what we did and no right to continue pretending otherwise.

THERE HAS BEEN NO ESCAPING the war for me.

It meant far too much, and I was in far too deep to just let it drop, so it has lingered nearby for the twenty-odd years since the last American caught the last chopper out of Saigon: lingered largely unaddressed, on the horizon one day, on my chest the next, a war that is over but nowhere near done.

I still cannot listen to the whump of helicopter rotors without recalling now middle-aged evening news footage of American boys, armed to the teeth, arrogant and terrified, leaping through the downdraft and into the tall grass, ten thousand miles from home. Most came back, many came back in pieces, and some did not come back at all. I remember and, like many who lived through the war, I remain suspicious of power and have never regained much respect for the exercise of force. I still have little use for patriotic displays and no use at all for military conscription. I close my eyes and see wire-service photos of peasants in black pajamas huddling together in the hope of simply making it through the afternoon without being shot or burned alive, and I am still haunted by how easily we defiled and abused, devoid of reflection, hidden from ourselves by a veneer of geopolitics and a parking lot full of denial. I still assume deceit and hypocrisy whenever politicians start dispatching youngsters around the world to kill and be killed. Most of the boys I grew up with learned that lesson the hard way. Leaders eager to talk the talk did their best to send us to the far side of the Pacific when it came time to walk the walk, and there things turned a lot uglier and a lot more evil than we ever imagined. Our America debased itself out in that tall grass ten thousand miles from home, sowing pain over all hell and gone for no good reason, no good reason at all.

It was wrong, and nothing has been quite right for us since.

[from *Our War: What We Did in Vietnam and What It Did to Us*, 1996]

The Bloody End

*T*HEY MET AS DEAN AND STUDENT two decades ago at Stanford University. The older man was the assistant dean of men, a political-science teacher who sought out and attracted bright young men who lived in an age of American life when idealism flourished, when it was thought possible that personal commitment could make life better for the downtrodden. It surprised no one when the dean became mentor to the bright eighteen-year-old freshman.

Years later, after a period in American life that would indelibly change both men and their relationship, one would murder the other.

In 1961, Allard K. Lowenstein, the Stanford dean, had already developed, at the age of thirty-two, those qualities that would make his career in public life. His intelligence was obvious, his exuberance evoked intimacy, and his appetite for all-consuming endeavor was voracious. He dominated as a matter of course. Politically precocious as a child in New York, his heroes were Eleanor Roosevelt and Norman Thomas and, throughout his life, he saw himself as the modern champion of post–New Deal social democracy. Typically, both of his childhood heroes ultimately became his friends. A graduate of Yale's law school, he spent his twenties in a political apprenticeship, first as president of the National Student Association and later as national head of Students for Stevenson and as an aide to Hubert Humphrey. Lowenstein seemed to know everyone. That immense network of acquaintanceship, coupled with his personal charisma, would be responsible for making him a figure without whom no anthology of the decade stretching ahead of him at Stanford would be complete.

Back then, student life was marked by a preoccupation with penny loafers and beer kegs. In contrast, the assistant dean's telephone rang regularly with calls from the likes of Ralph Bunche and Adlai Stevenson. The effect on undergraduates who were looking for inspiration and guidance was one of irresistible attraction, even though Lowenstein himself did not have the look of an apostle. With a head that seemed too small for the body he had honed during his collegiate wrestling days, he might have appeared ugly and mouse-like except for the presence he exuded. His eyes were hidden behind lenses as thick as Coke-bottle bottoms. His standard wardrobe ran to khakis, skintight T-shirts, and a "Yale" jacket. When he had to wear one, his tie was always askew. But no one paid much attention to any of this once he opened his mouth. To this day, Allard Lowenstein is remembered by many who listened to him as the most convincing human being they had ever heard.

One of those he persuaded to his thinking about the issues of the time was Dennis Sweeney, a scholarship student from Portland, Oregon, a former varsity basketball player and the class-day speaker at his graduation from Clackamas High School. Six feet tall, topped with thick brown hair, he had a cherub's face in those days. An only child whose natural father had died in a military plane crash when he was just a youngster, Dennis arrived at Stanford self-conscious about his working-class origins. The assistant dean of men was one of those responsible for pulling the shy young man out of his initial state of intimidation. Throughout his life, Allard Lowenstein singled young people out of the crowd to become his protégés. Dennis was among the first. By 1963, he had become an interdisciplinary honor student and speaker of the Stanford Student Congress. His Stanford contemporaries remember him as "sweet," "endlessly sincere," and "devoted to Al."

Lowenstein left the Stanford dean's office after a year, but the distance did not affect his connection to Sweeney. As he would with hundreds of other locales throughout his life, Lowenstein returned to visit Stanford regularly, and Sweeney often drove him around, between appointments, in a borrowed car. The burning issue then was racial justice in the American South, and Lowenstein's passion on the subject was immediately shared by Sweeney. What is now remembered as "the sixties" was about to begin, and if Allard Lowenstein was not exactly a father figure, he was at least the role model that Dennis Sweeney had been looking for.

I, too, had been a Lowenstein protégé during that decade and a friend and roommate of Dennis Sweeney's for two years after that. Eventually, all of us broke away from each other over politics. It seemed inconceivable that the culmination of the Lowenstein-Sweeney relationship would occur seventeen years later with a fifty-one-year-old Allard mortally wounded and Dennis holding the murder weapon. Back in the early sixties, dreams of making the world better were still envisioned as simple things that were inevitably redemptive for both the country at large and for the individuals who exercised them. No one had yet seen visions warp under the weight of the reactions they would produce. That experience was still over the horizon, waiting at the end of a decade that would leave Allard Lowenstein a legend and Dennis Sweeney a refugee from the person he could have been.

THE HORROR OF THAT EVENTUAL culmination has by now frozen both the accused and the victim in stereotype: Allard K. Lowenstein as the liberal champion of selfless democratic principle who deserved much better than he got, and Dennis A. Sweeney as the vindictive flotsam of a failed revolution who had become irretrievably lost along the way. In fact, both were too singular to define so pattly. To varying degrees, the realities that were both men have been obscured in the myth-making process. Allard Lowenstein lived a life that defied easy definition: He was at once both insider and outsider, selfless and yet self-obsessed, while Dennis Sweeney was both victim and executioner, a man whose madness might have derived as much from a medical tragedy—a random biological accident—as from the weight of experiential overload. The intersection of their lives, and of the history they shared, is a story of irony—of mutual respect and painful enmity, of obsessional truth and homicidal consequence. There are no neat packages here: Neither man succeeded, and neither man failed. Nothing changed, but everything was different.

By 1963, the focus of the politics of Lowenstein and Sweeney had become the civil rights struggle in the state of Mississippi. Lowenstein had first traveled there the previous year. One of the connections he made was with the Student Nonviolent Coordinating Committee, the shock troops of the Freedom Riders and the predominant civil rights organization in the state. SNCC distrusted white liberals; Lowenstein epitomized them. That they came together at all was a tribute to the needs of the moment. SNCC was considering plans to bring in Northern white students and, through his campus connections, Lowenstein was in the best position to supply them. The result was the Mississippi Summer Project of 1964, a pivotal event in the civil rights movement and one out of which grew the Freedom Democratic Party. Lowenstein's role in the project was to recruit and to advise. His differences with SNCC along the way eventually framed the Lowenstein-Sweeney divergence as well.

Sweeney was one of Lowenstein's first recruits. Allard arranged for Dennis to work in the SNCC office in Jackson. Dennis spent portions of the 1963–64 school year driving in and out of Mississippi with his mentor. In those days, Allard and Dennis were the closest they would ever be.

That closeness had totally disintegrated by the time the Summer Project was over. Even before the project had begun, Lowenstein's breach with SNCC had become so wide that he had initially decided to stay out of the state altogether. He changed his mind when the first three civil rights workers were killed. By then, his protégé Dennis Sweeney had been designated to accompany regular SNCC staff members into McComb, Mississippi, to work in the heart of Klan country.

Only the bravest went anywhere near McComb, whose reputation among civil rights workers throughout Mississippi was that of a rabid dog. The reality of McComb greeted Sweeney shortly after he arrived. He and the rest of the SNCC workers were asleep in the Freedom School, where they had been living, when a bomb was tossed into the front room. Dennis was closest to the explosion, but he was saved by a thick plywood bed board. The next issue of the local *McComb Enterprise-Journal* ran a front-page picture of the twenty-year-old Northern invader named Sweeney. The face it showed was handsome, the expression intense. The only visible imperfections were the teeth. They had spaces between them, and one seemed damaged.

After five more years of intense civil rights work, Dennis would look remarkably unchanged—except for those teeth. The front ones had been replaced with immaculate bridgework donated by a New York dentist who, like Sweeney, had volunteered to go south at the urging of Allard Lowenstein. But by 1973, the bridgework, which had been anchored to dental crowns, had been torn out by Sweeney's own furious hand, leaving little more than filed-down stubs, a sight that Sweeney would try to hide by keeping his upper lip pulled down like a shade over the unsightly gap. To those who experienced it, the terror of McComb was strangely reinforcing. It established a tight bond with his comrades that was closer than anything Dennis Sweeney would ever experience again. One of the consequences was Dennis's increasing attachment to SNCC's style of Jacksonian participatory democracy, to the exclusion of Allard's post–New Deal social democracy. The culmination of that distancing occurred during the 1964 Democratic National Convention in Atlantic City. The Mississippi Freedom Movement came north to demand that the Democrats unseat the "whites only" Mississippi delegation in favor of an integrated one. It was a move that Allard had long supported, arguing that the future of civil rights for black people should and would be decided in the political process. In the end, the Democrats offered the integrated delegation two of Mississippi's dozen seats, which the Freedom Movement delegates refused. Dennis Sweeney, like many young white volunteers, felt that the Democratic Party's failure to seat the delegates was perceived by the black student activists as evidence that the political process was part and parcel of what was wrong in America.

To Allard, it was a sign only that the task was difficult. The disagreement exemplified a fissure that ran through the entire civil rights movement, and Dennis and Allard quickly took positions on opposite sides. The split marked the end of the specialness of their relationship.

The dissolution of Sweeney's protégéhood was hard on both parties. For Dennis, the pain was that of abandoning a role model and setting out on his own. Instead of returning to Stanford, he stayed in the cauldron of McComb for another year as a SNCC staffer, earning $10 a month; his commitment was total. He would be arrested twice and harassed repeatedly. In the process, he felt betrayed, if not by Allard the person then certainly by Allard's politics. They were, in Dennis's view, responsible for distorting and manipulating the Mississippi Project to the ends of Northern white liberals and the Democratic Party.

That Lowenstein also felt personally betrayed is a matter of public record. By now, his split with the radical SNCC had moved into the open. He accused SNCC of undermining "the viability of American society." According to him, SNCC had become "destructive," "radical," "increasingly racist," and "insufficiently anti-Communist." One of the voices challenging him in the controversy was that of Dennis Sweeney.

The way Allard remembered it, a little less than three years before his murder, "Since Dennis and I have been quite close friends, it became a very, very personal thing. . . . During the period when I was becoming the . . . villain in their eyes, [he] became very much the spearhead of their campaign against me."

According to several of Sweeney's SNCC contemporaries, Dennis disagreed with Allard, but he never served as any kind of "spearhead." They say that Allard had a way of taking political difference as personal assault. In their eyes, his later description of events was both "paranoid" and "self-serving."

Eventually, when Dennis left the South and SNCC, Allard described what had happened. Dennis, as he saw it, had been "thrown out of SNCC because he was white. . . . They ended up accusing him of all the things they have accused me of. . . . It very,

very badly damaged him." Without commenting on the question of damage, Sweeney's contemporaries again disagree. They say that a consensus was reached that whites ought to return to their own communities and organize there; they say that expulsions didn't begin until long after Sweeney had left Mississippi.

THERE IS NO DISAGREEMENT that by the summer of 1965 the community in which Dennis Sweeney had found himself had dissolved. The civil rights movement had turned toward Black Power, and young whites began focusing on the war in Vietnam. Sweeney spent that last summer in Natchez working with a filmmaker on a documentary and preparing himself to return with his civil-rights-worker fiancée to life at Stanford University as a married student.

That same summer, Allard Lowenstein visited Bogalusa, Louisiana. He and another student protégé, who was driving with him, talked about Sweeney. To Allard, Dennis was a symbol of what had happened in Mississippi. Allard said he was going to write a book about his relationship with Dennis, and the two different directions they'd taken. Allard pictured it as a sad story and, for the first time, he referred to his former protégé and future assassin as a "victim."

IN RETROSPECT, LOWENSTEIN'S 1965 picture of Sweeney was at least premature. The Vietnam War increasingly dominated all other issues, and Sweeney certainly involved himself in it. After the quick breakup of his marriage, Sweeney committed himself full-time to the draft resistance movement. Lowenstein was uneasy with all disobedience to conscription, but by now his positions were rarely discussed by Sweeney and his friends.

One of the few times that Lowenstein's name came up was when *Ramparts* magazine in 1967 exposed the connection between the Central Intelligence Agency and the National Student Association. Neither the story in *Ramparts* nor any subsequent published investigation ever alleged that Lowenstein was party to the deception. But he had been NSA president in 1951—the year preceding the inception of the connection—and he had been a dominant force in NSA politics then, and ever after. That history was sufficient evidence to Sweeney and his friends that Lowenstein had known what was going on.

Throughout his life, Lowenstein laughed off the CIA charges. "I was the one they hid it all from," he would explain. To him, the allegation was just one more piece of "distorted" flak from the left. That direction always spelled conflict for Lowenstein, and in many cases it involved former protégés.

Despite a lifetime spent trying to alter its product, Allard Lowenstein saw himself as champion of the two-party electoral process. In 1967, he set out to prove that the system could correct its mistakes. He planned to unseat an incumbent Democratic president and to seat a new one who was opposed to the war.

It is a tribute to the breadth of his influence that Lowenstein could even attempt the effort, which he called the "Dump Johnson" movement. He moved endlessly back and forth across the country, sleeping in fifteen-minute intervals, subsisting on pound cake and Coca-Cola, fetching his tie out of his bag for one more rumpled appearance among his fifteen of the day. His unremitting energy, and his belief in his plan, inspired a chain of other believers and engendered a movement that began multiplying into a series of front organizations and student groups by the fall of 1967. Lowenstein tried to get Robert F. Kennedy and George McGovern to run, but neither one was willing. By November, Eugene McCarthy was in the race, backed by Lowenstein's youthful shock troops, among others. Within four months, Lyndon Johnson had announced that he would not run for reelection. The toppling of Johnson, though not entirely his handiwork, would become Allard Lowenstein's landmark in American political history.

It is somehow typical of both Allard Lowenstein and the decade he did so much to shape that success only seemed to produce a new dilemma: Whom was he to support now that Bobby Kennedy had made a belated entrance into the Democratic primaries? The move had left Lowenstein stranded in a political no-man's-land. On the one hand, he was a public supporter of McCarthy. On the other, his heart belonged to Bobby. Lowenstein tried to sidestep the worst of the political crossfire by returning to New York, where he and Jennifer, his wife of two years, bought a house on Long Island, and he announced himself to be a candidate for Congress.

Lowenstein was in the midst of his Long Island campaigning when Bobby Kennedy won the California primary. Kennedy tried to reach Lowenstein before going down to his victory celebration in Los Angeles's Ambassador Hotel, but missed him. He left a message, and told an aide that they would phone Allard again as soon as the celebration was over.

Instead, the call that finally came from Los Angeles brought the news that Bobby had been shot. Allard caught the first plane to Los Angeles.

The events of that night pitched Lowenstein into as deep a sense of personal loss as anything in his adult life. The story was one he would tell regularly to friends throughout the next decade. He reached the hospital and passed through the Secret Service cordon into Kennedy's corridor just as the doctor announced the death. Lowenstein and several others accompanied the body down to the ground floor in an elevator. Everyone was crying. As Lowenstein would later tell it, he turned to Ted Kennedy during the ride and said all he could think to say: "You're the only hope we've got left, and you're not good enough."

Lowenstein would always feel cheated by Bobby's death. He blamed the assassination for robbing the country of its rightful future.

For the rest of the year, Lowenstein mostly concentrated on running for Congress. That November, he won his first and only successful bid for elective public office. It was the personal highlight of his political career.

Meanwhile, Dennis Sweeney's life was bad, and headed for worse. The draft resistance movement had spent itself by the time Allard Lowenstein was sworn into Congress, and Sweeney and several others moved into an apartment in San Francisco. At first, Sweeney drove a taxi late at night, mostly hauling tourists to houses of prostitution. The work disgusted him, so he tried for a job in the post office. Shortly after he was hired, he was visited by two FBI agents. They just wanted to tell him, they said, that they knew where he was and that they would not bother him as long as he kept his nose clean.

The Nixon years were beginning, and hatches were being battened down everywhere. In something of a tribute to the coming decade, the signs of Sweeney's deteriorating mental condition were at first hidden by the suspicions shared by nearly everyone participating in anti-government protests. Until he finally talked about his encroaching madness, no one noticed.

Sweeney first revealed his emotional instability in San Francisco during the spring of 1970. He was planning to move to Boston and went to a park with a woman to say goodbye. They made small talk until Sweeney mentioned, in a calm and offhand manner, that he thought someone might have planted an "electrode" in his body in order to monitor and control him. The woman shrugged his words off as a bad joke.

Later, in Sweeney's accounts to friends and acquaintances, this "electrode" would acquire transmission qualities and would flood his head with messages for increasingly longer periods of the day.

After Lowenstein's assassination, Sweeney was typified as a casualty of the sixties who eventually broke under the weight of traumatizing experiences and bitter disappointments. The principal shortcoming of this characterization is its divergence from the working conclusions of modern psychiatry.

All known analyses of Sweeney's disorder thus far have concluded that he is a paranoid schizophrenic of the chronic type. The disease's symptoms are extraordinarily alike in all victims: hallucinations; the unwilling visitation of the afflicted by voices; delusions of persecution; and the development of elaborate and convoluted logic systems to explain all the symptoms. Two present theories speculate that the cause of the disorder is either a combination of genetic predisposition and/or enzyme malfunction, which may or may not be triggered by stress, or a virus of the central nervous system.

The meaning of Sweeney's progress from protégé to assassin breaks the easy stereotype. As much as being someone who finally cracked under the weight of emotional battering and sixties malaise, Sweeney was a person whose procession of bad luck was topped with a random calamity.

TYPICALLY, IN ANY ONE random month out of Lowenstein's thirty years of adult life, he might have given speeches in fifteen cities in ten states. A thousand phone calls would be sandwiched in between, as he touched base with dozens of protégés and old friends. Allard Lowenstein managed to rush headlong through three decades without slowing down. Such enormous energy is indicative of a driven quality. Lowenstein was generous and caring to a fault, yet found it difficult to sustain an interest in conversations he didn't dominate. He had absolute faith in the superiority of his own judgment but always made everyone else's case better than he made his own, in failed political races and in the adoption of lost causes. He cared little for titles, but spent much of his life pursuing them. Selfless server of causes, he arranged his life so that 95 percent of the situations he encountered centered on his own presence.

In most cases, a resume might provide additional perspectives in the comprehension of a public figure's life, but in Allard Lowenstein's, it proves to be woefully limited. Son of a doctor turned restaurateur, Lowenstein eschewed the Ivy League after Horace Mann School and attended the University of North Carolina in order, among other reasons, to compete on the wrestling team. After his NSA presidency, he enlisted in the United States Army. Later, he was an assistant dean of men at Stanford and a lecturer at several universities, served one term in Congress from Long Island, and did brief duty as an ambassador for special political affairs at the United Nations.

A more complete understanding of Lowenstein's importance on the American political scene relies on information that is apocryphal and told in anecdotes: He introduced John Kennedy to Eleanor Roosevelt at the 1960 Democratic National Convention. Adlai Stevenson broke away from a crowd of admirers to greet a strolling Allard on the Atlantic City boardwalk in 1964. Allard would have been Bobby's right-hand man. Some claimed Allard smuggled himself into Biafra in a last-ditch personal attempt to negotiate an end to the civil war. Allard bragged he was No. 7 on Richard Nixon's "enemies list." On one occasion, Allard apologized for being late, saying he had been in Northern Ireland and it had taken him longer to find a "solution" than he'd expected. Allard was the only Democrat William F. Buckley ever supported for Congress, or anything else. At the age of forty-six, Allard was still going down to Chapel Hill to work out with the University of North Carolina wrestling squad. The variety of the tales told by him and about him is endless.

Just exactly who and what Allard Lowenstein really wanted to be is an unanswerable question. The record suggests an ambivalence not uncommon among extraordinarily talented people. Like all historical creatures who are nine parts presence and only one part position, Lowenstein will probably be appraised, finally, as much by his reflection in those he touched as by his individual achievements. In that accounting, Lowenstein shows signs of faring quite well. Already, more than fifty young people who were introduced to politics by him sit in state legislatures.

Lowenstein, like Dennis Sweeney, suffered when the sixties ended. After being redistricted in his first bid for reelection, he lost. After that, he ran for Congress twice within four months in Brooklyn, and lost both times. Then he returned to Long Island, and lost again. After that came a divorce, and then he entered two congressional races in Manhattan within a year, both defeats.

For the first time in almost a decade, Allard Lowenstein saw, during one of his campaigns in 1974, the man who eventually killed him. Dennis Sweeney came to Lowenstein's house. There was a noticeable gap in Dennis's mouth, where the bridgework had been torn away by his own hand. He told Allard that someone had wired his false teeth so that they picked up messages from outer space. It was an encounter, not a confrontation.

BY THE TIME OF HIS VISIT to Allard's home, Dennis Sweeney had clearly slipped his tether. Since the onset of his illness, the voices in his head were speaking with increasing frequency; it was difficult for him to concentrate. When the voices did not stop, Sweeney shared his dilemma with his mother and his stepfather. They attempted to have him committed to an Oregon state mental hospital in 1973. He was held there for part of a week, but the diagnosis was insufficient to warrant confinement.

Afterward, it was obvious to Dennis that the forces trying to prevent him from removing his transmitter were greater and more sinister than he had first thought. Certainly the CIA had some kind of hand in it, he told friends. In Portland, he concluded that he would have to leave the United States to find a doctor who was willing to buck these powerful enemies. Before leaving, he wrote letters to a number of old movement friends.

"I am at the lowest ebb of my life now because of the psychological warfare that is being made on me," he wrote one of them. "I am simultaneously attuned to and programmed electronically . . . [unable] to sort out my own thoughts from the impulses running through my skull. I am fairly certain that I have software I wasn't born with."

Sweeney made it as far as Paris but, when he could not find work, quickly returned to Boston. There he ran the grill at a hamburger stand, and then worked in a mattress factory. Sweeney's social contacts were limited, but he got in touch with a few old friends living in Massachusetts. Among them was the filmmaker with whom he had worked in Mississippi during the summer of 1965. When the voices in Dennis Sweeney's head began to be identifiable as those of real people, the filmmaker's would be the first he would set out to track down.

That he had been unsuccessful at eluding his demons was obvious in a 1975 phone call he placed to Allard Lowenstein in Newark. His tone was much more hateful than it had been the last time.

There were people watching him, Dennis said, and Allard was responsible. He told Allard to call his dogs off.

"Dennis," Allard pleaded, "let me help you. I know people who can help you. I want to put you in their hands."

"So—you too," Sweeney growled in response.

It was the last conversation between them before they kept an appointment in Manhattan late on the afternoon of March 14, 1980.

In between, Dennis Sweeney became obsessed with the Natchez filmmaker, then in Boston. There now seemed to be a lethal edge to his actions. The filmmaker noticed it as soon as Dennis arrived for his next visit. That 1975 meeting remains the fullest available picture of the former civil rights worker's rapidly escalating paranoia.

Sweeney entered the filmmaker's office like a snarling dog. For the next four hours, the filmmaker would be too frightened of provoking Sweeney to ask him to leave. Sweeney said he had had it. He said the filmmaker, the filmmaker's wife, and even the filmmaker's five-year-old son had been broadcasting to him twenty-four hours a day. He "knew" the filmmaker was part of the "killer elite, on the run since Watergate." It was an "international Jewish conspiracy." The filmmaker, Dennis hallucinated, was trying to force him to "marry a Jewess."

He had not had a woman in years, Sweeney said, because the voices were "exhausting" him. He could not understand why they were doing all this. Sometimes, he told the filmmaker, he became "radioactive," other times "transparent." His thoughts were being "communicated to other people," and the voices in his head kept telling him to do "terrible things."

As soon as Dennis Sweeney left, the filmmaker, who had been a gun-control advocate, bought a pistol. He then briefly left Massachusetts, and on his return he kept his address a secret and got an unlisted telephone number. All the while, Sweeney kept making regular telephone calls to the filmmaker's office. The filmmaker finally decided that the only way to get Sweeney off his back was to meet him face-to-face. They arranged to do so on a street corner in Cambridge; the filmmaker brought two friends along as protection.

Sweeney approached directly and, when he was within arm's length, ordered the filmmaker to take his glasses off. Then Sweeney began pummeling him. When the filmmaker's friends pulled Sweeney off, the former civil rights worker made no move to resume. Instead, he issued a warning.

"The next time you've got a message for me," he screamed, referring to the imaginary transmissions inside his head, "deliver it to my face!"

With that, he turned and headed for the subway.

Thoroughly terrorized, the filmmaker attempted to send a warning message through intermediaries to Allard Lowenstein, telling him to avoid Dennis Sweeney.

The effort, apparently, came to naught.

SWEENEY'S EXPLOSION ON THE Cambridge street corner evidently redirected his obsession from its focus on the filmmaker and sent it reeling even more deeply into his past to single out Allard Lowenstein. Sweeney moved to Mystic, Connecticut, and lived there for the next two years, earning his way doing carpentry jobs. He kept to himself but once told a fellow boarder that he picked up signals "from Mars."

In July 1979, he moved to a rented room in nearby New London. His stepfather died of a heart attack at the end of February 1980, and by the time Sweeney returned from the funeral in Portland, he seemed to be under the impression that he could detect Lowenstein's hand in the death.

On March 11, Sweeney walked into Raub's Sporting Goods in downtown New London and made an application to purchase a seven-shot Llama .380 semiautomatic pistol costing $120. He signed forms attesting that he had never been convicted of a felony and had never been committed to a mental institution. Five days later, he picked up the weapon and a box of ammunition. By then, he had told his landlady he would be leaving Connecticut soon. He also made an appointment to see Allard Lowenstein at his office in the law firm of Layton & Sherman in New York City at 4 p.m. on Friday, March 14.

That Lowenstein made room on his schedule to see Sweeney is both tragic and typical. Lowenstein felt uncomfortable in abandoning anyone. When he was with people he'd known as a Stanford dean, he made it a point to mention Dennis Sweeney and the madness that had descended upon him.

Certainly Lowenstein could have easily told Sweeney he was too busy to meet with him. In 1980, he had not slowed down. For the first days of his last week, he was in New Hampshire campaigning for Ted Kennedy's presidential bid. He returned to New York on Wednesday with the usual circles under his eyes. His assistant met him at LaGuardia Airport, and during the drive to Manhattan, Lowenstein looked over his mail. One of the enclosures was a picture from a kaffeeklatsh that he had attended several days earlier.

"I look like Frank Graham [United States Senator from North Carolina] did a month before he died," Lowenstein said. "Do you think I've only got a month left?"

The assistant filed the remark away with a lot of similar speculations about his own death that Lowenstein had made in the past few years. It was a trait that was shared by many men fresh to their fifties.

Lowenstein showed no signs of unease about his scheduled appointment with Sweeney. Afterward, he expected to meet with a man running in the upcoming congressional race on Manhattan's East Side; he planned to tell him he would be in the race as well.

By noon in New London that Friday, Dennis Sweeney had finished packing all his possessions. Later, when police searched his room, everything was neatly stored in boxes for transporting, and there was a fresh change of clothes laid out on his bed. Sweeney drove his pickup truck onto the lawn of his rooming house to load it more easily. But when he came back outside, wearing Levi's, boots, a plaid shirt, and a blue nylon windbreaker, he got in without loading a thing and drove off. Later that same day, police would find the truck abandoned in Midtown Manhattan.

As he sat in Lowenstein's Rockefeller Center waiting room, Dennis was remembered as being expressionless and seemingly calm. He had, apparently, hidden the Llama .380 in his jacket. He and Lowenstein shook hands before disappearing into the office behind a closed door.

There is no record of the two men's final conversation. Some of those in the waiting room think it lasted more than ten minutes. What is known from the fragments pieced together by the police after questioning Sweeney is that, after their talk, Dennis stood up and shook his former mentor's hand again. Allard, no doubt, thought that Dennis was about to leave. Instead, according to police sources, Dennis announced:

"Al, we've got to put an end to this obsession."

Then he pulled his $120 pistol.

Allard shouted, "No!" and threw his left arm up to protect himself.

Dennis Sweeney fired all seven rounds. Five shots hit Allard Lowenstein. Sweeney then walked back into the waiting room, laid the empty weapon in the receptionist's letter tray, took a seat, and lit a cigarette. He said not a single word, just sat there.

By the time the ambulance arrived, Lowenstein was unconscious, bleeding profusely, but still alive. "He's been controlling my life for years," Sweeney finally told the police. "Now I've put an end to it."

ALLARD LOWENSTEIN WAS NEVER one to give up early in any battle, and the one he waged with death was no different. As usual, the odds were long. Lowenstein arrived at Saint Clare's Hospital with his left arm broken and his entire left lung shot away. Two slugs had pierced his heart, one leaving a hole an inch and a half across. It took five and a half hours to sew him back together. He survived all of that. There was hope in the waiting room, and among those in the crowd on the street, when hours passed and people remembered Lowenstein's indomitable will and his wrestler's body. But this time, these would not be enough. After half an hour in the recovery room, Lowenstein's heart stopped pumping. When the news of his death reached the sidewalk outside the hospital, sobbing was heard on all sides. It was said that Allard Lowenstein had died a hero's death, fighting every inch of the way.

That stature seems confirmed by his final resting place. On March 19, Allard Lowenstein, a former congressman, was buried with full military honors at Arlington National Cemetery, about as close to John Kennedy's grave as is the grave of Kennedy's own brother Robert.

DENNIS SWEENEY IS CURRENTLY imprisoned at the Rikers Island detention center in New York's East River, charged with second-degree murder. The corridors at Rikers are lonely and mean, but they pale in comparison with the madness into which Dennis Sweeney first stumbled ten years ago. He has pleaded not guilty, by reason of insanity, and is being kept under medication in the mental observation unit at Rikers, awaiting the judgment of a psychiatrist as to when, or whether, he will stand trial. His hair is still thick and luxuriant, his body trim. Only the teeth give him away. They sit on his face like relics from an age of trench warfare.

Despite the charges against him, Sweeney still does not think his victim is dead and claims Allard's voice continues to echo in his head.

[*New York Times Magazine*, August 17, 1980]

Author's note, April 2020: Dennis Sweeney was incarcerated in a New York State mental hospital until 2000, when he was released on parole. He now lives in Oregon, where he grew up.

Behind America's Marijuana High

ON WEDNESDAY, AUGUST 31, 1977, twenty-seven Mexicans and six Americans boarded the Mexicana Airlines 8:30 a.m. flight to Oaxaca from Mexico City International Airport. The tall, smooth gringo in a tan leisure suit and shades who boarded right before the doors closed went more or less unnoticed. He wore a deep-blue polyester shirt patterned with red and orange blossoms. His tourist permit listed him as one Henry Amazon, a vacationing insurance agent from Denver. Amazon had paid for his ticket with two crisp American $20 bills and had lied about being on vacation. The journey he was starting over the Sierra Madre del Sur and into the highland Oaxaca Valley was a business trip, and Amazon's real business had nothing to do with insurance.

Henry Amazon is a smuggler of fine marijuanas, and his pseudonym is just one aspect of his trade. Over the last ten years, he has had papers identifying himself as Henry Amazon from Denver, William Spence from El Paso, Morris Wilson from Dallas, and Hector R. Cruz from Oklahoma City. He has also been known, less formally, as "Fast Eddie," "Chorizo Sam," and "El Tortuga." The only nickname that provides any real information about Henry Amazon is El Tortuga—the snapping turtle. It hints at the fierceness running beneath his pleasant, almost gentlemanly presence. More than anything else, that force is responsible for the American's survival for a decade as what the Mexican police call a *traficante*, a drug trafficker. The Tortuga nickname had been hung on Amazon in a Zapotec Indian village six miles off the highway from Oaxaca (pronounced wa-HA-ka) to Puebla three years earlier. Amazon had driven there in May looking for a farmer named Ramón with whom he'd done business the previous November. Ramón's crop had been destroyed by the *Federales*, but the farmer said there were two strange Indians from the coast who were around with superfine leaf. Normally, Amazon did business only with Zapotecs, but he was anxious to get the truck loaded and on the road. Ramón arranged an introduction.

The two Indians were members of the Huave tribe from Puerto Escondido, and the small sample they showed the American was of A-plus quality. The surface of the cannabis was greasy with resin that balled up between Amazon's thumb and forefinger when he stroked it. The long hairs on the face of the leaf had turned a deep red, and the few seeds in the sample were a dark, mottled khaki color. As usual, Henry Amazon said friendly things to the Indians in his broken Spanish. Amazon is a quiet man who smiles a lot. The two five-foot-tall Huaves mistook his style and thought he was one more gringo they could sucker punch. It was a critical mistake.

The strange Indians told the American that their load was up the mountain a way, and they offered to take him to see it that night. They said he should bring his money. At 11 p.m., Amazon started up a two-lane dirt road leading out of the village in his rented Volkswagen van, with the two Indians sitting behind him in the cargo area. They climbed the road steadily through the black evening and were soon skirting a sheer drop of two hundred feet to their left. The Indians were talking to each other and did not know that Henry's Spanish was a lot better than he let on. The Huaves were discussing where to kill him and take his money. It was clear to Henry Amazon that he was going to have to do something quickly.

When he saw a third-class bus roaring down the slope toward them, Amazon whipped the VW across the bus's lane and jumped out the passenger side of the van. The bus driver blasted his horn and slammed on the brakes. Smoke spewed from the bus's brake drums as it rattled to a halt twenty feet from the van in a swarm of dust, and the beam from the headlights flush on the cargo door. The first Indian to jump out was blinded by the glare. He had a short knife in his hand. Amazon took the weapon away and punched the Huave unconscious. The second Indian was carrying a short length of wood. Amazon tore the stick out of his hand, picked the Indian up, and threw him over the nearby cliff. The bus pulled around the van, blasting its horn. Then Henry Amazon found the other unconscious Huave in the dark and threw him over the cliff, too.

The story of what happened to the two Huaves got around, and the Zapotecs began to say that the grande gringo looked as if he were asleep but would snap your head off if you made a false move: El Tortuga. Henry Amazon used the name a lot. Being known as the Snapping Turtle was a good reputation to have in Oaxaca.

As marijuana smugglers go, Henry Amazon ranks among the turtles of the business, not among the hares. Other Americans with a lot less experience than he has are dealing in buys of thousands of pounds worth millions of dollars, but Amazon has kept his a small business. Henry and his one junior partner rarely use more than four or five other people in a smuggle, and rarely move more than three hundred pounds at a time. At that rate, he nets $300,000 a year. Amazon's income supports a wife, four children, and a handful of needy friends. He owns his 360-acre Colorado ranch and four trucks outright, and pays all his bills in cash. Over the years, the *traficante* has converted his extra capital into precious metals, old coins, jewels, and antique china that he keeps hidden under the floorboards of his two-story house.

Amazon got his start in the business shortly after his discharge from the Marine Corps in early 1968. His first supplier was another veteran who worked for the United States Border Patrol. Flashier *traficantes* have come and gone from Oaxaca since Henry Amazon started, but few have lasted as long as he has. Henry Amazon stays close to the ground and remains hard to notice. The police detection systems are designed to catch braggarts, fools, and folks working over their heads. The hotshots get caught up in greed and the thrill of the game, make a mistake, and disappear from the face of the earth. During the month before Henry Amazon's flight to Oaxaca, four Americans whom police have called *traficantes*—Paul Raymond Smith, Teresa Kelly Ward, Douglas Michael Dighero, and

Timothy Robert Trout—had been shot to death in Oaxaca under mysterious circumstances.

For those who are caught by Mexican police with more than an ounce of marijuana, the minimum prison sentence is five years, three months. *Traficantes* captured while hauling their loads are virtually guaranteed a police torture session at the site of their arrest. *Traficantes* say that if they are caught carrying money on the way to a buy, they have a way of just disappearing, never to be heard from again. Henry Amazon had boarded the Mexicana flight that day with $7,000 in American twenties and another $3,000 worth of Mexican pesos in his bag. With luck, Amazon would have turned his ten grand into nearly $90,000 in the space of two weeks.

The standard profit margins of the business are a considerable temptation. Few smugglers multiply their investment any less than five times in a single venture, and some clear more than 1,000 percent. The statistics that document American marijuana use are varied, and the numbers are only approximations. The National Institute on Drug Abuse, a federal agency in Washington, D.C., estimates that there are fifteen million regular marijuana users in America. Recent public opinion polls suggest the figure is higher than that. If the polls' estimates are true, twenty-eight million adult Americans—20 percent of the adult population—consume an ounce of marijuana every two months, and another seven million— 5 percent of adult Americans—smoke at twice that rate.

There is, then, a market for something like fifteen million pounds of marijuana a year. Taking into account the markups along the way as crops in the fields become salable ounces in the street, in the average year a minimum of $10 billion changes hands in payment for marijuana on the American market. The nations from which the most marijuana is exported to America are Colombia and Mexico. Most of the Colombian product enters the country along the Gulf Coast, or on the Atlantic side of Florida. Most of the Mexican marijuana arrives by land, over the border anywhere from Texas to California. Marijuana is grown throughout the Republic of Mexico, but the states of Sinaloa, Guerrero, and Oaxaca are renowned for the high quality of their crops.

The smuggle that Henry Amazon commenced on August 31 was not an unusual venture, as typical as any activity in a freelance business can be. It took six days for Henry to get his load of marijuana together, and another four days to get it across the American border. This reporter accompanied Henry Amazon throughout his business dealings in Oaxaca, and followed the shipment as far north as Guerrero.

I

On the Mexicana Airlines Boeing 737, Henry Amazon was sharing a row of seats with an old Mexican in a black suit who crossed himself and mumbled Latin as they took off over the high brown scud covering Mexico City. Strangely enough, the part of the smuggle that Henry dreaded most was the forty-five-minute plane ride into Oaxaca. Planes made Amazon uncomfortable, and Mexican planes left him terrified. The air over the 9,000-foot mountains was never very steady, and on bad days Mexicana's planes experienced sudden drops and shuddering bumps that left Henry digging his nails into the armrests. When the plane skipped and fluttered, the pressure in Henry's stomach made him squirm. Amazon ignored the stewardess's offer of orange juice and rolls, and tried to ease his stomach by chewing Dentyne. He stared out the window and tried to watch the clouds.

As the Boeing dropped through the overcast, Amazon could see that the brown ridges snaking together in a lacy pattern on the ground below were dropping and getting steadily greener as the forests on their sides thickened. Gradually, the steep forest was interrupted by an occasional cultivated patch nestled in a hollow or on the side of a ravine. The plane skimmed along the belly of a gray hammerhead cloud and began descending as the ground below got flatter and flatter. Tilled fields now covered the widening space between ridges in a green patchwork.

Amazon began to relax when the 737 crossed over the last high peak and the Oaxaca Valley opened up ahead. The pilot announced in Spanish and English that the plane was passing over the ruins of

Monte Albán, ancient capital of the Zapotec nation, first excavated in 1931. The ruins appeared as a few quick arrangements of stone on the crest of a peak passing suddenly far beneath the wing, and then the Boeing began a slow turn around the city of Oaxaca, approaching the runway south of town. Amazon rolled his gum in a ball and stuck it under his seat.

The plane touched down with a sharp rubber slap and taxied toward the one-story terminal. The sun was burning off the last of the morning mist. Yoked oxen were working the fields around the airport. August is the last full month of Oaxaca's rainy season, and the runway tarmac was splotched with puddles. The Mexicana flight came to a halt opposite a detachment of four soldiers in full combat gear. The soldiers were carrying automatic weapons and lounging around a sandbag emplacement, guarding three blue-and-white helicopters. One private was sitting on an oil drum, balancing his Belgian machine gun between his feet while he threw pebbles at a stringy brown dog. The rest were standing, or leaning on the bags. The helicopters belonged to the Policía Judicial Federal, Mexico's national drug police. The *Federales* used them to hunt marijuana and to pursue *traficantes* all over the Oaxaca Valley and into the surrounding hills. The choppers looked like locusts squatting on the asphalt. Henry Amazon let his breath escape between his teeth with a hissing sound, then made his way up the aisle, out the exit, and bolted down the stairs for solid ground.

2

Henry Amazon's first piece of business in Oaxaca was to meet his partner, Zoro CeAttl. After the incident with the Huaves in the van, El Tortuga had decided to give up working as a loner. Through a friend, he had found Zoro in the state of Guerrero, where he lived. Zoro CeAttl had paid for his large ranch by running wetbacks into California. Zoro CeAttl was half Mixtec Indian and could get along in four of the Zapotec language's twenty or more dialects. He was good with Indians and kept track of the local marijuana market. After three years of heavily shared risks, Zoro and the American were as close as brothers. On their last trip, Zoro, Amazon, and a Zapotec driver had hidden in the jungle along the coast for two days and nights. They were waiting for the soldiers at the army roadblock three miles up the road to pack up and go back to base. When they did, and Amazon's 206-pound load reached Colorado, Henry and Zoro made arrangements for their next meeting. They would make contact on the last day of August at a favorite diner of theirs along the Mexico City highway.

Amazon rented a Ford LTD from Hertz at the airport and started across Oaxaca. To Henry, driving in Mexico was a game. When in doubt, his rule of thumb was to accelerate, with his hand on the horn. The technique was especially effective in an LTD. No one wants to run into one. The big Fords are the Coupe de Villes of Mexico. Virtually all of the vehicles on Mexican roads are made inside the country under manufacturing agreements with major automakers. Mexican Ford trucks, Volkswagens, Toyotas, and International Harvester–licensed Dina flatbeds dominate traffic. Prohibitive duties exclude cars manufactured across the border. In a country where most of the people move on burros, oxen, or their own feet, an LTD is a sure sign of money and, therefore, influence.

Henry Amazon looked both ways and pulled onto the two-lane highway that leads from the airport to the city. In five minutes, he reached the outskirts of town. The burro traffic along the edge of the road had appreciably increased. The beasts around the airport had lugged towering mounds of freshly cut alfalfa on their backs, but as he approached the city, Amazon saw more and more men with machetes who were driving burros laden with one- and two-inch-thick lengths of stick. These men cut the wood out in the countryside and then wholesaled it in Oaxaca to vendors who quartered each stick, chopped the quarters into one-inch blocks, and then sold the blocks six or eight at a time in the squatter settlements as cooking fuel. Amazon turned off the highway, cut through the streets on Oaxaca's edge until he reached the Mexico City road, and followed the signs toward Matamoros.

After half an hour of driving, Henry Amazon's Ford pushed up a gentle rise. A brick house with a cane roof sat off to the right, with a thirty-foot flowering tree by the front gate. The flowers were bright and burgundy-colored. A little more than a mile ahead on the left was a light-green café and a bus stop. Amazon parked the Ford on the road shoulder out in front of the café and went inside to wait for Zoro.

Zoro CeAttl arrived twenty minutes later on a third-class bus. Henry Amazon could hear it coming five minutes before it arrived. Mexican buses are all equipped with an exhaust system of three-inch pipe that runs straight from the engine under the length of the carriage and up the back to the roof level, with no muffler anywhere along the way. While accelerating, the buses emit a tenor "blaaat" that can be heard for miles. By law, there are no bus companies. Each bus is owned by a driver who has a license to ply a given route. Ticket prices are controlled by the federal government, and each bus has its own name and decoration. The one Zoro rode on was orange, and "El Tiburon" (The Shark) was painted in purple on each side. A crudely brushed line of green waves ran the length of the vehicle, the bottom half was splattered with mud, and the roof was piled high with baggage. Zoro CeAttl got out, climbed the ladder to the cargo rack, and tossed his suitcase down. The two amigos greeted each other with big smiles and claps on the shoulders.

Zoro was hungry and ordered a dish of mole (chunks of meat in a thick brown sauce laced with chocolate) from the old woman who ran the diner. The two smugglers sat in the corner of the room at one of the two oilcloth-covered tables, while the proprietor heated her mole in a pot braced over a small mound of glowing one-inch wooden cubes. When Zoro asked for coffee, she produced a bowl of hot water and a jar of Nescafé. CeAttl and Amazon soon stopped chatting and got down to work. Henry wanted to locate 250 pounds of marijuana as quickly as possible. They knew that Flacco, the Zapotec they had dealt with the last time, had close to 100 pounds, and he'd mentioned a farmer on the west side of Ocotlán who had 100 pounds more. CeAttl said he knew another Indian named Jesús on the San Dionisio road who could round the load out with some very high quality leaf. Zoro would leave a message for him. Zoro CeAttl paid the woman, went outside, and threw his bag into the

LTD trunk. In the bag, Zoro had a Browning .45-caliber automatic and two Smith & Wesson .38 Specials that he and Amazon planned to trade for weed.

The Oaxaca Valley is shaped roughly like a three-cornered star. Oaxaca, population 120,000, sits at the star's axis, 240 miles south of Mexico City and 900 miles south of San Antonio, Texas. One corner points toward Puerto Ángel, another toward Tehuantepec, and a third toward Puebla and Mexico City. After an hour's drive in the valley toward Puebla, the elevation rises from Oaxaca's 6,000 feet to close to 9,000. After three hours of driving the other way, toward Puerto Ángel, the road drops into tropical jungle, full of avocado trees and mangoes.

Most of the state of Oaxaca's 2.5 million citizens are Indians. There are approximately 250 Zapotec villages in the valley of Oaxaca. The largest are full of small brick and adobe houses with stuccoed walls and cane or tin roofs. The smaller villages are collections of one-room cane huts back in the bush. The police are rarely seen outside Oaxaca City, and then only in the larger villages. The Zapotecs live on the valley floor and on ever-higher levels that reach up into the mountains. The Zapotecs in established houses stay in one place and farm with oxen and wooden single-blade plows. But after you pass the sixth village back from any dirt road, you can find small clusters of Indians still living as they did two thousand years ago, in the cycle of camping for a season, planting, and then moving on into the depths of the Sierra Madre del Sur to camp and plant again.

What always amazed Henry Amazon about the Zapotecs was how many of them there were, and how hard they were to see. As he and CeAttl sped onto the Mitla road, Henry stared ahead at the green valley walls that rose on the horizon. The tops of the far mountains were obscured by formations of angry gray thunderheads advancing on toward the Pacific Ocean, ninety miles away. In Colorado, the scene would have been called a wilderness, but in Oaxaca the seemingly unpopulated landscape is actually dense with Indians. There are few places to go in the daylight in Oaxaca where you cannot be seen by someone. Under the trees, in the shade of rocks, and along the ravines, families of Zapotecs cluster. Once members of a noble and thriving civilization, the Indians are now at the bottom of Oaxaca's economic ladder. Their poverty has created political unrest in every corner of the valley.

According to the Mexican labor department, 74 percent of all of Oaxaca's families live on less than 200 pesos ($8) a month. A quarter of them have electricity, and fewer than that have running water; 87 percent live in one or two rooms and cannot afford to buy milk, eggs, or meat. Their principal nourishment is corn and beans. The price of beans has risen 310 percent in the last two years, and the cost of corn tortillas has quadrupled. Most Zapotecs try to survive by growing corn and maguey cactus. Many cannot even produce enough corn for their own consumption. The maguey plants take ten years to mature. The leaves are then discarded and the heart of the cactus is boiled down into the drink mescal, which can be consumed as it is or further refined into tequila. A truckload of mature maguey hearts yields $10—a dollar a year—to the family that grows it. Some of the villages earn extra money from weaving and from handicrafts, but without their marijuana crops, a lot of Zapotecs would have no cash income at all.

Cannabis is grown throughout the valley and up in the Sierra Madre del Sur. Plots are largest deep in the mountains. The two-acre to ten-acre plantations back there are guarded by Indians who carry automatic weapons and have been seen drinking Coors beer. Some of those crops are serviced by airstrips cut into the mountainsides. However, most of Oaxaca's marijuana is grown in family patches of twenty to fifty plants, or in village crops of up to five hundred. If thirty of a family's B-quality plants reach reasonably lush maturity, their sale will net some $600, almost six times the average family's total yearly income from other sources. Since the temperature in the region rarely drops below 60 degrees Fahrenheit, a fresh marijuana crop can be harvested every four months. The best harvest of all is at the end of the rainy season in late August and early September.

Zoro CeAttl was counting on the Indian Jesús for the best leaf. Jesús had relatives in a village back in the mountains that was famous for its *sin semilla*, mature female marijuana plants that have never been pollinated and therefore have no seeds. In their unpollinated frustration, the virgin plants exude resin in large quantities that coats the leaves, making them sticky to the touch. Jesús had said he would have some when Zoro returned. It was of triple-A grade. Henry Amazon could sell that kind of marijuana for more than $1,000 a pound in Colorado.

About four miles past Mitla, Zoro began looking for the place where Jesús had said to leave messages for him. The highway had risen over the crest of a ridge, and when the LTD reached the first dirt road on the downhill side, Zoro motioned for Henry Amazon to turn onto it. After traveling another two hundred yards, he told Henry to stop. Next to the road, someone had planted a straight line of eight maguey. Behind it, the countryside was covered with low trees, tall grass, brush, and cactuses. Zoro collected several stones the size of his fist, piled them in front of the first maguey, and hopped back in the car. Jesús would see the signal and get in touch with Zoro through a Zapotec in town. For all the *traficantes* knew, the Indian was watching them at that moment.

"Now let's go find Flacco," CeAttl said. Amazon drove back to the highway and continued down the hill. Nearly twelve miles later, he turned right onto a dirt lane and slowed to twenty miles an hour. Stones rattled off the LTD's underbelly. After five minutes, the road dipped as it entered Flacco's village, a mescal village. Maguey hearts were boiled here. The edges of the street were dotted with heaps of processed cactus pulp, and the fresh piles were still steaming. Flacco's village stank. The boiling of maguey releases an odor like that of gangrene. Henry Amazon sucked some air into his lungs and rolled the Ford's window up. A matted white dog yapped after the LTD. A double-axle Dina truck loaded with mescal barrels was approaching from the opposite direction, and the two vehicles met at a spot where a small creek crossed the street. Henry Amazon came to a full stop in the muddy creek bottom as the truck squeezed by, reeking of maguey juice and splashing slop on the side of the rental car. The white dog attacked the oncoming Dina's wheel and was run over.

The two smugglers stopped at the storefront on the next corner, where a Zapotec family sold groceries and soft drinks. Henry and Zoro got out of the car and asked for some orange-flavored Tehuacán mineral water. Henry Amazon's eyes began to smart from the shock of the mescal factories' stench. The man behind the counter took their order and sent his daughter to fetch the bottles from the cooler. He remembered Zoro from before and was very friendly. Zoro told him to tell Flacco to get in touch "the usual way," and to tell him Zoro was in a hurry. The man said he would, and that Flacco had left something there for him. The storekeeper produced a newspaper-wrapped parcel the size of two fingers. Zoro slipped it into his boot in one quick movement and thanked the man. The two smugglers took their drinks and drove back out of the village. The dead dog was still in the road. Henry wanted to go around it, but there was no room. So he accelerated over the carcass, drove to the highway, and turned toward Oaxaca, planning to check into a motel room and wait for everyone to get in touch.

When they crossed back over the ridge, Zoro opened Flacco's package, rolled a joint using the marijuana sample inside, and lit it up. The leaf was of B quality, with decent flavor and a sneaky punch that came on slowly. The LTD wound its way down the mountainside. Off to their right, the northeastern end of the valley spread out under an enormous sky full of thin gray silk, rushing along in patches. Zoro CeAttl stared west toward Ixtlán and in five minutes had spotted one of the *Federales'* helicopters. It was a blue-and-white speck ten miles to the northwest. Zoro watched as the chopper darted over a ridge, circled a ravine, and climbed to surmount the next ridge and hunt again. When the pilot sights weed, the area is bombed with defoliants and noxious chemicals. The number of Indians who have been poisoned during or after this procedure remains an unrecorded statistic. Loads of weed coated with herbicides have recently begun to appear in the New York, Boston, and Toronto marijuana markets. The National Institute on Drug Abuse has just begun to study the problem but as yet has no idea what the long-term effects of smoking poisoned marijuana may prove to be. Those who have consumed defoliant-laced pot experience severe headaches and occasional vomiting.

3

The effort against marijuana cultivation is the sole concern of the Judicial Federal. The Policía Judicial del Estado de Oaxaca (state police), the other major police force operating in Oaxaca, concerns itself with the rest of criminal activity. Political action is at the top of its list. During the last week of August and the beginning of September, six different high-ranking officials from Mexico City flew in to confer with the *jefe* of the Policía Judicial, Jaime C. Palencia Jiménez. Palencia, a thirty-one-year-old *huero*—a white Mexican—from Mexico City, had been appointed to his provincial post five months earlier. The visitors, who came from the division of the Mexican attorney general's office that concerns itself with political crimes, were apprehensive not only about Indians but also about students. Several months earlier, the state had been in open turmoil. The governor had been removed for having let things "get out of hand." Palencia was imported as part of the new administration. The trouble had begun at the university on Oaxaca's north side. When a Communist slate was victorious in the student body elections, the former governor had refused to let it assume office and had imposed his own set of student officers. The result was a series of demonstrations that became a running battle, one that left more than forty people dead. The governor was finally replaced by an army general who allowed new elections to be held. This time, the winning leftist student slate was allowed to assume office.

In the course of the struggle at the university, the police had picked up reports of numbers of *huero* and mestizo (Mexicans of Indian-Spanish extraction) students making contact with insurgent Zapotecs in the south end of the valley and in the surrounding Sierra Madre. It was this alliance that bothered the political officers who came to visit the *jefe*. They worried about a replay of the events of the early seventies, when the neighboring state of Guerrero had been torn by guerrilla uprisings. Things there had subsided only after an extensive campaign by the army that broke the rebel bands and sent scattered remnants fleeing south into the state of Oaxaca.

The leader of the Guerrero *guerrilleros*, Lucio Cabañas, was finally ambushed and killed in December 1974.

Historically, the Zapotecs have been a rebellious people. Barefoot Oaxaca Indians fought in the armies of José María Morelos, the half-breed priest who led southern Mexico against the Spaniards in the early 1800s, and they fought under Gregorio Meléndez when he rose up in 1835 against the "despots" who had "betrayed" Mexico's new independence. Benito Juárez, the founder of the modern state of Mexico, was a full-blooded Zapotec. When Juárez nationalized the holdings of the Roman Catholic Church, Mexico was soon occupied by a French army. Zapotecs—half of them unarmed—in white cotton "pajamas," *huaraches*, and black felt hats with red bands fought the French and the *hueros* of the conservative Catholic militia outside Juchitán in September of 1866. Led by a chieftain named Nine Lives, the Indians pushed the French back past Tehuantepec. Zapotecs were used by both sides in the civil wars following the revolution of 1910. They are a people short in stature, but they fought with the desperation that only those who live on next to nothing a month can feel.

Guerrilleros have been a part of life in the Oaxaca Valley since before the arrival of Cortés, and they are still a part of it today. The modern guerrilla bands are scattered and largely isolated from one another. Most of the rebels are Indians whose opposition is fueled by their poverty and resentment of the rich *hueros'* domination of Mexican life. The guerrillas have little political leverage and are struggling to rearm and regroup after four years of military reverses. The most famous of the local guerrilla leaders is called El Coyote, a Zapotec *brujo* (medicine man) from deep in the mountains. Some of the bands are Marxist-Leninist, some are *bandidos*, but most are just groups of Indians who are tired of being at the bottom of the pile. The *guerrilleros* are usually on the move, traveling as far south as Guatemala and then journeying north again along the ridge of mountains that runs along Mexico's spine. Some of the marijuana plantations in the South Sierra Madre pay for the military efforts of the more organized bands. Airstrips are used by *traficantes* who fly in and barter crates of weapons and ammunition for A-quality weed. The strongest of all of Oaxaca's armed political splinter groups is the Unión del Pueblo. The political officers from Mexico City who visited Jaime Palencia were worried that the UDP had recruited student members through contacts in the Communist villages around the south valley. Walls in neighboring Ocotlán are dotted with crudely splashed hammer-and-sickle graffiti.

The state police exercises its political concern from a distance. It lacks the helicopters and other sophisticated equipment used by the *Federales*, and state policemen are prone to treat their own safety as their first priority. Rarely do they or the *Federales* risk moving around the valley after dark, and then only with an army escort.

4

Early Thursday morning, Zoro heard the sound of the *Federales'* helicopters again. He was sleeping in the bed nearer to the motel-room window when the droning pried his eyes open. It was 6:30 a.m. Zoro CeAttl swung his legs onto the floor and rubbed his face. Henry Amazon was still asleep on the other bed. They had holed up in a three-room establishment in the south end of the valley, 120 pesos ($5) a night. Zoro lifted one of the slats in the Venetian blinds and peered out. Two choppers were heading farther south, specks on the far mountains. Zoro grinned. During June, two Indians had shown him the remains of another helicopter that was wedged into a ravine in the southern foothills, in Zapotec territory. The blue-and-white paint was burned off, and the helicopter was a twisted wreckage among the rocks. The Zapotecs said the guards at the nearby fields had shot it down. Two *Federales* were killed, they said. After the crash, they maintained, another of the blue-and-whites came and, with the machine gun in the side door, killed everyone in sight of the ravine. The Indians claimed that twenty-six men from their village had been shot.

Zoro liked the idea that the men in the choppers were targets, too. Zoro CeAttl had come to hate the police of the Judicial Federal. He considered them to be murderers and thieves who, in his experience, shot people only when they could not shoot back. Officially, the

Judicial Federal is the Republic of Mexico's federal police force. Half of the organization's three hundred agents perform functions roughly similar to those of the American FBI; the other agents concern themselves with drug-control efforts. The *Federales* came into their own under former president Luis Echeverría. A formal training program was established, and selected agents were sent to Washington, D.C., for additional instruction. As the American government made more and more money available, both for training and in direct grants, the Judicial Federal began to take its role against the *traficantes* more seriously. The federal agents usually operate in squads of eight or ten, never for extended periods of time in any one location. An agent will work the frontier along the American border for a month, then move to Guerrero and head on to Veracruz. The Mexicans work closely with the American Drug Enforcement Agency and with INTERPOL, the international police organization. The DEA maintains its headquarters in the American embassy in Mexico City and fields thirty-two agents, who work in pairs dispensing "technical assistance."

Money for the *Federales*' effort is appropriated as part of the State Department's budget for international narcotics programs. Since drug-enforcement efforts were accelerated under the Nixon administration, the *Federales*' appropriation from the United States has grown each year to the present annual level of nearly $16 million. Much of the money is spent on blue-and-white helicopters, on radios, and for other machinery. Another part of the appropriation is plugged directly into the *Federales*' salary ladder. Federal agents live very well by Mexican standards. In Oaxaca, they work out of an office over a funeral parlor near the *zócalo*, the central square in the heart of the city.

As August became September, the agents of the Judicial Federal knew it was harvesttime, too. Teams from Mexico City, from the frontier, and from Guerrero, along with DEA agents, had been coming in and out of Oaxaca steadily all month. The *Federales* kept their choppers in the air, and occasionally went out with army units at night to set up roadblocks. During the last few weeks, the Indians said, a federal team had been cruising the valley in a van with soda-pop advertisements on the sides. The *Federales* do not wear uniforms but seem to be most comfortable in polyester suits and open-collar shirts. *Federales* are either mestizos or *hueros*; no one in Oaxaca has ever seen a full-blooded Indian *Federal*. Zapotecs say the *Federales*' eyes give them away. According to the Indians, they have "bad eyes," and the Zapotecs will look in another direction if they see *Federales* face-to-face.

5

Shortly before noon on Thursday, after Henry Amazon awoke complaining of insect bites, he and Zoro drove to a spot twelve blocks from the Judicial Federal office to pick up their messages. The drop spot was a stall in Oaxaca's downtown market, where an old Indian woman sold shirts and woven belts. The downtown market fills two buildings, each a half-block square, and overflows into the streets for another two blocks. Zapotecs from all over the valley take third-class buses into town, their goods tied to the roofs, then unload and set up shop. The market smelled of blood and leather, laced with the smoke from twenty cooking fires. Henry and Zoro made their way past sheets of thin beef hanging on hooks, buckets of shrimp from the coast, piles of serapes, oranges, discount *huaraches,* tortillas, and black pottery, looking for the old woman.

Zoro had first met the woman's husband the year before, when he had stopped in their village for an orange Tehuacán. Zoro had heard music, drunken laughter, and the sound of gunfire and had gone around the corner to investigate. There appeared to be a party going on, and there was lots of shouting and shooting of *pistolas* into the air. Zoro CeAttl asked one of the men squatting by the wall what they were celebrating. The Indian said it was a funeral. A young child had died, he explained, and when the young die they have not lived long enough to accumulate much sin, so they are assured of going to heaven. There was no reason to be sad. The man invited the stranger to drink mescal, and Zoro ended up staying there all day. After two more visits from Zoro, the Indian agreed that his wife would take CeAttl's messages for 100 pesos ($4.40) a month. When Henry and Zoro found the woman, she said that both Flacco and Jesús had checked in. Flacco would meet the two *traficantes* on the Teotitlán road at four that afternoon. Jesús said that they should come to the usual place at midnight on Saturday night, and that they should be ready to do business. Zoro and Amazon headed back for the LTD.

On the street outside, Henry Amazon complained to his partner. "This is slow, Zoro. I mean *slow*. We're gonna have to goddamn sit around all day. It's gonna take a week to get the load."

CeAttl shrugged. "What can we do, amigo? It will speed up. You'll see."

Henry didn't answer. The biggest part of a *traficante*'s time is spent waiting, but Henry still hated it. Amazon and CeAttl wasted an hour drinking coffee on the terrace of the Hotel Marqués del Valle across from the *zócalo*, went back to the market to buy a few blankets, and then decided to visit Monte Albán. Amazon had toured the ruins at least thirty times before, but he was still fascinated by the rich history of the nation of marijuana growers.

At its height, Monte Albán was the capital of a Zapotec nation that controlled the entire valley, and at times extended as far south as Tehuantepec on the Pacific coast. Monte Albán is six miles southwest of the modern-day city of Oaxaca, on an isolated group of hills that rise out of the countryside near the hub of the valley. The view from the ruins commands Oaxaca and most of the surrounding countryside. Until Mexico's leading archaeologist, Alfonso Caso, began digging there in 1931, Monte Albán was just a cluster of brush-covered hills that had lumpish outlines. Caso's excavation immediately began uncovering a series of ancient tombs on the tallest hill. At first, the diggers found few artifacts, but when they broke through a fitted stone roof into a room divided into four chambers, Caso uncovered one of the richest archaeological finds in the New World. The tomb was the burial place of eight chieftains who had been laid to rest surrounded by carved jade figures, gold diadems, pearl earrings, turquoise mosaics, thirty strips of intricately carved jaguar bone, a solid-gold mask, and much more. Five hundred pieces of treasure were shipped to Mexico City under military guard, and the artifacts were returned to the valley only after the State of Oaxaca fought a lengthy court battle against the federal government.

The excavation of Monte Albán has continued fitfully, until today the entire Great Plaza on the crest of the hill is open to tourists, who come there from the rest of Mexico, the United States, Canada, and France. The Zapotecs themselves seem to have lost any sense of connection with the ruins, and only the sleaziest of Indians appear there to sell trinkets and phony artifacts to *turistas*. Few if any Zapotecs can afford the 10-peso admission charge.

The Great Plaza is a group of seven buildings of varying sizes surrounding a central rectangle, connected by inside passageways and outside steps. This is only a small fraction of the ancient city that once covered more than twenty-four square miles. The "classic epoch" at Monte Albán lasted from the sixth to the twelfth centuries A.D. The Monte Albán Indians were master craftsmen and left behind beautiful carved jade, polychrome frescoes, and clay urns. The ancient Zapotecs worshiped a variety of gods. A special favorite was Quetzalcoatl: "Plumed Serpent," "The Breath of Life," the lord of the creative forces, the sky and the wind. Quetzalcoatl was the god of peace, art, wisdom, and prosperity. The third son of the Lord and Lady of Substance, Quetzalcoatl disguised himself as an ant, discovered maize under the mountain Popocatépetl, and gave the seeds to the Indians. He also invented the arts, science, and the calendar. Quetzalcoatl had many incarnations. In one of his most glorious, he made a raft from snakes and sailed to Tlapallàn, where he immolated himself. Quetzalcoatl's ashes turned into birds, and his heart became Venus, the morning star. On ceremonial occasions, Zapotec nobles wore jaguar-head helmets topped with long feathers from the bright green quetzal bird.

Monte Albán was finally abandoned when the civilization could no longer support the city's magnificence. The Zapotecs had built a sophisticated and extensive urban culture, but their agriculture could no longer keep pace with their population. The Indians left their city and moved to the other side of the valley. In the fourteenth and fifteenth centuries, while the Indians were trying to stave off the onrushing Aztec empire, Zapotec culture flourished briefly again at Yagul, Mitla, and as far away as Tehuantepec. In 1465, the Zapotec army was surrounded by Aztec legions in the fortress atop Guiengola Mountain. The Zapotecs broke the siege by sneaking down the mountain at night, kidnapping Aztecs, and carrying them back to the Zapotec lines, where they were butchered and eaten. The Zapotecs were finally conquered in 1495, only to be "liberated" twenty-six years later by the Spaniard Hernán Cortés.

At first the Zapotecs welcomed the advent of Cortés as a means to throw off the control of the Aztec empire and revenge themselves on their Mixtec neighbors. Within twenty years, the Spaniards turned on their former Indian allies and proceeded to crush all Zapotec outposts. Dominican friars dug out the ritually buried corpses of past chieftains and dragged them through the streets. Native Zapotec music, poetry, and dances were forbidden. Indians caught with ancient hand-painted hieroglyphic scrolls were tortured, and the scrolls destroyed. The dominance of Spain and her church were complete. The evidence is still visible from the heights of Monte Albán today. In village after village, one-room brick huts with cane roofs cluster around three-story Catholic churches complete with forty-foot ceilings, mahogany pews, and gilt altars.

6

After three hours of sitting on the ruins and looking out at Oaxaca, Henry Amazon's watch indicated that it was time to meet Flacco. He and Zoro drove down the mountain toward Mitla. It took half an hour to reach the Teotitlán road. Shortly after, Zoro spotted Flacco's truck pulled off the dirt in the thick brush bordering a cornfield. Henry Amazon pulled in behind.

Flacco was thin as a rail and came up to Henry Amazon's shoulder. His teeth were stained a deep brown color near the gums. The brown paled to yellow the closer it got to the chewing edge. His upper lip was covered with a sparse mustache. The Indian wore a T-shirt, twill pants, and an ancient pair of *huarache* sandals. His heels were knobbed with a thick wall of calluses. Flacco owned his bright yellow Dina truck with his father and four brothers. It was theirs by virtue of long years of hauling maguey, thanks to lots of marijuana cultivation, and a small but usurious loan from a man in Mitla. By Indian standards, the truck represented a great deal of wealth, and Flacco's family was considered well-off. The Dina's cab was fringed in red tassels that dangled inside the entire width of the windshield. The grille was covered with a welded network of steel pipe designed to act like a locomotive's cowcatcher and called a *tomba burro* (donkey dropper). Loaded trucks in Oaxaca do not stop for livestock on the road. After everyone had said *"mucho gusto"* and got reacquainted, Flacco broached the subject of money. He wanted 800 pesos ($35) a pound. Zoro CeAttl translated. Henry Amazon coughed and shook his head. He lowered his voice and spoke in a hard, negotiating tone.

"Tell him not for that shit he left with the Indian," Amazon instructed his partner. "That ain't worth six hundred [$26]." Flacco responded that the sample had been offered just to show them what else was around. His was much better. Flacco produced another packet from his pocket and handed it to Henry to examine. The Indian said he had ninety-eight pounds of it. Amazon unfolded the paper, picked the cutting up by its stem, and smelled the marijuana carefully. The leaves were stickier than those in the last sample, and had dried a deeper green with a gold tinge. "That's worth seven hundred [$31]," Amazon told Zoro. Zoro translated and Flacco looked hurt. He said that anything under 750 ($33) was impossible. Amazon immediately answered that he would pay 750 if Flacco would carry it with them as far as Guerrero. Flacco was a little taken aback. He did not like to risk his Dina. Henry Amazon sensed the Indian's mood and reached into his boot for the clincher. The gringo pulled out a chromed snub-nosed .38 and handed it to the startled Zapotec, butt first. Flacco rolled the weapon between his hands and hefted it.

"Tell him we'll throw that in for him to keep now, since he's taking a risk," Amazon told Zoro. "But we don't pay for the weed till the other end of the line."

Zoro translated and Flacco agreed. The only way for an Indian to get a gun in Oaxaca is for a *traficante* to sell it to him. Gun possession is dealt with harshly by the authorities. Flacco said he would meet them at 8:30 that night with the other Zapotec he had mentioned, the one who had a fresh crop. Flacco tucked his new *pistola* in his pants and mounted the family Dina. Amazon and CeAttl went back to the motel for a nap. An hour later, a curtain of rain began working slowly up the valley from Monte Albán. It fell in silver streaks, forcing the goat herds and the cruising red wasps to seek the protection of bushes and trees.

7

At 8:30 on Thursday evening, September 1, the two smugglers were sitting inside their LTD with the windows rolled up, across from the produce market on Mitla's main street. The Zapotec women in the market stalls were beginning to pack up their wares under the pale glare of a string of bare bulbs. Electricity came to Mitla two years ago. It was still raining outside. A one-tent entertainment, the Frank Brown International Circus, was in the village for the night, and Mitla rang with the sounds of hurdy-gurdy music. The first show was scheduled for 9 p.m., and Zapotec families huddled under the market awnings, waiting.

Mitla is the Zapotecs' ancient "Abode of the Dead." Called *Yoo-paa* in their native tongue, it was the Indian empire's spiritual heart. The high priests lived there in low, flat-roofed temples that, the Spanish missionaries wrote, were "prouder and more magnificent than any seen in New Spain." The central temple was built on four levels, three of which were underground. The ground level was reserved for the gods. The first floor below that was a burial chamber for high priests. The level below the priests' floor was a burial place for kings. The lowest level was a common burial site for Zapotecs who died in battle. In the fourteenth and fifteenth centuries, sick and unhappy Indians of all kinds went to Mitla to beg to be allowed into this last chamber, so they could die there and enjoy eternal bliss. Legend has it that when the Dominican priests arrived, they discovered a tunnel leading out of the bottom chamber going even deeper into the earth. The priests started to explore the passageway but were overcome with fright. Calling the tunnel a "backdoor to hell," the Dominicans sealed it up so well that, the legend says, no trace of it can be found today.

At 8:50, Zoro and Amazon spotted Flacco's yellow Dina splashing down the street. The Indian pulled in behind the LTD and got out. The Zapotec accompanying Flacco was taller and even narrower. The other Indian's name was Victorio, and he had not yet grown a mustache. His deep brown face, like Flacco's, was dominated by a broad nose and eyelids that appeared to droop. While the four of them huddled under an awning and talked, Victorio's fingers pinched the seams of his khaki pants. The Indian had never done business with a gringo before. Henry Amazon and Zoro CeAttl tried to put him at ease, with little success. Victorio smiled in greeting, but his face quickly returned to its flat set. He carried a machete in his belt. The smugglers explained that since they had not done business with Victorio before, they would want to see his load when they talked price. The Indian said it could happen in six hours, at 3 a.m. Flacco suggested that they meet in a gully that ran along the San Dionisio road. Amazon agreed and leaned against the wall with Zoro while the Indians beat back up the street against the deluge. The hurdy-gurdy music made the adobe wall behind the smugglers vibrate.

"He sure was nervous," Henry said.

"Sure he was," Zoro answered. Henry Amazon's partner spoke the "s" with a "ch" sound. "Who wouldn't be?"

The last month had been a very bad one for smugglers, and everyone in Oaxaca knew it.

8

Late Saturday morning, July 30, 1977, a Zapotec farmer from the southeastern end of the valley had walked into the local police office in the village of Ocotlán and recounted a grisly story. He had been approaching the village of San Miguel on his way from

San Dionisio. At a spot where the road dipped and a creek crossed it, there was a wash, a dry streambed. The farmer had seen smoke down the wash, investigated, and had come across the remains of two Volkswagen combis (vans). Both had been burned and were still smoldering. A mutilated gringo was lying dead a little ways down the wash, and a dead mestizo was sprawled near one of the combis. Inside the other van was a mound of charred flesh. The Indian didn't know how many people were in there. He didn't want to go too close, because of the smell.

The gringo down the wash was immediately identified by the Oaxaca state police as a *traficante* from Fort Bragg, California, named Paul Raymond Smith, age thirty-four. Smith had had a hard time of it before he died. According to the state police, his hands had been bound and he had been tortured with a long blade that had been dug into his pectoral muscle and twisted. After an unknown period of torture, Smith had somehow run 120 feet from the van before he had been shot twice in the back with a .22-caliber weapon. When he was sprawled on the ground, dying, one of Smith's murderers had driven a combi back and forth over the American's head, mashing the side of it and distorting his face. The Mexican corpse was identified as that of a small-time hustler from the city of Oaxaca, Luis Alberto Villagómez Hernández. He too had been shot to death.

The state-police detail that was sent out to fetch the bodies and inspect the scene on Sunday, July 31, was under the personal direction of *jefe* Jaime C. Palencia Jiménez, of the Policía Judicial. The police were armed with handguns and with automatic weapons. The investigators got what they needed and left quickly. During the entire time they were there, the cops' activity was watched from afar by a barely visible line of sixty Indians on the ridge overlooking the road. A number of the watching Zapotecs were carrying rifles and shotguns. The police determined that there were four more bodies in the second combi. All had been cooked by a fire hot enough to melt the combi's engine. Two of them were eighteen-year-old Americans who, like Smith, were from Fort Bragg, California. One was a woman, Teresa Kelly Ward. Before the burning, a bullet had been fired at point-blank range into the back of her skull. She was identified by her dental charts. The police tentatively identified the American male next to her as one Douglas Michael Dighero, although his dental exam was inconclusive. He was killed with a .765 Mauser rifle. The two incinerated mestizos were shot with a Mauser as well. One was named Manuel Hinojosa Hernández. The other, Alberto Aurelio Ortiz Mendoza, was also known as El Tasajo (Piece of Meat). El Tasajo was identified at the city morgue by an old woman who sold food to the Oaxaca whorehouse where Tasajo's girlfriend, Nanci Gama Cortés, worked. She recognized Tasajo by the wristwatch cooked into his wrist.

The murders made headlines all over Mexico. American tourists began leaving Oaxaca steadily on the two daily flights out of town. By Monday, August 1, Raul Mendiolba Sereno, director of the Judicial Federal, had flown to Oaxaca from Mexico City to assume command of the investigation. Shortly thereafter, the identification of the third Mexican body was withdrawn. According to fresh police announcements, this body only appeared to be that of El Tasajo. The wristwatch that the old woman recognized, they said, had been put on that body to throw the police off the scent. El Tasajo, the police maintained, was the real killer. He had been the middleman in a big dope deal, and had got greedy. According to the Judicial Federal, at the time of their deaths the gringo *traficantes* had been carrying $60,000 in American cash.

As the Judicial Federal investigators reconstructed the case, Paul Smith was the leader of a ring of California smugglers, six of whom—the state police gave their names as Richard and Darrell Peller, Donna Lynn Lefever, Betty Eggleston, and Ralph and Mark William Smith—were waiting for Paul Smith, Dighero, and Kelly Ward in the Mocambo Hotel in Veracruz. The Veracruz contingent had two Ford campers that had false bottoms in which the load was to be smuggled north. Paul Smith and the two eighteen-year-olds were apparently planning to purchase the marijuana and drive it to meet the campers on the Caribbean coast. If the Americans indeed intended to spend $60,000 on marijuana, they would be hauling almost a ton of weed. One of the burned VWs had been in Veracruz on July 20 and had been driven over the mountains to Oaxaca by Dighero and Kelly Ward. Paul Raymond Smith flew into Oaxaca on Mexicana Airlines and rented the other combi on July 27. The Oaxaca authorities say that the Americans made contact with El Tasajo shortly after their arrival and arranged a deal. The police version of events has the Oaxaca hoods luring the Americans out into the countryside and murdering the three of them along with three other Mexicans who went along for the ride. *Jefe* Palencia theorizes that El Tasajo had one accomplice. Tasajo and the accomplice got the jump on everyone else, and then tortured Smith until he told them where the money was. After the two conspirators had killed the five others, Tasajo turned on his accomplice so he would not have to share the loot. Tasajo then supposedly burned the vans and made it back to Oaxaca on foot, where the police claim he was seen at 9:30 a.m. Sunday. Tasajo's accomplice, the police say, was the unnamed third charred mestizo.

The Zapotecs in and around San Dionisio tell a story that differs in virtually every respect from that of the authorities. They believe the *Federales* were behind it all. Somehow the Judicial Federal had found out about the deal, and agents were waiting for Smith's party when it headed out for San Dionisio. The Indians believe that the *Federales* kept the money for themselves, telling Smith to run, then shooting him as he did so. The original coroner's report on the bodies stated that Smith had been tortured with a bayonet, a weapon that normally only the army and the *Federales* have access to. This report was withdrawn before becoming official. Two months later, there was still no official statement from the coroner on the results of Smith's autopsy. The police insist that Smith was tortured with a sheath knife he had been carrying on his belt. No knife or scabbard was found at the scene of the crime.

No one in San Dionisio stepped forward as an eyewitness to the murders, but several Zapotecs claimed to have seen events that, they say, took place the day after. Early Sunday morning, July 31, 1977—before the police claim to have had any information about the bodies lying dead in the wash—according to the Indians, a team of Judicial Federal police drove into San Dionisio looking for the man who had arranged to sell *sin semilla* to Smith and company. The suspect was not home, but they discovered three barrels of airplane fuel in his house, obviously stashed to supply planes at a hidden airstrip somewhere in the hills. The Indians claim the Judicial Federal officers then proceeded to burn the house down and arrest the missing Indian's thirteen-year-old son. According to the Indians, the boy escaped when he jumped out of the *Federales'* truck along the road to Ocotlán, and the youth went into hiding.

When asked about the Indians' version, the local Judicial Federal officials consulted their superiors in Mexico City, refused to comment, and directed all questions to *Jefe* Jaime Palencia Jiménez of the Policía Judicial del Estado de Oaxaca. Palencia denied the validity of the Indians' charges with a wave of his hand and a nervous laugh. When pressed, he refused to comment further.

9

One of the many people in Oaxaca who believed the Indians' story was an American named Timothy Robert Trout. Timmy Trout was a *traficante* from way back. Timmy left Oaxaca for several days immediately after the deaths of Smith, Kelly Ward, and Dighero, returning early the next week on a private plane that landed deep in the mountains. When he returned, Trout told his friends in Mitla that the *Federales* had killed Smith. Trout claimed to have known the dead American under the nickname "Huichol Pete." Huichol Pete, a.k.a. Smith, was a big mover whom Timmy had helped on deals over the years. Trout was visibly nervous. He stayed in the village and remained indoors. He kept repeating that the DEA was identifying big smugglers and giving their names to the *Federales* to kill. Trout was sure they were after him next. Timothy Trout was registered at the Hotel Mitla under the name Charles Nasey. Trout, a.k.a. Nasey, was wanted in California for evidence in several narcotics cases and was also being sought by the state of New Mexico for the armed robbery of an Albuquerque grocery store on May 15, 1975, and the subsequent assault on a pursuing police officer. Trout had begun smuggling in the late 1960s, when he was an Albuquerque hippie with hair down to his knees. Since then, he had filled out some and had his hair cut and styled; but Trout's business remained the same.

The people who knew Timmy Trout well swear that what happened on the morning of Thursday, August 11, 1977, was at heart an act of suicide by Timmy Trout. Instead of continuing to hide out, Timmy Trout got drunk and drove into the city of Oaxaca to walk around the *zócalo*. His friends say Timmy just got tired of waiting to be killed and made himself a target. Timmy, they said, could not resist tempting fate.

According to the Oaxaca state police, at 2:30 a.m., Thursday, August 11, Timothy Robert Trout, alias Charles Nasey, was staggering around downtown Oaxaca under the influence of an unknown drug, firing a .38 Special into the air. Elements of the 22nd Safety Patrol were, the police say, attempting to disarm the American when he fired on them. Timmy Trout was killed at the intersection of Mier and Terán Streets, five blocks from the *zócalo*, by a shot in the back from an M-1 carbine. No policemen were wounded, and no damage was done to their van. Several weeks after the incident, police said Trout's gun was not a .38 Special, as first reported, but a 9-millimeter automatic. According to Oaxaca press accounts shortly after the incident, the paraffin tests instituted as a part of the preliminary coroner's examination indicated that Timothy Robert Trout had not fired a powder-burning weapon at any time during the evening of August 10 or in the early morning of August 11. When questioned, the police confirmed these press accounts. This report, too, has yet to be made official. The Oaxaca police have no explanation for the fact that there were no powder traces on the American's hands.

Both the Drug Enforcement Agency and the Judicial Federal deny that they had any knowledge of Timothy Robert Trout until after they read reports of his death. Both agencies deny executing *traficantes* and deny all charges of stealing evidence or money. Trout's body was shipped to his lawyer in Albuquerque. Timmy's Mitla friends were not sure how he was actually killed, but they were skeptical about the official version of his death. The most common theory was that Timmy was kidnapped by the *Federales*, questioned, and eventually executed. They believed that the body was dumped after death at Mier and Terán Streets, and arrangements were made with the Safety Patrol to concoct a cover story. Most of those who knew Trout in Mitla quickly joined the outward flow of gringo tourists that increased as news of their countryman's death got around Oaxaca. It was only three weeks later that Americans began to return in their usual numbers, with Henry Amazon among them.

Henry Amazon had known Timmy Trout in the old days around Brownsville, Texas. Henry had always thought of Timothy Robert Trout as a "mean little gila monster son-of-a-bitch who'd off a cop in a hot minute." Henry Amazon could not believe that Timmy would fail to take any police with him if he had a gun.

10

At 2 a.m., Friday, September 2, Henry Amazon wheeled the LTD through the darkened village of Ocatlán. He and Zoro had napped at the motel and wakened to Henry's travel alarm. The rain had slowed to a constant film of mist drifting toward earth. There was no wind at all. Amazon was wearing a dirty brown serape and a ten-gallon hat. The LTD circled the Ocotlán square, sped along the street on the other side, and headed into the rolling hills. The road they followed touched the corner of San Miguel and ran on along the flats next to a stream. At around 2:30 a.m., the two smugglers passed the combi rented by Paul R. Smith the month before. The charred combi lurked in the mist, and water dripped where the windshield used to be. The departing state police had towed it out of the wash to high ground, stripped off its wheels, and abandoned it. The other van, with the bodies inside, had been hauled back to the city as evidence. Twenty minutes after passing the combi, Henry Amazon pulled the LTD into the brush and turned off the lights. The stream beside the road had turned, and it ran under a rough stone bridge. Henry and Zoro walked upstream and quickly lost sight of the road. Zoro led the way with a flashlight. When the two partners reached a tree that had fallen across the stream, Zoro switched the light off and they sat on a log.

"This is the spot," CeAttl whispered.

Henry Amazon couldn't see his hand when he held it in front of his face. He only sensed Zoro's presence nearby. It was like being locked in a closet. Henry pushed the button on his digital wristwatch regularly. Usually the glowing green numbers read exactly as they had the last time he had looked.

Henry Amazon jumped half a foot when a hard hand grasped his shoulder. "*Mucho gusto,*" a voice said. It was Victorio. Henry Amazon had no idea how long he had been standing behind them.

The Indian led Henry and Zoro down a trail that seemed to die in the underbrush on the other side of the log. Victorio kept pressing on through the branches, and they stumbled into a cave at the side of the streambed. Flacco was inside, standing beside a mound of burlap bags. His new pistol was tucked in his belt. Each bag was stuffed full of two-foot-long marijuana cuttings. Zoro flashed the light on the pile while Amazon opened one of the sacks. The air in the cave was saturated with the sweet odor of recently cured weed, a presence that seemed thick enough to cut. The marijuana had no red hairs on its leaves, and it had been harvested just a little too soon, but it was sticky green and colored gold around the edges: A-minus weed. The smugglers and Victorio quickly settled on a price of 700 pesos a pound, with a 25-peso-a-pound finder's fee for Flacco. Henry and Zoro arranged to meet with Victorio the next night at a spot off the Tehuantepec highway where they could exchange money and goods. Flacco would meet them at the same place with his loaded truck. As soon as their business was completed, the smugglers returned to the LTD. Henry Amazon could hardly keep his eyes open during the drive back to the motel, and he slept until Friday noon.

II

When he awoke, Zoro was already dressed. After Amazon showered with cold water, he and CeAttl got back in the car and drove up the highway to talk. Henry Amazon made it a rule never to discuss business in a rented room. Outside, the rain had given way to a bright afternoon. The only clouds that could be seen were toward Tehuantepec, and all else was a fluorescent blue. Henry Amazon was in a good mood. The load was coming together quickly. When it came time to move, he told Zoro, he figured the best way to do it was to divide the weed between Flacco's truck and the trunk of the LTD, but they would need another truck to cut the trail. The third—empty—truck would drive ahead of the two loaded vehicles. If it encountered roadblocks, the others would have enough warning to turn and run for it. Zoro said it was a fine plan if the "bell cow" knew what it was doing. Henry claimed he knew just the man for the job. His name was Rascon, and he lived in a village off the Mitla road. In half an hour, they had parked the LTD in the Indian's yard.

Rascon's wife came out of the house, where she had been making tortillas. She said Rascon was down at the field playing ball, and gave them directions. The game the Zapotecs play is called *mano fría* (cold hand). The ball field is a flat patch of dirt forty yards long and fifteen yards wide, bounded on each side by cornfields. Each player of *mano fría* is equipped with a glove attached to a knob five times the size of a large clenched fist. The knob is hard as rock, the accumulation of countless wrappings of leather strips. The average glove weighs twelve pounds. The surface of the knob is studded with the exposed heads of two hundred nails. The ball is the size of a cantaloupe and made from unprocessed rubber. The court is divided in half, eight men to a side, and the ball is delivered from the serving stone, a two-foot-high flat piece of rock with a slanting top. The server balances the ball on the head of his glove, drops it on the stone, and clubs it over the midline. *Mano fría* is a game of long volleys. The rubber ball is hard, and it reaches a velocity great enough to break an unprotected shoulder. Errant shots run through the corn like cannon fire. To the tourist's eye, the game resembles a sort of cave man's tennis. In the ancient version of the game, the ball was heavier and capable of crippling a player for life. At special games in Monte Albán, the entire losing team and the captain of the winners were ritually executed after the matches. They counted it a great honor.

Rascon was his team's champion server. When he saw Amazon and CeAttl standing on the sidelines, he shouted to them that only one game was left. His team won easily, and Rascon walked back to the village with the two smugglers. Rascon had good teeth and a mustache that ran the length of his cheek down to his jaw. When they reached his house, Rascon had his wife serve some hot soup made from chicken livers and bits of scrambled egg. They discussed business in his dining room. It had a dirt floor, a table, and a single bench. One end of the room was dominated by the family altar, a brick shelf holding several pictures of the Virgin of Guadalupe that had been clipped from magazines. At night, the Zapotec, his wife, and six children slept on mats rolled out on the floor.

Rascon wouldn't make the run for the money that Amazon offered. He said that 1,400 pesos ($60) wasn't enough. Who knew what would happen to his truck if there was trouble? Henry Amazon was in hurry and didn't know who else he could get for the job, so he upped the offer. He could give Rascon 1,400 pesos and a gun. The American slid a shiny .38 down the table to Rascon's bowl. The Zapotec smiled. After extracting promise that the smugglers would also pay the cost of gas for the truck, Rascon agreed. He would be waiting, in a spot they decided upon, at 2 a.m., Sunday, September 4.

Zoro and Henry were all smiles on the way back to the motel. The load was located, ready to be paid for and picked up. He and Zoro would buy as much of Jesús's *sin semilla* as they could afford, and they would then meet Flacco and Victorio, pick up Rascon, and get on the road to Zoro's ranch in Guerrero. All that was left for them to do now was to wait, being tourists for the next day and a half.

At 8:30 Friday evening, Amazon and CeAttl went to the *zócalo* for dinner. The Oaxaca State Band was giving a concert in the Victorian bandstand at the center of the square. The band members wore khaki uniforms with Sam Browne belts. The two smugglers took their dessert of fresh coconut ice cream at an outdoor table in front of the Hotel Marqués del Valle. The band music was loud enough to fill the whole city. The Mexican, French, and gringo tourists were lounging on the park benches or walking in the crowd that slowly circled the square on its sidewalks. The ritual is known as "The Dance." Everyone strolls and watches everyone else. Mingled in the crowd were hustlers, Zapotecs, gigolos, *Federales*, and smugglers. Amazon amused himself by trying to pick out the *traficantes*. They strolled by in twos and threes, looking just a bit too relaxed, and seemingly giving every passing face their personal *Federales* test.

One likely *traficante* locked eyes with Henry Amazon and quickly turned away. Henry watched the American walk on by and heard him talking to his friends and motioning toward Amazon's table as if the lanky American sitting there ought to be watched out for. A wrinkled Indian woman approached Amazon's table trying to sell a peso's worth of pumpkin seeds from her basket, but Amazon ignored her and listened to the brassy tones of the Oaxaca State Band echo off the surrounding mountains. They were playing the United States Marine Corps Hymn.

12

Twenty-four hours later, at 10 p.m., Saturday, September 3, 1977, Henry Amazon and Zoro CeAttl pulled out of the motel parking lot. They said little to each other. The air was full of thunder, and lightning flashed, but no rain was falling. Amazon could feel a pool of fear in his bowels. He and his Mixtec partner were about to run the gauntlet. The next few hours were the most dangerous part of the business, and the two of them had been smuggling long enough to know they could not help but be scared. Death might be waiting for a *traficante* on the other side of each approaching curve.

Their destination was along the dirt road that crossed fifty miles of rolling terrain to connect the Tehuantepec highway with the one leading to Puerto when they turned from the pavement onto the dirt road. The LTD advanced through the darkness with a steady crunch of pebbles under the wheels. Zoro peered into the fan of light cast by the Ford's high-beams, looking at the edge of the road for a formation of four boulders that had the shape of a pregnant woman. They reached it in fifteen minutes and pulled the car off on a shoulder. The hillside dropped off to the smugglers' left, and Zoro located the narrow trail that ran down it. They stepped from the car and Henry Amazon plunged into the solid darkness, following his partner's flashlight. The air was charged with the power of the approaching storm. A little way down the hill, the trail reached a clearing near a cane-roofed and adobe-walled hut. As the two smugglers approached the building, figures began to emerge from the darkness behind them. A few carried shotguns, and all were armed with machetes. Zoro and Henry turned and smiled.

"*Mucho gusto,*" Zoro opened.

The Zapotecs responded and said Jesús was inside. The two *traficantes* ducked through the doorway and their flashlight immediately fell on Jesús, squatting against the far wall. Next to him was another man in *huaraches* and wearing new twill pants. He was not an Indian. Zoro introduced Henry Amazon to Jesús, and then Jesús introduced the smugglers to his friend.

"*Mi amigo, el Cubano,*" Jesús began. ("My friend, the Cuban.")

Henry Amazon's eyes lit up. "So," the American said to himself, "this dude Jesús is connected to the Cubans. Hot damn." Henry Amazon had been hearing about the Cubans in the hills, off and on, for five years. He did not know what they were about, but he knew they were there. Amazon had seen Cubans in Oaxaca the previous November twice when he had been the middleman in a big weed shipment for two Canadians. The deal had been struck in a remote south-valley village. The Cubans had been there when the money was exchanged, and again at a hidden airstrip when the pickup was made with a Lockheed Loadstar. The village that supplied the weed was known to be under the protection of a sizeable guerrilla band. There were eight of the Cubans, dressed like Indians, but with different faces and different behavior. The Cubans and the Zapotecs carried carbines slung over their shoulders. All that Amazon could find out about them was that they came from much deeper in the Sierra Madre. The Cubans might have been Communists who had filtered in over the years or remnants of some broken exile army whose members had become soldiers of fortune enlisting with the local *guerrilleros*. The only thing Henry knew about the Cubans was that they were connected to high-quality leaf. This man's presence was a good omen.

The *traficantes* got right down to business. They had *sin semilla* on their minds. The Indian responded that he had twenty-four pounds left and wanted one hundred American dollars per pound. Jesús called out through the open doorway and another Zapotec entered with a long rectangular box, the kind used for shipping eggs. He handed it to Amazon and left immediately, while Jesús lit a candle. Henry Amazon opened the box and found a dozen small bundles of gorgeous brown leaf covered with red hairs. The marijuana was sticky and seedless. Amazon said that for all twenty-four pounds he'd give them $2,250, plus a gun. Henry pulled the Browning .45 automatic out of his boot and passed it to Jesús. The Zapotec hefted the weapon and handed it on to his Cuban friend. The Cuban popped the clip out and tested the action. He handed it back to Henry and engaged Jesús in a rapid, whispered Spanish conversation.

"Other Americans give two of those for a pound," Jesús finally told Zoro. "We just want more cash, in American." The statement had a final note to it and the *traficante* did not argue. Henry Amazon put the gun away and pulled a wad of twenties from his other boot. By the light of the candle, he counted out $2,400 worth. Jesús handed the cash to the Cuban, who stuffed it in his pants. Jesús blew out the light and they all stepped out into the clearing. The night was warm and stuffy. Lightning was still flashing. Three Indians were waiting with five more egg boxes. The *traficantes* exchanged goodbyes with the Cuban and Jesús and followed the Zapotecs up the hill to the LTD. The cartons were loaded in the trunk, and Amazon turned the car back toward the highway.

"One down, two to go," Amazon said to Zoro.

Victorio was supposed to be waiting in a wash that branched off the next dirt road on the left. It was 1:30 by the time Zoro CeAttl and Henry Amazon found the place. There was no sign of either the Indian or Flacco, who were both supposed to have been there a half hour before. Amazon and his partner stepped out of the car and waited, leaning against the front fender. The dark was swampy and quiet, except for the thunder echoing across the valley. Henry Amazon checked his watch. At 1:45, the *traficante* heard a noise behind him and turned to peer into the black. It was Victorio. He had two other Zapotecs with him. They were wearing machetes.

The Indian said he had not seen any sign of Flacco but didn't want to wait. His two friends began carrying burlap bags and loading them in the LTD's trunk. Only half would fit. The other bags were piled by the side of the wash, to await Flacco's truck. The delivery totaled 103 pounds. Amazon counted out the Indian's money, and a smile broke over Victorio's face. As he handed the full payment to the farmer, Henry asked Zoro to ask the Zapotec if he was planting another crop. The Indian said he was, and Amazon pulled the Browning. The movement startled the Zapotec, but he quickly relaxed when the *traficante* handed it to him, butt first. "Tell him it's a down payment," Henry said. "His new crop belongs to us. And tell him to wait a little bit longer before he harvests—until the hairs get red." Victorio nodded agreement, told Zoro how to find him the next time, then melted into the shadows with his two friends.

Zoro and Amazon had to wait another two hours for Flacco. They paced next to the LTD and grumbled. Amazon checked his watch regularly. When they were about to give up on Flacco, the two smugglers saw headlights approaching on the road. Zoro and Henry hid in the brush at the side of the wash as the truck pulled in next to the LTD. It was Flacco.

"Where the fuck have you been?" Amazon demanded.

Flacco said it had taken a long time to load the truck. He had covered his load with maguey hearts to camouflage it. Amazon told him to get ready to unpack, because they had more weed to put on the pile. Flacco smiled weakly and jumped down from the cab. It took the three of them an hour to move the maguey, to add the remainder of Victorio's weed to Flacco's, to cover it all with a plastic sheet, and to load the maguey back on top. It was 5:30 a.m. before the convoy reached the highway for Oaxaca. Henry Amazon hated to run loads in the daytime, but he liked the idea of waiting for the next night even less. A film of pink light had appeared over the eastern mountain slopes, and daylight was approaching rapidly. They were to meet Rascon at the Caves of the Devil.

13

The Caves of the Devil are group of fissures in the face a three-hundred-foot cliff one hundred yards from the highway. The Zapotecs believe they are openings in the underworld. Indians who think their dead relatives have gone to hell climb to the caves and burn candles in their memory. Rascon was parked at the base of the cliff. His Ford flatbed had a deep green cab and a *tomba burro* painted a powder blue. "*Numero Uno*" was painted in blue script on the driver's door. Amazon woke up Rascon by pounding on his window.

"Let's move!" the *traficante* shouted.

Rascon started up his Ford and led off. The signals remained the same as the last time he and Amazon had worked together. Two flashes of the brake lights meant "watch out"; three, "danger"; and four flashes meant "run for it." Rascon cruised at least a quarter mile in front of Flacco, and Amazon and the LTD were another three hundred yards behind. Zoro rode in the cab with Flacco. To get over the coast road into Guerrero, the convoy had to cut across the outskirts of Oaxaca. Morning traffic had begun, and the city was alive with cooking fires and ambling burros. It took twenty minutes to get across town. Amazon was glad to leave the streets behind and, finally, to hit the countryside. Sweat had soaked through the armpits of his leisure suit. There was one last moment of worry near Ocotlàn, when Rascon flashed twice, but the reason was soon obvious. A truckload of soldiers passed them going back toward town after an all-night roadblock. Most of the privates in the open truck bed were asleep. Several dangled their legs over the back lip of the truck. They did not give either the Zapotec vehicles or the LTD a second look.

The rest of the trip was uneventful. As the road began dropping toward Puerto Ángel, the storm that had been rumbling all night finally broke. Rain fell in waves that cascaded over the nose of the

Ford with such force that the windshield wipers could barely keep pace. The roadside quickly became a mass of puddles, and the trucks threw sheets of spray off their rear wheels. The deluge lasted for two hours and shattered the day's sultry heat. When it finally stopped raining, the loaded convoy was running along the road with jungle on each side. Henry Amazon rolled his window down and listened to the high chatter of the monkeys and the sounds of the tropical birds. He wanted to sleep, and slapped his cheeks to stay awake.

After two rest stops, the *traficantes'* caravan reached Zoro's ranch in Guerrero close to 1 a.m. on Tuesday, September 6, 1977. Rascon was paid off as soon as they arrived at Zoro's, and he departed immediately. When Flacco and the two smugglers unloaded Flacco's truck, Zoro and Henry discovered that Flacco's load wasn't the second grade-A sample he'd shown them but was of the same grade as the B-quality package Flacco had left for them with the Indian in the mescal village. Henry had to be persuaded not to break Flacco's jaw. After an hour of argument, Henry finally paid Flacco a dollar a pound less than they had agreed on and sent him on his way. On Tuesday morning, September 6, the two partners loaded their 225 pounds of marijuana under the floorboards of Zoro's cousin's third-class bus. Zoro rode with it, and his cousin, to Mexicali. Amazon drove the LTD to Acapulco, turned it in at the Hertz desk, and caught the first flight to the States. Zoro unloaded the weed in Mexicali and stored it in his cousin's garage. On the night of Saturday, September 10, Zoro drove the load out of Mexicali in a Dodge Power Wagon with a camper on the back, crossed the Colorado River at a remote spot, and drove into Arizona. He and Amazon met six miles from the border and transferred the marijuana. Henry Amazon drove his loaded Pace Arrow motorhome to Colorado. The weed sold quickly, and at good prices.

On Thursday, September 22, Henry Amazon and Zoro CeAttl met again in Tijuana to split the profits. Zoro CeAttl made $44,130; Henry Amazon recouped his original ten grand, and made $44,130 more.

[*New York Times Magazine*, October 18, 1977]

Busted in Mexico

*P*AUL DICARO AND DEBORAH FRIEDMAN left Guadalajara on Thursday morning, January 22, 1976. Three weeks of camping on the Pacific beach at Puerto Vallarta and visiting Paul's American friends at Guadalajara University in west-central Mexico had reduced the couple's finances to their last $40. Paul and Debbie were anxious to return to their Sonoma County, California, home. DiCaro, 29, installs winery irrigation systems, and Friedman, 26, helps run their fifty-five-acre co-op farm. Paul and Debbie have been living together for three years. The two Americans spent most of Wednesday night packing their 1963 Volkswagen. Debbie carefully hid the remains of an ounce of marijuana she had bought to smoke on the beach inside two cards sealed in envelopes and addressed to their house in Healdsburg, California, U.S.A. Debbie threw them in among fifteen other letters in her bag, and she expected to mail the whole batch somewhere along the way. By 7:30 Thursday morning, Paul DiCaro and Debbie Friedman were on Highway 15 headed north across the state of Jalisco, one thousand miles south of the American border.

The first few hours had all the earmarks of another mellow Guadalajara day. It was 80 degrees when they crossed the mountains and dropped down the long run through the cactus to Tepic. The sky was solid blue. Debbie was driving while Paul stretched out in the back seat and relaxed, or got loose, as he put it. Getting loose was something he rarely did in Mexico. This was his third visit in four years, and every time he went south, he tied his over-the-shoulder hair up on top of his head and hid it under a wide-brimmed hat.

The Mexican authorities dislike longhairs, and Paul DiCaro wasn't looking for trouble. But that day he did not expect to get out of the car for another twelve hours. He took off his T-shirt, combed his hair out, and fell asleep in the back seat.

When he woke up an hour later, the day had changed drastically. Debbie was calling him from the front seat:

"What's this? What's happening?"

Paul shook himself to attention. They were north of the town of Magdalena and had been surprised by a roadblock. A stop sign was planted in the middle of the two-lane road, and uniforms were milling around the cars parked on both sides of the blacktop.

"*Aduana*," Paul answered.

Aduanas are a series of checkpoints set up along the Mexican highway system. The police camp there in sporadic twenty-four-hour shifts and check all vehicles for guns or dope. Debbie stopped their VW next to the brown khaki *Federal* straddling the dotted line with an M-2 carbine strung over one shoulder. He bent down and put his face in the window.

"*Por favor*, your papers, *señorita*."

Debbie did not have them and had to ask Paul. The *Federal* looked at Paul's hair and stared while Paul handed forward their passports, visas, and car insurance papers. The *Federal* thanked Debbie and looked at Paul again before going over to the group in uniforms on the road's shoulder. When he finally returned, the policeman spoke rapidly in Spanish with an occasional English word thrown in. The couple's papers were in order, but there was still some problem. The *Federal* wanted them to pull over to the side. He said he would have to detain them "for a moment." It was 9 a.m.

That "moment" is the subject of this account. By 11:30 a.m., DiCaro and Friedman would be found to be in possession of an envelope containing marijuana—thirteen and a half grams, to be exact. Had they been stopped with the same quantity of contraband in California, they would have been issued a citation and fined $25. Instead, by 5 p.m., they would be charged with buying, possessing, trafficking, transporting, and intending to export dangerous drugs, and they each would face a possible fifty-seven years in prison.

They would join some six hundred other Americans in the Mexican prison system, the largest single group of this country's citizens imprisoned in any foreign nation. Most of the arrests have been on drug charges, however a good number have been for minor violations, and it is the treatment of those arrested or imprisoned that is the focus of attention and concern. This account was drawn from interviews with Paul DiCaro and Deborah Friedman and with dozens of others, as well as from documents and records in the Mexican court system and offices of both American and Mexican immigration and diplomatic authorities.

Paul and Debbie's nightmare began with a single marijuana seed that Paul says did not belong to them. Debbie had spent an hour the night before on her knees looking for seeds in the car's upholstery. He says the seed belonged to the Mexican Federal Judicial Police.

That Thursday the Magdalena *aduana* was being manned by eight *Federales* armed with automatic weapons and two plainclothes federal agents. Three *Federales* began combing through the car's carpet, and two others stood beside Paul and Debbie, fifty feet from the car. Finally, Paul said, a young agent, wearing a bright polyester shirt, sunglasses, and pointed boots, looked at Paul for a moment, walked to the car, bent over the doorway for ten seconds, and then stood up with his hand over his head. *"Mira!"* he shouted. "Look at this." He was holding one marijuana seed.

The "discovery" gave the police license to search everything. Paul was handcuffed with his hands behind his back and told to get down on his knees. Paul DiCaro got up off his knees twice in the next two and a half hours. The first time was when the agent came over to ask, in Spanish:

"Do you have any contraband in your car you want to tell me about?"

"No," Paul said, struggling to his feet. Paul DiCaro wanted out of the vise he felt tightening around him. He continued talking in stumbling Spanish. *"No inglés, amigo,"* the agent said. "It makes no difference," Paul said. "You can have it all. *Sabe?* The whole thing. The car. The sleeping bags. Everything." Paul motioned with his head at the VW surrounded with brown uniforms. "It's all yours.

Just take us to the bus station and let us buy a ticket north."

The agent laughed and pulled a fat wad of bills out of his pants pocket. "*Muchos pesos,*" he grinned before walking off. Paul took the response as a simple statement that the price was a lot more than an old VW and two sleeping bags. A *Federal* motioned Paul back to his knees with the barrel of his carbine. DiCaro got on his feet a second time when the agent discovered the hidden weed. The agent was going through the mail in Debbie's bag again and noticed that two of the unopened letters were addressed to herself in her own handwriting—apparently an obvious giveaway. He shouted and ripped them open. The agent was on Paul in a flash. DiCaro had just enough time to stand up before the first blow landed.

"You lied to me, gringo motherfucker!" the agent shouted. "You lied to me twice." Then he swung at Paul's head. DiCaro tried to back up, but a *Federal* had moved behind him and there was suddenly nowhere to go. The blow slid off the American's ear.

"Wait a second . . ." As Paul recounts the story, he tried to talk through the pain ringing in his head, and as he did so, the agent swung a foot at the gringo's testicles, threw a series of body blows, and then another kick. "You can have it all. You don't want to bust me . . ." The plainclothes agent hit Paul DiCaro in the middle of the face.

Deborah Friedman ran toward them. "*Mi esposo!*" she shouted. "*Mi esposo!* You can't beat him like that!"

The agent laughed, took one more kick at DiCaro's crotch, and had the *Federales* chain Paul to the Volkswagen until a car could be sent out from Guadalajara to pick the Americans up. A black 1974 Lincoln Continental with a red light on the roof arrived three hours later. Paul was put in the back seat, and two agents drove him south. Debbie followed without handcuffs in the VW, driven by a third agent.

The Lincoln carrying DiCaro stopped for a little excitement along the way. The car had been moving through the outskirts of Guadalajara at a fast clip when a Chevrolet passed them going even faster and cut them off. The agents were furious and began chasing the Chevrolet. After weaving through traffic for three blocks, the

Lincoln caught the Chevy and forced it to pull over. The two agents drew their .45s and got out of the car. One grabbed the Chevy's driver by the collar, and the other put a pistol to the driver's head. They said he ought to learn some respect. The driver protested, pulling the arm of his jacket down and showing them the insignia on his khaki shirt. He was a *Federal*, too. The plainclothesmen said it did not matter. He still ought to learn respect. They slapped him a few times before returning to Paul. The rest of the trip was uneventful.

At 4:45, the Lincoln Continental pulled into the garage under the Palacio Federal, the center of law enforcement in the state of Jalisco, in downtown Guadalajara. As soon as Debbie arrived in the VW, the agents took them both to the sixth floor, where they were told they would be interviewed as soon as Captain Salinas returned from dinner. That took three hours.

In the meantime, Paul and Debbie waited on a bench with no idea of what would happen. Their legal knowledge, restricted to high school civics and TV cop shows, had hardly prepared them. They would not be allowed a phone call for a week. Their requests for a lawyer were ignored until after they were interrogated twice. They would not be fed for four days, and then only because another prisoner shared some beans her mother brought on visiting day. The interrogation began at 8 p.m., and it set the tone for what was in store. DiCaro and Friedman were not shown any identification by their interrogator, but they are certain that he was called Captain Salinas, though Mexican authorities whom I have since queried now insist that there is no such captain.

The captain was sitting behind his desk when DiCaro was brought into his office. He motioned for Paul to sit. Two agents in plainclothes stood at parade rest behind Paul's chair. One held a two-foot-long hard leather baton. Throughout the interview, he twisted the leather in his hands, and it made a high squeaky sound behind the American's left ear. Salinas toyed with the edge of a folded newspaper on his desk. The captain wanted Paul to explain the marijuana.

Paul asked for a lawyer instead. The captain refused. Paul asked for an interpreter from the consulate. The captain said it was not necessary. Paul asked for a phone call, and Salinas smiled.

The agent on Paul's right bent over and suggested he ought to get on with his story. The captain was a busy and very important man. DiCaro took the agent's advice and did not ask for a lawyer again until Salinas closed the interrogation by sliding a piece of paper across the desk. This was Paul's statement, and the captain wanted him to sign it. The paper was typed in Spanish on both sides. DiCaro understood only every tenth word.

"If you don't mind," Paul explained in a polite voice, "I'd like to have my lawyer read it before I sign."

As soon as the words were out of DiCaro's mouth, the room filled with tension. The agent on DiCaro's right bent over nervously and advised signing right away. The agent on his left increased the volume of his leather squeak. After an appropriate pause to let the enormity of the moment sink in, the captain proceeded to teach Paul DiCaro the rules of the game. He opened the newspaper in front of him and revealed a .45-caliber Colt automatic pistol. The captain placed his palm on the weapon and turned it until the barrel pointed straight at DiCaro. Paul stared. With a slow motion of his thumb, Salinas drew the Colt's hammer back. Paul DiCaro reached forward, took the pen off the desk, and signed his name. The captain smiled and said he had to sign both sides. Paul DiCaro smiled and signed his name a second time on the back.

DiCaro and Debbie Friedman were quickly learning the workings of Mexican law. It and the Yankee variety are built on different principles. The theory behind Mexican Justice is the Napoleonic Code, a legacy from the reign of Emperor Maximilian in the nineteenth century. Under this form of legal organization, the accused are, in effect, assumed guilty until they prove their innocence. There is no effective Bill of Rights, and arrest is the equivalent of indictment. There are no juries, and trials are not usually open to either the general public or the defendants themselves. The judge decides largely on the basis of the case description written by his own secretary. Lawyers rise to be secretaries, and secretaries eventually become judges. Legal business is conducted in very small rooms, and there are no verbatim transcripts of the proceedings.

The daily application of the Napoleonic Code is shot full of *mordida*, the homegrown expression signifying the practice of gaining influence or getting results through bribery. Whom your lawyer knows and what his friends will do for you are as important as the law itself. Those who have risen to high position expect their assistance to be rewarded in proportion to their stature. The result is *mordida*. Lawyers who know the judge or his secretary are in great demand and figure the price of bribes into their fees.

There are thousands of tiny passageways through the legal maze built by Napoleon and *mordida*. But these passageways were invisible to Paul and Debbie, whom Salinas ordered off to the city lockup. On the arch over its front door are inscribed the words *Procuraduría de Justicia*, literally translated as "where justice is procured." The sign means exactly what it implies.

It was 30 degrees in Guadalajara that night, and the jail was cold. There was no food. On the women's side, Debbie was able to borrow a blanket. On the men's side, Paul slept in a T-shirt on the floor. Both felt they were being buried alive and prayed that someone would rescue them.

On Friday night, January 23, DiCaro and Friedman had a visitor. They had no idea how he knew they were there. His name was Hale, and he was a representative from the American consulate. He patiently explained that his job was to help them get a lawyer, contact relatives in the United States, and help arrange for them to receive money from home. Nothing more. He had no advice to give and no influence to wield on their behalf. Hale produced a list of Mexican lawyers and asked Paul to choose three of the unknown names. The consulate would contact their choices directly.

Blindly, they selected Gustavo Ramírez Gómez. If they had not been such newcomers to Mexican justice, they never would have hired him. Gustavo Ramírez's *mordida* was minuscule. He had begun life as a *campesino*, a peasant; after the family farm was foreclosed, he moved to the city to work as an auto mechanic. Gustavo Ramírez learned the law at night school. He was full of resentment for the system and the way it worked. Ramírez was a very principled man who believed the law was the law and ought to be bigger than anyone who practiced it. He wanted $1,000 to take the case, to be paid when they were released.

Paul and Debbie hired him because he looked straight in their faces and seemed to know his business. Small *mordida* or not, Gustavo Ramírez was a smart attorney. He was the first to tell DiCaro and Friedman about articles 524 and 525 of the Federal Penal Code. These provisions established a legal classification of marijuana "addicts" who trafficked for use only. According to articles 524 and 525, possession of up to forty grams is considered an addict's habit and constitutes grounds for dismissal of criminal charges. Ramírez recommended pleading addiction and would approach the judge with this argument immediately. He was sure the charges would be dropped without a hearing. Gustavo Ramírez assured them, optimistically, that the process would take no more than seventy-two hours.

Ramírez was wrong. Seventy-two hours later, Paul DiCaro and Deborah Friedman were still in the lockup. Ramírez apologized for their disappointment and explained that the judge was about to be promoted and did not want to jeopardize his possibilities by seeming to be lenient on gringo marijuana addicts. They would have to wait for a formal hearing in two weeks. Paul and Debbie winced, tried to stifle their panic, and buckled down for their wait.

One full week after the arrest, the two Americans were transported to the Jalisco State Penitentiary, outside Guadalajara. The prison was in an uproar when they arrived, and soldiers were patrolling the grounds. The army had reinforced the prison guards after a daring breakout the day before. Six political prisoners had killed two guards with pistols and gone over the front wall. A bus with sandbagged windows had been waiting for them and raked the front of the prison with automatic-weapons fire. Two more guards died on the front steps.

The Jalisco State Penitentiary did not feel much like home, but Paul and Debbie recognized it was going to be just that for another two weeks at least, if Gustavo Ramírez was right. DiCaro and Friedman did not want to think about how long they'd stay if Gustavo was wrong a second time. The car dropped Paul at the main entrance and Debbie around the corner at the women's gate.

The walls at the Jalisco State Penitentiary are twenty feet tall and four feet thick. Built in 1926 to hold fifteen hundred prisoners, it now houses more than thirty-five hundred. Twelve blue-shirted guards walk the wall with carbines during the day, and the shift doubles at night. The women's section is a small compound, 90 by 150 feet, housing one hundred prisoners. With the addition of Deborah Friedman, three of them were American citizens. Jane Barstow (like all the names of American prisoners described here, except those of DiCaro and Friedman, this is a pseudonym) had been arrested for possessing two hundred seeds in her car. She would end up staying four months and spending $4,000 to get out. The other American citizen, Elaine Gavin Sanchez, was married to a Mexican who had been arrested on kidnapping charges. Elaine knew nothing about it but was arrested anyway. At the Palacio, she said she was strapped to a table while a *Federal* interrogated her with applications of an electric cattle prod to her breasts, vagina, and rectum until she passed out. Like everyone else, the American women spent their days wandering around the central compound and then at night they were locked into one of four large sleeping rooms. Only half the women had beds, and the rest slept on the floor. Debbie, Jane, and Elaine slept on the floor. No one would sell them beds.

The Men's Prison takes up the rest of the penitentiary's fifteen acres, except for the administrative offices and the separate political compound. The Men's Prison is more like a village, with a population of 3,400. It has a soccer field, rubber factory, basketball court, and a dozen assorted shops and cafés. On the night he arrived, Paul DiCaro met the prisoner who owned Javier's Café, which is between the mess hall and the front office. Javier befriended the American and told him Jalisco State Penitentiary's first commandment: "*Con dinero baila el perro*"—with money, even the dogs will dance.

Javier knew what he was talking about. Every male prisoner at Jalisco State sleeps in one of six sections according to the state of his finances. A single cell in Department 6 costs a flat fee of $25. Department 5 rises to $45, and Department 3 on up to $75. Department 4 is simply called "H" and, at $100, is the last of the flat-fee cellblocks. Departments 1 and 2 have eighteen-by-eighteen-foot cells with eighteen-foot ceilings, arranged into suites, and rent by the month. Half of the prisoners cannot afford a cell and sleep in the hallways in either Departments 5 or 6, where they pay an appropriate "street fee" to the inmate "street sergeant." The street sergeant takes a small piece of his rents and passes the rest on to the department captain, also an inmate. The six department captains take another small cut and deliver the remainder to what is called the prisoner *jefe*, or boss, Don Calistro, an old man doing twenty-seven years for cattle rustling. This *jefe* keeps a herd of cattle inside the walls in a corral he himself rents from the warden.

Paul DiCaro began his stay in prison sleeping on the floor of Department 5. He explained to the sergeant that he had money on its way from the United States and would pay his fee when it arrived. After four days, the money had not come and DiCaro was transferred to the floor in No. 6, the second worst. (The worst is the Pit, to which a prisoner is sent as punishment. The Pit's ceiling is four and a half feet high and its residents are chained to a floor that the guards slosh with water every two hours. After one miserable night on the street in No. 6 listening to the sounds of four hundred very poor people creeping around in the dark looking for something to own, Paul DiCaro knew he was going to have to get some credit right away. To do that, he would have to talk to Don Calistro, the *jefe*.

Don Calistro was not exactly suffering. He kept his cattle down by the soccer field and sold them to the prison butcher shop, which he also ran. The shop supplied the mess hall, the cafés, and the restaurants, one of which was Don Calistro's. He had a handsome suite where he lived with his wife and children. Paul DiCaro approached him there on February 3, the thirteenth day after his arrest. He told the *jefe* that the money was sure to come. Don Calistro relented and DiCaro moved back to No. 5. Two days later, a money order arrived from Paul's brother in Chicago. Paul DiCaro paid his debts and bought a cell in H right away. It had showers and toilets. Six of the ten other Americans in the Men's Prison lived there.

Like DiCaro and Friedman, the rest of the Americans in the Jalisco State Penitentiary were small fish. Throughout the 1970s, the United States has applied heavy pressure on Mexico to stop drug traffic. Good enforcement statistics have been rewarded with financial aid and gifts of equipment. The result has been thousands of arrests and an increase in traffic. The major dealers who move marijuana by the ton and 90 percent pure heroin in kilo lots are rarely arrested. They have the requisite cash for some very heavy *mordida*. The small fish are used to fill the statistical breach. Once he had met some of these other Americans, Paul realized just how lucky he and Debbie had been.

Mort Brainard was the only one besides Paul who did not tell stories about having been tortured. Brainard and his wife had been busted at the Magdalena *aduana*. The *Federales* found four and a half kilos of marijuana in the car and, Mort said, stripped his wife naked on the spot. He was told she would be raped if he did not sign a confession.

Bill Frye and Sam Russell had been arrested in the cab of a truck hauling three hundred kilos of marijuana. The two Americans said they were chained to a tree at the scene of their arrest for two days and beaten at regular intervals. When they finally reached the Federal Palace, they were cattle-prodded around their genitals, beaten with clubs, and immersed head first in a fifty-gallon drum of water. Frye is sure his testicles were permanently damaged. Originally sentenced to two decades apiece, $30,000 in bribes and legal fees had reduced their terms to eight years.

The Patterson brothers, James and Dennis, were awaiting sentencing for marijuana transportation. James had been worked over so viciously at the Palace that he almost died; his interrogator had beaten on his chest with a mallet and split open his rib cage. He was never hospitalized.

Robert Gordon's questioning was conducted by the usual team of four *Federales* in a room right off the Federal Palace parking lot and lasted thirty days. He reported being given the full treatment of water, cattle prods, and clubs. Gordon was originally arrested when the police kicked down the door of his Guadalajara apartment. They were looking for cocaine. No cocaine was ever found, he said, but he was charged with selling it nevertheless. His confession was signed after the interrogating officer placed a loaded .45 against his head. Gordon had been in the prison for three years.

No one was worse off than Alan Cummings, who had been caught with LSD. This seemed especially infuriating to the *Federales*. Two months after they were through beating him, a tumor had begun growing on the back of his head. In prison more than two years, he had once been hospitalized for a week, but only after he had passed out on the floor of his cell and seemed to be dying and the rest of the Americans pooled their cash and bribed the jailer to take Cummings to the infirmary. Alan was married to a Mexican woman who came to sleep with him every two weeks and she was pregnant. He seemed to be slowly dying in the Mexican prison yet had never even been sentenced. The other three Americans there were not well known by the rest.

Frye and Russell had bought a three-room suite for $500 when it had become clear that they were going to be in Jalisco State for some time. It was one of H's nicest. During his first few days in that department, Paul spent a lot of time there, listening to their stories. They explained that there were no guarantees even *mordida* would work. One American arrested for possession of a marijuana cigarette had spent $10,000 over the last year and was still inside Santa Marta prison. All the Americans told stories about their countrymen. One was of an American citizen named Hernandez, from Tucson, who had been giving the Guadalajara jailers a hard time, and they were said to have administered a fearsome beating with their leather batons. Two days later, on Christmas Eve 1975, Hernandez was rumored to have died from his injuries. Paul DiCaro soaked up the talk, and felt worse with every story.

He and Friedman next saw each other on the regular day when the women were allowed to visit the men. The couple walked across the plaza outside H, and Debbie shuddered as her eyes fell on the Snail, a Mexican prisoner who had tried to commit suicide by jumping off the two-story administration building. He had failed and only broken a leg. Rather than set the bone, the prison authorities amputated it above the knee. The Snail could not afford crutches, and he made his way through the dust by pulling himself along with his arms.

The two Americans' hopes for the judge's hearing on Monday, February 9, fell flat. The judge was unwilling to do anything more than reduce the charges. He said he needed more evidence about their addiction. Ramírez apologized for this further disappointment and delay but reassured his clients that it would be only a short while before they were freed. Paul and Debbie had their doubts.

So did Hannah Friedman and Tod Friend. Tod Friend is a member of DiCaro's and Friedman's Sonoma County co-op and shares their house. Hannah Friedman, Debbie's mother, is a housewife in Waukegan, Illinois, with a long history of community service. At this point, they joined forces to try to rescue Paul and Debbie. Before they were done, $10,000 had been spent in bribes, lawyers' fees, and expenses. Relative to the sums paid by other Americans, it was a bargain basement.

As soon as Debbie's mother had heard from the consulate, she had wired money and guaranteed the lawyers' fees. She and her husband, a suburban physician, had flown to Guadalajara and visited the couple on Sunday, February 8. Hannah Friedman had been so sure of Paul and Debbie's imminent release that she left them two plane tickets home, told them to stay out of trouble, and flew back to Chicago that night. When she heard that her daughter was still behind bars, she felt Debbie and Paul were being swallowed in legal quicksand. She was not sure what to do.

Tod Friend had heard that it was possible to call the prison directly and talk to an inmate. He did and got Debbie on the phone. She said things did not look good. Friend called Hannah Friedman, told her he was going south, and promised to call her from Guadalajara.

He rented a room in the Hotel San Jorge and began visiting Paul and Debbie every day he could. Most of the visits took place in a small room in the front of the prison, but on two days a week he was allowed to be locked in the men's side with Paul all day long. Paul figured they needed a new lawyer. He liked Gustavo Ramírez but thought he was too naive and did not have the necessary connections. Paul had a replacement in mind: Francisco Gutiérrez Martín.

Gutiérrez Martín was said to be a legend behind the walls of the Jalisco State Penitentiary. Martín's extraordinary influence grew out of a long career teaching law at Guadalajara University. Three of his former pupils sat on the Jalisco State bench, and the old professor was said to be making great sums of money. Paul had seen one example of Martín's influence firsthand. Two seventeen-year-old Mexican kids had been brought to the prison after being arrested while harvesting an entire field of marijuana. They were cocky and bragged that Gutiérrez Martín was their lawyer so there was no reason to worry. Two days later, the kids were released. Many people told Paul that he and Debbie would have been home by now if they had hired Gutiérrez Martín. Paul was convinced and sent Debbie a message to call Martín, who said he could, indeed, get them out. It would cost $12,000 cash in advance.

Twelve thousand dollars in cash is a lot of money, and it took five days for Tod to persuade Hannah to bring it down. When she finally arrived in Guadalajara, Mrs. Friedman planned to see Martín and make the arrangements as soon as she had registered at the Hotel Fénix. She would have if there had not been a sudden change in plans. At the last minute, Paul and Debbie decided to stick with Gustavo Ramírez. The change of heart grew out of a conversation with an imprisoned lawyer in Javier's Café while Tod was spending the day. The lawyer's name was Abraham, and he agreed to look Paul and Debbie's papers over. Abraham concluded that it was a waste of money to hire Martín.

"Gustavo has done all the work," Abraham explained, "so why Martín?" The prison lawyer said the charge reduction was a first step to freedom and told them not to worry. Gustavo had all the right law on paper.

Tod reached Hannah with the news after she had contacted Martín and made an appointment. She called Martín back, canceled the appointment, and deposited her $12,000 certified draft (on a Waukegan, Illinois, bank) in the hotel vault. The decision saved money but would eventually cause Paul and Debbie plenty of trouble. The smell of cash was around their case now, and a lot of folks in Guadalajara have a nose for the smell of cash.

In the meantime, Gustavo Ramírez put the final touches on their case. Friends of Paul, Debbie, and Hannah in the United States sent letters asserting that the couple were genuine marijuana addicts and had been treated for their addiction for years. The last piece of the puzzle was their official certification. To get this, Paul and Debbie were taken out of the prison to a clinic near the Federal Palace. They both passed the examination with flying colors.

The other Americans had clued Paul in that the tests picked up traces of marijuana resin in the mouth and on the fingertips. Their mouths and hands would be rinsed with a solvent to collect samples. On the recommendation of his countrymen, Paul bought a little weed on the plaza and smoked half a joint on the morning of the tests. He hid the remainder in his pants and passed it to Debbie on their way to the clinic. She asked to relieve herself before she saw the doctor and smoked the rest of the weed in the bathroom. The next day, Dr. Natzahualcoyotl Ruiz Gaitao sent a memorandum to the Third Judge of the Distrito en el Estado certifying that the accused, Paul Francis DiCaro and Deborah Lee Friedman, "are habitual drug addicts in the use of marijuana . . . requiring at least three to six cigarettes a day."

With that document, Gustavo Ramírez was ready to go back in front of the judge.

A few days after Gutiérrez Martín's aborted contact with Hannah Friedman, Ramírez began to encounter signs of Gutiérrez Martín's continued presence. Martín had evidently not lost interest in the possible $12,000 fee.

Gustavo was worried. He explained that Martín and the judge's secretary had been talking. Ramírez had picked the story up on the courthouse grapevine. Martín was said to have told the secretary that the DiCaro and Friedman case had money attached to it, and that if it could just be held up until the Americans changed lawyers, there could be $400 in it for him. The news of Martín's presence had left Gustavo Ramírez ready to quit. He thought he ought to leave the case. Martín was impossible to fight.

The Americans disagreed. Hannah and Tod wanted to know why Gustavo did not just take $800 to the same secretary. Gustavo said they should not need a bribe. They were clearly in the right under the law. The Americans agreed but said they'd rather see Paul and Debbie free. Ramírez responded that it was exactly this *mordida* that had made Mexican law a joke, and he wanted no part of it. Gustavo Ramírez was a man of intense belief. He refused to eat meat because it symbolized the fat Mexico of the cattle barons. He refused to drink soda pop because it symbolized Mexico's addiction to the Yankee Coca-Cola culture. Gustavo kept a photo of Che Guevara over his file cabinet. It took Tod and Hannah half an hour to change Ramírez's mind about bribing the secretary. Finally, the challenge of beating Martín and his desire to get Paul and Debbie released overwhelmed Gustavo's reluctance. The bribe was offered immediately and consummated with cash during the next week. On the morning of Friday, February 26, 1976, the judge signed the documents dropping criminal charges. Gutiérrez Martín subsequently denied any involvement in the case.

The news reached DiCaro around 10:30 a.m. He was not expecting it. Paul DiCaro had begun assuming that nothing would work out and was preparing to serve five years and three months, the minimum sentence for drug-related convictions. On Friday morning, DiCaro was all set to play third base in a prison baseball game. One of the young boys who hung out on the plaza brought Paul the message. He thought the American's freedom papers had arrived. Paul tipped the kid a peso and hurried to the prison building, where a guard told him to go back to H and get his stuff. Paul DiCaro was being released. Debbie was given the same news on the women's side half an hour later. Then they waited. The guard said it was only a matter of signing some final papers. Paul sat in the visitors' room for three hours. During that time, Tod, Hannah, Gustavo Ramírez, and Ramírez's son Carlos arrived to welcome them out. They all waited together. When the guard finally gave Paul his release certificate and official papers, there was great jubilation. The rescue team was laughing when they left to pick up Debbie.

The laughter came to an abrupt halt as soon as they walked out the front door. Two agents from the Department of Population were waiting on the steps. The Department of Population's jurisdiction includes foreigners inside Mexico. The agents approached Paul and explained that before his release was final, there were some more papers to sign downtown. Paul was stunned. The agents handcuffed him and hustled him into their waiting automobile. The rescue team tried to follow the car but lost it. Shortly after, the agents grabbed Debbie at the women's gate. None of the rescuers had any idea where Paul and Debbie were being taken. Once again, Paul DiCaro and Deborah Friedman had disappeared into the morass of Guadalajara law.

Gustavo Ramírez's best guess was that they had been taken to the city jail, and the rescue party drove straight there. The lawyer went into two different offices to inquire and was told that there were no Paul DiCaro and Deborah Friedman in the city lockup. Gustavo was headed back to the car when he spotted a policeman friend of his in the hall. The friend assured him in confidence that he had seen the Americans in the building not ten minutes earlier. Gustavo came back to Tod and Hannah looking angrier than they had ever seen him. He said he was going to find the judge and would drop them back at the Hotel Fénix.

Gustavo's friend had good information. Paul and Debbie were in the basement sharing a cell. For the last thirty-six days, DiCaro had prided himself on his composure, but that was all behind him now. Paul and Debbie had quickly perceived that all the talk about signing papers was a hoax, and DiCaro was furious. He spent three hours kicking the door and screaming about all the rotten chickenshit *cabrones* who had kidnapped him. He screamed down the hall that he wanted to talk to someone, goddamn it. No one came until 11 p.m. By that time, DiCaro had calmed down and he and Debbie were in their sleeping bags on the cell floor.

The visit was from Señor Gabriel Romero Barragan, the head of the Department of Population of Jalisco. He identified himself by flipping out a gold badge with papers and a photo. Romero stood on the other side of the bars flanked by two bodyguards. He had evidently just come from dinner. One of his bodyguards reached up and wiped a spot of enchilada sauce from his lapel.

"Buenas noches," Romero began. He understood the whole case, he explained in English, and he knew that the two Americans had their freedom papers, but that did not matter. Under the law, the Department of Population had the authority to hold them for thirty days before deportation. If, on the other hand, their friends were to make an arrangement with him, Romero could sign their deportation papers immediately and put Paul and Debbie on a plane. He gave the couple a scrap of paper with his phone number on it. Romero said he would instruct the jailer to give Paul and Debbie two phone calls the next morning. They should call their people and have them contact him directly. He would be in his office between nine and noon.

"Tell them to bring their best offer," Romero added with a smile.

Paul and Debbie were ready to pay whatever it took. They knew that if they were not released by Saturday at 6 p.m., all the legal machinery would shut down until Monday. By then every jackal in Jalisco would be onto their case and they would be buried in payoffs. February 26 was the worst night the couple had spent in jail. Their prospects seemed miserable.

As it turned out, they had seriously underestimated Gustavo Ramírez. Ramírez was not about to be walked on by Señor Romero, head of Population or not. Ramírez found the judge coming out of a movie at close to midnight. He explained what had happened and pointed out that Population had no legal authority over DiCaro and Friedman. The charges had been dropped, so no deportation was in order. Population was totally out of bounds. Not only that, the lawyer argued, it was an obvious insult to the judge himself. When a judge ruled, it was final, and Population should not think it could overrule him. The judge agreed and called his secretary. Instead of meeting Romero the next morning, Ramírez huddled with the judge's secretary. The incentive of another $800 cash for "bail" was enough to persuade the secretary to accompany him to the Palace and file charges against Romero and everyone else involved in the two Americans' illegal detention. They arrived at the Guadalajara lockup's main desk at 11 a.m.

The secretary threw six different files full of charges on the counter and demanded the immediate release of the Americans, DiCaro and Friedman. The act drew a lot of attention. Secretaries to the judge of Distrito en el Estado do not visit a prison lockup except on very special occasions. The first clerk took one look at the secretary and the papers and called his superior. The superior approached the papers with a smile but lost it as soon as he began leafing through them. He retreated to the phone and called the Weasel. The Weasel was the lockup's resident legal expert. He had a thin face and a long, twisted nose that twitched a lot as he read through the files. The Weasel got back on the phone and made calls for the next hour and a half. During the last and longest of them, he did little but listen to a loud Spanish voice and answer "*sí*" and "*no sí*." After hanging up, the Weasel called down to the cellblock and told them to send the two Americans up.

Like every other process they had been through for thirty-seven days, this last one took some time. Paul and Debbie had to wait half an hour at the cellblock door. The turnkey explained that he was on his lunch break and could not open the door until he was done. They watched him eat burritos until Debbie started pulling her hair and screaming. This apparently moved the jailer to finally open up, and then he returned to eat his lunch in peace. Paul and Debbie waited another three and a half hours in the front office while Gustavo, the judge's secretary, and the Weasel shuffled papers and signed documents. At 5 p.m., Paul DiCaro and Deborah Friedman walked out the Federal Palace's front door. After thirty-seven days behind bars, the late-afternoon Guadalajara streets felt electric.

The party celebrated in the Hotel Fénix dining room. Gustavo was paid his $1,000, plus a $1,000 bonus, and put the dinner celebration on his tab. He wanted Paul and Debbie to stay in town to testify against Romero, but Paul, Debbie, Tod, and Hannah were ready to leave. Hannah suggested that they do so before Population had a chance to counterattack, and she devised a plan. The Americans made plane reservations departing the next day from both Guadalajara and Mexico City—then, in a rented car, they drove to Monterrey, changed cars, and drove on to Texas. They crossed the Mexican border at Nuevo Laredo shortly after midnight on Sunday, February 29. On their way to the San Antonio airport, the party stopped at the Alamo. It was 5 a.m. Tod, Paul, and Debbie kissed the monument's wall.

At the airport, Paul bought a Sunday copy of the *San Antonio Light*. The front section was dominated by a two-inch banner headline: U.S. SUICIDE IN MAZATLAN JAIL. The story, by Larry D. Hatfield, was about a young American jailed in the state of Sinaloa who had "committed suicide . . . rather than face torture for his part in an aborted escape attempt." Paul DiCaro and Deborah Friedman didn't need to read further. They closed the paper, boarded the plane to San Francisco, and counted themselves lucky to be north of the Rio Grande.

[*New York Times Magazine*, May 1, 1977]

The Battle of Coachella Valley

ALICIA URIBE REMEMBERS the 16th of April like she remembers her feet or the fingers on her hands. The day is built into her body now. It has been ever since it first happened. She and a hundred others started the 16th lined along the hot dirt shoulder in front of the Mel-Pak vineyards. The road behind them slid six greasy miles east to Coachella and Indio. Alicia cocked her union flag over her arm and let it slop sideways like wash on the line. The 90 degrees around her kept lifting off the valley floor in thin slabs. Each way Alicia looked, the world had a warp to it and a shimmer, like the air was dribbling sweat.

The 16th didn't feel all that different from any other spring day in the Coachella Valley. At ten, the heat pushes past 100 and the asphalt on the far side of noon bubbles like cornmeal mush. Three o'clock cooks spit before it has a chance to touch ground. Without deep wells and old age, the Coachella Valley would be one long griddle of sand, anchored with greasewood and horned toads. As it is, forty thousand people live along its bottom and rising sides. The old ones built Palm Springs to comfort their rich arthritis; the young ones dug enough deep wells to cover patches from the San Jacinto Mountains to the Salton Sea with grapes, date palms, grapefruit, melons, and sweet corn. If it were a year like any other, Alicia Uribe and her hundred friends would have been up to their shoulders in Thompson Seedless. But 1973 hit the east end of Riverside County like a bizarre snowstorm. The trouble and the crops came in together. A lot of folks guessed the trouble was coming, but no one knew it would show up quite the way it did.

From the 16th on, the Coachella harvest was as plain as the nose on Alicia Uribe's face.

She remembers a red pickup truck and a white sedan spitting rooster tails behind their tires. The two shapes bounced along the ranch road, through the fields, and toward their line.

"Los Teamsters," the woman next to her said.

As the word jumped from ear to ear, the pickets began shouting and waving their red-and-black flags. The truck pulled even with Alicia, and a fat man in the passenger seat jerked a .38 out of his pants. He let the sand billow over the tailgate and used his mouth to shout back.

"Eat shit!" the fat man rumbled.

The white sedan slumping along in the fat man's tracks was quiet. Its upholstery was covered with four men in clean shirts. Making a sudden skip on the loose dirt, the car swerved right, and one of the shirts in the back window leaned out and laid a pair of brass knuckles along the side of Alicia Uribe's head. Ever since, her face has had a little dent to it. The blow fractured Alicia's cheek, broke her nose, and dug a scratch across her right eyeball. The white sedan turned left and disappeared toward Palm Springs.

Lying there in hot sand mixed with her splatter of nineteen-year-old blood, Alicia Uribe became the first casualty in a war that has bubbled out of every tin-roofed shed within forty miles of downtown Indio. The fight is all about grapes and the people who pick them. It has three parties and two sides. On the one hand is Alicia Uribe's sixty-thousand-member United Farm Workers Union, AFL-CIO. Their three-year contract with the desert grape industry expired April 15. On the other side, the twenty-seven growers who own the valley's 7,100 acres of table grapes sit with the two-million-member International Brotherhood of Teamsters, Chauffeurs, Warehousemen and Helpers of America. The Teamsters own the red pickup, the white sedan, the brass knuckles, and a fresh set of contracts that give them claim to represent the valley's thirty-five hundred vineyard workers. The International Brotherhood and the growers have signed each other up, and the UFW is striking them both. It is no small fight. Before the summer's over, it could grind its way across America's produce counters and perhaps even reach the outskirts of Washington, D.C.

NONE OF THIS WOULD BE happening if it were not for the United Farm Workers. Ten years ago, they were a truck-stop joke up and down Highway 99; now they are nationally known. There were lots of reasons for the union's rise, but the biggest was the pure and simple need for it. Since the Okies left to fight World War II, farm labor had belonged to a lot of Mexicans and a few Filipinos and Arabs. Telling one from the other wasn't hard if you just looked at check stubs. The Southwest had a white man's wage, a Mexican wage, and a lot of distance in between. Most Americans paid little attention, holding comfort in the knowledge that Mexicans did not need much money seeing as how the price of beans was so cheap. White folks commonly understood dollars were a fortune in Spanish and trusted the honky legend that was sure all the wetbacks took their earnings south and bought steel mills on the outskirts of Tijuana.

As a result, the nation's three million agricultural laborers worked an average of 119 days a year, with an annual wage of $1,389. One out of every three farmworker houses had no toilet, one out of every four no running water. The average worker lived to be forty-nine years old, and a thousand a year died from pesticide poisoning in the fields. If there was anything the people with those lives needed, it was a union.

And they knew it. Since the Spanish missions, California's produce has been worked by people who followed their dreams across a border and figured they deserved a whole lot better than they ended up getting. In 1884, Chinese hop pickers waged the first strike in Kern County. They asked for $1.50 a day and ended up with an ass-whipping and a broken union. After that it was more of the same. Growers are very powerful people with big bags of money, plus a command of both the language and the local police. At the same time, the world is full of people who are hungry, poor, and desperate enough to chase their dreams to California. Together, the two make a magic combination all the way to the grower's bank. Once you've paid your last peso to get there, California's a hard place to get back from and an easy place to starve. Over the years, the bosses have made a practice of hiring a new dream if yours gets slow or uppity. The technique's been enough to make a lot of folks swallow their bitch and tote that sack. The man who signs the paycheck is called "yassuh, boss" and thanked for the opportunity to sweat in his fields.

Filipinos, Japanese, blacks, Mexicans, Okies, and Arabs all followed in the Chinese footsteps. The IWW tried to organize a union, the CIO tried, the AFL tried, and then the AFL-CIO tried again. All of those efforts failed. When, in 1935, the National Labor Relations Act recognized the right of working men, farm labor was excluded. Each succeeding minimum-wage bill had agriculture in a special place all to itself. Some growers took to economizing by dropping wages every time they broke a strike. For a man picking grapes, 1884 and the 1962 Delano that Cesar Chavez drove into looked a lot alike. Farmworkers used just one picture for both their pasts and their futures. It was worn on the edges, sore, and ate whenever it could.

Not that Chavez was shocked. His family lost their Arizona farm in 1938. Cesar and the Chavezes moved the length of California, living in hovels, missing shoes in the winter, and working when the labor contractor said it was all right. By 1952, Chavez lost his patience, went for a break in the clouds, and became an organizer for the Community Service Organization at $35 a week. He did that for the next ten years. Chavez wanted to go into rural California and build a union, but the CSO decided against it. So Cesar took his 1962 life savings of $900 and went to his brother's house in the San Joaquin Valley.

The dream in Chavez's mind took root in tiny houses, with whatever circle of workers could be collected. When the talking was over, the hat made its way around the room and Cesar lived out of it, picking grapes each time the sombrero came back light. Soon the house meetings called themselves the Farm Workers Association. By 1965, the organization supported itself with dues and fought two small strikes. Then the dream blossomed. In September of that same year, the Filipino Agricultural Workers Organizing Committee came to Delano to work grapes and had no taste for the $1.20 an hour being offered. AWOC struck, and the FWA had to stand on one side or another. Eight days after the Filipinos set up their pickets, the Farm Workers Association voted unanimously to jump in with both feet. Together, they called themselves the United Farm Workers and started off into the biggest fight they had ever imagined.

The UFW spent five years on strike and boycotting to win their original contracts with the table grape industry. Before the union's victory, base wage in grapes was $1.20 an hour, with a ten- to twenty-cent kickback to the labor contractor. The 1970 union agreement started at $2.05 and created the first hiring hall in grape-growing history. It also forced the growers to accept pesticide regulations much stiffer than the State of California's, plus an employer-financed health plan, banning workers under sixteen, and no firing without just cause. The contract lasted three years. Today's troubles started when it came time to sign a new one: Negotiations never passed the first point of discussion. It wasn't just the union's proposal the growers didn't like. Most of them plain could not stand the union. "It's too goddamn democratic," is the way one described it.

All union members are on crew committees, which elect representatives to a ranch committee and then the ranch committee negotiates. At contract time, that means the growers sit face-to-face in a $50 hotel room with the people who work for them, listening to them talk in Spanish, and eventually giving in—none of which are too popular among rich growers and corporations. When the talks started this year, it was not long before the UFW understood the growers had Teamster contracts in their pockets and the tiny United Farm Workers was in for a brawl with the largest union in the Western world.

"The Teamsters and growers have joined together," explains Chavez, now UFW national chairman. "They are trying to destroy our union and force the workers to accept a union they don't want."

For his work as chairman, Chavez receives $5 a week plus food, gas, and shelter. To look at him, you would not think Chavez has an age. His face is full of soft creases sitting sidesaddle on a collection of bumps. Behind it, his mind perches on his short body, flicking, watching, and poised like a cat. And that is all of Cesar Chavez that shows to the outside observer. There is more, to be sure, but the rest has turned in on itself, grown into its dark brown root, stewed there, and sprouted into a crowd of red-and-black eagle flags. Chavez is more than meets the eye and less than a nation of movie magazines and talk shows has come to expect. He gets up in the morning and scratches himself like everybody else, but the boundaries we call personality are not so sharply drawn. In some strange way, Cesar Chavez does not exist. His laughter and the fear on his eyelids are his own, but the shadow he casts has long since become the shape of a long sweating line of desperate humans inching out of Mexico. When he talks, the voice always sounds bigger than the face it speaks with; it is as though the words come from somewhere over his shoulder. Chavez behaves like a bulge in the hide of a thousand years' history. When he looks up, he seems embarrassed by it all. The nerves in his fingers betray him. They grapple with each other under his conversation. The words glide along in their own self-conscious way, full of stumbles and wide enough to touch the ears of every López in California. He is the leader of his people more than he is anything else. The meat on the surface is Cesar Chavez, but the stuffings are 100 percent union. It makes him hard to know and easy to believe.

Over the years, Chavez has acquired the habit of meaning most everything he says. He calls the Teamster move "fearful and dishonest." "They're afraid of the farmworker," he explains, "because they don't control him."

"We have offered elections to let the workers decide which union they want, if any. The Teamsters have refused, and the growers, of course, have held out. They know if the workers are given the choice, they will be put out of the fields by a very large majority. Instead, the Teamsters hired goons in Los Angeles and brought them to Coachella with the idea of scaring our pickets away. They're slowly finding that the workers are not afraid of them.

"I can understand the employers," Chavez continues. "They're employers and acting like employers. When it comes to the Teamsters Union, that's a different question. They're supposed to be a union and are acting in concert with the growers to destroy us. It's a shameful act and they won't succeed.

"The Teamsters claim to have signed forty-five hundred workers in the Coachella Valley. We know they haven't," Chavez chuckles. "There aren't forty-five hundred grape workers in the valley. You see, the Teamsters don't organize workers. They organize employers. They're very successful at organizing employers but very bad at organizing workers."

George Meany, president of the AFL-CIO, put it more simply in his own stern tone. He got on ABC's evening news and called the Teamsters "strike breakers."

WHEN TEAMSTER PRESIDENT Frank Fitzsimmons heard the comment, he announced on nationwide television the next night that Meany was "senile." It was a smart move. If he had not chosen that tack, Fitzsimmons might have had to stand on the Teamster record, which isn't a very smart thing to do. Of course, Frank Fitzsimmons did not get where he is by being anybody's dummy. His presidential paycheck reads $175,000 a year, plus travel and maintenance for himself and his wife. The Teamsters national headquarters is equipped with a limousine plus driver, a full-time barber, a full-time masseur, and two French chefs, not to mention the president's private seventeen-seat jet. All that, of course, does not change the union's record, starting with the president and working its way down.

Fitzsimmons's predecessor, Jimmy Hoffa, had a problem common to Teamster history. He was sentenced to fifteen years in a federal penitentiary for tampering with a jury. (His sentence was later commuted by Richard Nixon.) Since taking the reins, Fitzsimmons has had his own brushes with the law. Last February, an FBI stakeout spotted him meeting with alleged L.A. Mafia members Peter Milano and Sam Sciortino at a golf tournament in Palm Springs. Before the golf balls were gone, Fitzsimmons had talked with Lou Rosanova, allegedly of the Chicago Mob, as well. Four days later, he and Rosanova met again at a health spa in San Diego County. When their meeting was over, Fitzsimmons went north to San Clemente and hitched a ride back to Washington with Richard Nixon on Air Force One. Wiretaps later revealed a contract in the offing allegedly designed to bleed the union pension fund with a mafia health care plan. The mob's kickback was reported at 7 percent. When it came time to renew the wiretaps, Attorney General Richard Kleindienst refused permission and the investigation was dropped.

Some said it was a case of the old Teamster solution again. The Teamsters were the first union to endorse the Republican ticket, and rumors in Washington hold that Fitzsimmons had veto rights on the secretary of labor. The daily *New Hampshire Union Leader* has charged that the Teamsters invested better than half a million dollars in the secret Watergate campaign fund. When special counsel to the president Charles Colson retired from public life a few months back, he joined a Washington law firm that had begun handling the Teamsters' seven-figure business just the month before; needless to say, Fitzsimmons, Kleindienst, Colson, Milano, Sciortino, and Rosanova have denied all charges of wrongdoing.

At the bottom rung of the International Brotherhood, the record is no better. The Teamsters had no foothold in fieldwork until the last half of 1970. Two days after the UFW won industry-wide contracts in grapes, the Teamsters signed five-year agreements with a frightened set of Salinas lettuce growers. The UFW responded by shutting down the lettuce fields with a walkout of seven thousand workers.

When the Teamsters appealed to the courts to invoke California labor law and stop the UFW from striking, they won an initial injunction. Two years later, the California Supreme Court reversed the findings of the lower courts. The justices ruled that the law forcing compulsory arbitration only applied to two unions representing factions of the same working force. The court found the international union guilty of accepting the growers' invitation and making deals without worker representation. The Teamsters were, in the terms of the law, ruled a "company union," organized by the management to do the management's bidding.

Since the Teamsters arrived in Salinas, three of their "organizers" have been charged with violations of the Gun Control Act of 1968; half a dozen more are in court charged with felonious assault. Teamster Frank Carolla has told the federal grand jury that grower representatives delivered $5,000 packets of fresh bills to Teamster officials each week at the Salinas airport.

The only agricultural successes the Teamsters have enjoyed are in the packing sheds and canneries, both of which are under uncontested Teamster jurisdiction. Even on its own turf, the big union has had its problems. Committees of Chicano workers have formed in the canneries all over California. One recently filed thirty-six charges of racism against the Western Conference of Teamsters. The Equal Employment Opportunity Commission upheld all thirty-six and issued a cease-and-desist order to the Teamsters.

That's not the first time the International Brotherhood has been called racist. Such talk is all over Coachella and Salinas, and the Teamster leadership has done little to dispel the rumors. After three years of "organizing" in the Salinas fields, the Teamsters have failed to deliver union cards to the largely Chicano membership. Without a card, a worker has no rights in the larger union. When Einar Mohn, head of the Western Conference, was questioned about Teamster plans for membership meetings in Coachella, he said it would be a couple of years before any were held. "I'm not sure," he explained, "how effective a union can be when it's composed of Mexican Americans and Mexican nationals with temporary visas. As jobs become more attractive to whites, then we can build a union that can negotiate from strength."

Despite this dubious record, the International Brotherhood of Teamsters continues to claim it best represents the workers of the Coachella Valley. So far, the Teamsters have committed over a million dollars to their effort. Agriculture is big business, and according to the Teamsters, only an International Brotherhood has the size to handle it.

Agriculture is indeed very big business. It accounts for one-third of California jobs and better than half of the state's accumulated wealth. If all the agricultural workers organized into a single union, it would be the nation's largest and have an importance beyond its size. Agriculture is rapidly becoming the keystone of the Republican economy. Faced with other industries' inability to compete, the United States has moved into an increasingly unfavorable position in world trade. This has blown the worth out of the dollar and lit a fire under Richard Nixon. He plans to escape the dilemma by increasing the production and export of farm products. Already, government production controls have been lifted and doors opened to the Russian and Chinese markets. Needless to say, Richard Nixon isn't too excited about including Cesar Chavez and the UFW in that strategy. He would sleep a little easier with it in the hands of his friends.

One such friend, Undersecretary of Labor Laurence H. Silberman, arranged for Frank Fitzsimmons to speak at last December's annual convention of the American Farm Bureau. The Farm Bureau is a growers' organization with a long history of calling unions Communist fronts, but they received Fitzsimmons warmly. He called Chavez a "revolutionary fraud" and got a big hand. A month later, the Teamsters signed an agreement with the Labor Contractors Association, and their representatives showed up in Coachella with an offer.

Their offer was ten cents an hour less than the UFW's, included no hiring hall, no special pesticide regulations, and was written in English. None of the Teamster rank and file have seen a copy of the contract yet, but the growers say it is attractive, fair, and about time. "It's nice to have somebody with a little strength on our side for once," commented one Coachella ranch manager.

THE TEAMSTER STRENGTH IN Coachella is hard to miss. Most teamsters average better than six feet high and two hundred pounds heavy. Some are red-necked truckers from Indio, the warehousemen from L.A. look like hippies, and the rest grease their hair into a duck's ass. They all get paid $67.50 daily from the union's organizing funds. Each day at 5 a.m., these "organizers" assemble in the Safeway parking lot off Highway 111. The fat ones like to stamp their feet on the asphalt and say one Teamster is worth five Mexicans. Those are just about the odds they work. It makes for long, hard days.

There are five times as many Mexicans, but they are mostly small and half are women and children. They start at 4:30, drinking sugared coffee in the Coachella park across from the hiring hall. As the picket captains pass the word on which ranches are working, the United Farm Workers huddle into caravans, then head out the highway and across county roads. The streets running east and west are all named after numbers, the ones north and south after presidents. The armies rarely get lost. They usually show up about the same time. Since Alicia Uribe's dented face, the courts have given the UFW the far side of the road and the Teamsters the side with grapes on it. The judge said the distance would keep things peaceful; Riverside County sheriffs cruise between the lines to make sure. But even the cops have not been able to keep the noise down.

Both sides have bullhorns and start using them when the first folks show up to work. The UFW calls them "scabs." To the Teamsters they are "brother Teamsters" and "good Mexicans." The old Fords and new Chevys that come in the morning bring a mild breed. These people do not talk a lot. When they do, they are "looking for work." After they find it, the roar does not diminish until three in the afternoon.

The United Farm Workers wave their flags and shout, *"Huelga"* into the fields. They stand in a solid line, on tops of cars and in roadside weeds. Most have no idea that James Buchanan was the fifteenth president of the United States. They know him only as a street in the Coachella Valley.

The Teamsters on the other side of the bumpy tar are spread thinner. They like to take their shirts off, flash their tattoos, and every now and then one threatens to drop his pants at the UFW. That always gets a big laugh. One slow morning, the boss Teamster stalked out into the fields, brought twelve workers out, arranged them by an American flag, and took their picture for the Teamster newsletter. When they got bored once, some Long Beach banana loaders stuffed a gunny sack, hung it as Cesar Chavez in effigy, and danced around it, spitting and calling the ex–potato bag fourteen kinds of motherfucker.

At three, the fieldwork stops, the United Farm Workers split for the shade trees in Coachella, and the Teamsters find an air conditioner. No one in the valley with any sense works past three. Both sides agree to let the sun carry the action until six. Then the battle starts all over again. The UFW uses the cooler evenings to spread out into the valley's sprinkling of little towns and labor camps.

On April 24, twenty strikers from the Coachella-Imperial Distributors Ranch took their leaflets and walked into the CID labor camp. The rest of the ninety-strong UFW pickets stayed on the road, by the line of gnarled cypress and the wave of sand pushing up on the camp's gate. The "camp" is a house trailer, a large single-roomed building with a bathroom in one end, and two cottages divided into two rooms apiece. The little houses are for families, and the big one holds thirty single men. The trailer is pulled by a semi and belongs to the camp manager, a short man with knobs of curly hair on his nose. On April 24, he never even came outside. As soon as he saw the strikers, he just grabbed the phone.

In ten minutes, the police arrived. While the sergeant and the picket captains discussed the UFW's right to be there, the Teamsters burst in. Minutes later all hell broke loose. The twenty Teamsters were led by Al Droubie and rushed up from the road. Droubie has not been very active in the last month, but in the first two weeks of the strike he kept busy enough to draw three different assault charges. Droubie paused momentarily at the sight of the police. But he was pissed off and began screaming.

"Get the fuck out of here!" he yelled. "Get these assholes out of here!"

Taking his cue, the pear-shaped Teamster behind Droubie threw a board into the circle of strikers and began to swing his bicycle chain. Droubie spotted Tom Dalzell, one of the UFW lawyers, in the front of the crowd. "Get him," he allegedly muttered, and the squat guy next to Droubie knocked Dalzell out cold with a right hand to his head. Droubie himself allegedly chased down UFW organizer Marshall Ganz and plowed him into the sand, screaming, "Fuck you, Ganz!" The Teamster had ripe sweat streaming down his face.

The twenty-man rush forced the UFW across the sand to the road. Once past the gate, they held their ground by the parked cars and sang *"No Tenemos Miedo."* That means "We are not afraid." The Teamsters stopped at the edge of the camp and punctuated the song with flying rocks that carried with a whistle and a thud when they slammed into the farmworkers' cars.

"Fuck you!" Droubie shouted from the cypress.

The most popular UFW response to the Teamster muscle has been on the picket line. As a group, the International Brotherhood of Teamsters, Chauffeurs, Warehousemen and Helpers has been shortened to *"los gorillas."* Some mornings, the pickets bring bananas tied to the ends of poles and dangle them at the Teamster line. The Teamsters have been carrying thick sticks, getting tans, and picking up Spanish. When they do, the shouting has been known to hurt their feelings. "I never called their mother none of them names," the one called "King Kong" said. "It ain't fair."

"YOU SEE, THESE CHAVISTAS are hypocrites," Ray Griego, Teamster Local 208, explains. Ray came out from L.A. after the first week of the strike. He likes to wear a flat black hat so he looks like Black Bart, and he loves to talk on the bullhorn. Griego is the only Teamster patrolling Karahadian and Sons Ranch who speaks Spanish, so he gets to be the Teamster voice every day. "Sometimes when I'm out here, I see them pray on their picket line, but only 25 percent of them mean it. One of the guys was flipping me the bird while he was supposed to be praying. I ask you, is that real?"

"We're just here to protect these people in the fields," is the way Ray Griego sees his job. Griego claims he has never laid a hand on anybody since he came out from his home in La Mirada.

"These people," he says, pointing back over his hat to the stooped shoulders in the field, "want to work. They got daughters and sons at home, but they're afraid to bring them to the fields because of these Chavistas. Since we've been here, they bring their kids.

"Do you know," Griego argues, "these Chavistas eat nothing but tortillas, beans, and potatoes all the time? That's all they eat, swear to God. Yesterday, one of them gave me a burrito. It was pure beans. It got me so mad that this man Chavez comes out here and feeds these people that shit morning, noon, and night. So what I did was buy some burritos myself. I came back and gave them a Teamster burrito. It was all meat. I ask you, what kinda union is it that makes its people eat beans? Those people inside the fields are eating beef in their burritos. They'll tell you they have to go with the people who put meat on the table, and that's us."

Pio Yerpes is a Filipino worker in the fields Ray Griego guards. Like most of the fifteen workers on his crew, he has been out of work much of his life. Farm labor is seasonal, but living is year-round, which means bills that only a paycheck can satisfy. In April and early May, the crew do what's called thinning. The bottom of the grape bunch is cut away from the stem, and six branches are left on top to make big, sweet Thompsons. If the job is done wrong, the grapes grow into water berries, bloated and tasteless. In June, the crews are tripled and they begin to pick. If the picking is done too slowly or too late, the grapes shrivel into raisins and droop on the vines, crusting into heaps. Whenever he works, Pio Yerpes uses his bandana to tie a straw hat to his head. Shade collects into a black apron under its brim and falls all over his eyes.

"I am a member of the Teamsters," he says. "I signed already. It seems to me it's good, but I don't know much about them yet. My boss, Mr. Karahadian, he sign with the Teamsters. Where shall I go? Shall I follow Chavez to strike? Without some money? And who will pay me? I'm supposed to follow my boss. Am I right? I have to support all kinds of things. Some of my car and everything like this and that. I go with them and what will happen? They will give me $5. Can I live on $5? It seems to me that's ridiculous."

K. Karahadian, the boss of Pio Yerpes and owner of the

fields Ray Griego guards, agrees. Karahadian made his stash in knit sportswear and moved out of L.A. in the thirties to own some grapes. "This Chavez made too goddamn many mistakes," Karahadian claims. "We tried to negotiate with this fellow clear back in November. He had a contract that was impossible to live with. About twenty negotiable items and we never got past the first one. In the meantime, we warned them. The Teamsters are in the valley, we said, but he wouldn't listen."

The 1965 strike hurt Karahadian, and thoughts of the new one jam his jaws together, so an occasional word beaches on one of his molars and rattles inside his head. "He . . . he simply pushed the workers away from his union. We didn't have nothing to do with it. If Teamsters came into our fields before negotiations, we chased them off. We kept out of the picture completely. We did the best we knew how to get along with this Chavez. Even then, his union was always har . . . harassing us with all kinds of stupid grievances, filling every day, just absolutely a bunch of nothings."

As far as Karahadian is concerned, the UFW is Cesar Chavez, and Cesar Chavez isn't much. "He's just not a labor leader," Karahadian says. "He's a revolutionist, or something like that. Those two don't go together. The Teamsters are in and that's all. That's the whole goddamn thing in a nutshell."

Rosario Pelayo used to work in Karahadian's fields before Ray Griego began to guard them. She tells a different kind of story. "The Teamsters never came into the fields to talk to us," she explains. "Our foreman was a Teamster and he signed us all up without telling us. The day before the strike, the Teamsters came and broke all our union flags. We had flags on our cars and on the grape rows, and they tore them all down. We went to the foreman. We told him that we were still under contract and that we did not permit him to come and molest us. The owner came up and said if we wanted to we could leave.

"The next day," Rosario recalls, "the union pickets came and called us to come out of the fields. We began to talk to the other workers. When we did, the son of the foreman picked up a grape stake and told me to leave. I said I was going to leave but that we'd all go together. We didn't agree with the union he wanted."

Rosario Pelayo claims she left the fields with eighty-five others. Her face is expressionless; she doesn't really smile or frown. She says the crew that replaced them is from Texas and northern Mexico. "The first time I ever got to talk to a Teamster," she continues, "was out here on the picket line. I told him that I didn't think their union was bad but it was very apart from our union. If they wanted to be our union, they should have talked to us. They don't represent farmworkers."

Rosario Pelayo, her husband, and their six children live on $50 a week strike benefits. "It's difficult," she admits, "but we have to struggle. It's our life."

SINCE APRIL 16, THAT LIFE has been a lot more dangerous than they ever expected. The Teamsters started a fear campaign sprinkled with beatings back in April and May. By June the situation became even more tense. June means picking in Coachella, and picking is a very touchy time. Grapes must be picked, packed, and sent to the cooler at the right moment. Left too long on the vine, the grapes begin to wrinkle, and each wrinkle means money out of a grower's pocket. June was slow this year and there were many wrinkles. Crews were short, the strike grew, and the crop began to burn around the edges. The UFW pickets numbered in the hundreds, and the Teamsters had to recruit fifteen-year-olds to do the work. The situation worsened and the Teamsters finally decided to cut the crap and get down to business. June 23, 1973, was the Battle of the Asparagus Patch.

The attack took shape at seven in the morning around the vineyard owned by Henry Moreno. A hundred United Farm Worker pickets got tired of standing next to Avenue 60 and decided to move into a clump of desert between the grapes and a field of asparagus, ninety yards farther on. The court injunctions said they had to stay sixty feet from the vines, so the pickets walked the long way and set up behind the field, with the asparagus to their backs. Most of the pickets were teenagers, women, and children. While they were making their way around the vineyard, seventy-five Teamsters crunched up behind the vines to watch. The Teamsters split into two groups, one facing the pickets, the other to their side and behind them. The International Brotherhood distributed pipes and tire irons. It was not long before they began to take swings and throw rocks at the stragglers in the UFW line.

The Teamster leader was known as the Yellow-Gloved Kid. The name came from the squash-colored gloves he never took off. He perched on the back of a white pickup, tugged at his wrists, and delivered hoarse shouts. Two fat Teamsters near him carried pistols tucked into their belts. The Teamsters were soaking up the heat like sponges, getting redder as they waited, and rubbing their hands in wet circles.

Then the waiting was over. The Yellow-Gloved Kid lobbed a firecracker toward the UFW picket. "Kill them!" he allegedly shouted. "Kill them!" That set the Teamsters in motion and their June offensive was under way. Three sheriffs stood between the two unions, but that did not even slow the Brotherhood's rush. The group to the side and back drew blood first. The ground they charged across was full of bumps. As the pickets tried to escape, they stumbled and fell into the Teamsters' path. A man named Tamayo hit the hardpan deck and two long-haired Teamsters allegedly split his head open with a pipe. It was as easy as swatting flies. For good measure, they spent five minutes kneading him with their size 12s. When Federico Sayre tried to help, he was knocked into the sand by a third Teamster coming up from behind.

All the United Farm Workers began to run, but there wasn't really any place to run to. The Teamsters had circled them on three sides. Some ran out the open side into the asparagus patch, only to be chased down. Before the police reinforcements arrived, several pickets got to sample Teamster benefits close up. A blond Teamster chased Roy Treviño with a tree limb and allegedly beat him to his knees. Each time Treviño staggered to his feet, the Teamster laced him with his piece of tree. When Joe Pavia finally helped him away, Roy's head was raining juice and he kept coughing blood in a thin dribble between his lips. Consuelo López found her son Ricardo by a pile of grape lugs with his face pushed in. The police helped the hundred limp back to the main road, but the Teamsters didn't want to stop. One called "Cat Man" chased a fourteen-year-old boy down the street and allegedly whipped him with a stick. Another ran across the road, opened a pickup door, pulled the driver out, and kicked his ass with a club. When the dust settled, five UFW members were in the hospital; twenty more were treated and released.

Before the June offensive ended four days later, eighteen Teamsters faced assault charges; a UFW member's house had been burned to the ground; Cesar Chavez was shot at; and four more UFW members were hospitalized after being "organized" with tire irons. When a priest had his nose broken by a three-hundred-pound Teamster in the middle of a crowded coffee shop, the shit finally hit the fan in the Teamster front office. Frank Fitzsimmons sent his own fact finders to Coachella and their report clinched it.

Murray Westgate was one of the men Fitzsimmons sent to help "maintain good relations with the press" and report back. On arrival, Fitzsimmons's emissary was quoted as saying there might be a "violence problem" in Coachella. Westgate was having dinner at the El Morocco Motel in Indio when he got the chance to investigate the problem in greater depth. Teamster Hank Salazar was with him. When a Teamster Westgate had never seen before approached Salazar and Westgate, Westgate looked up from his blue cheese dressing to introduce himself. The Teamster backed away from Westgate's handshake.

"I don't want to know you, you son of a bitch," the Teamster said. "Why the hell do I want to shake your hand? You think you can pull that shit on everyone? I don't like you. Get fucked." With that, the Teamster walked around the table, allegedly punched Westgate in the mouth, and then punched him once again to make sure he remembered the first one. "Don't try to pull that shit again," he said and left Westgate on the floor.

Westgate picked himself up off the carpet and the waitress brought his steak. Ralph Cotner, the Teamster area supervisor, approached him from across the room. "Westgate," he said, "there are four more guys standing over there who are madder than hell at you, and who are waiting to do the same thing unless you get the hell out of here right away." Westgate kept eating. As far as he could tell, everyone was angry about what he had told the press. The Teamsters wanted no publicity on the "violence problem."

Cotner bent over Westgate's shoulder again. "If you don't want that thing shoved down your throat," he allegedly said, "you'd better get the hell out of here." Westgate looked up and Salazar interceded. "Look, Murray," Salazar said, "you better get the hell out of here before you get killed." Westgate abandoned his steak and left.

Before the end of June, new orders came to Coachella. The Teamster "guards" were pulled out and sent to Arvin and Lamont, in Kern County. The director of the Western Conference's Agricultural Workers Organizing Committee, Bill Grammi, announced the move to the press.

"We're doing this," Grammi said, "because we believe that local law enforcement agencies have realized the need for increasing their forces to the point where their protection appears adequate."

BUT THE WAR CONTINUES. The bulk of table grape growers have signed with the Teamsters, and the UFW is still fighting for its life. Coachella is burrowed in front of its coolers now, waiting for November. The harvest is over. The UFW has gone north to Arvin, Delano, and Selma, striking all the grapes that are left to strike. It is a hard fight for the UFW to win by itself. They are a union of poor people—a union that has struck in table grapes, wine grapes, lettuce, and vegetables for eight years running. To win, the strikers must make their quarters do the work of a $5 bill. It's not easy, but their friends' help may make it easier.

Friends are one commodity the UFW has been able to count on. In the first five-year strike, it was the American grocery shopper who finally brought the growers to the table. When the demand for union grapes forced everything else off the fruit shelves, the UFW got a contract. The new boycott has already made this year's grapes worth $2.50 less if they do not have the black eagle—the UFW seal—on the box. Field production is 38 percent of last year's crop, and if the price dips much further, growers will be losing money with each box they ship.

The biggest farmworker friend has been the AFL-CIO. Three weeks after the strike started, George Meany announced that the 13.5 million member labor federation would tax its members four cents a head for three months and give the UFW a strike fund. The money has kept the UFW eating. In the meantime, a lot of grapes have turned brown, with puckers all over them like small prunes.

The shame of it all is that the money's wasted. All the money— the UFW strike fund, the Teamsters' million, the $250,000 spent by the Riverside County Sheriff's Department—could have been saved with the price of one honest vote. An election would sort out all the claims quickly, but it is not likely to happen soon. The Teamsters are not big on elections. They have run against the UFW three times in their agricultural organizing adventures and lost each time. The Brotherhood's attitude suits the growers fine.

It's the case of Keene Lersen that has most of the owners scared. Lersen is one of two Coachella growers who renewed their UFW contracts. In the first strike, he was a grower spokesman. Lersen went around the country telling whoever would listen that his workers didn't want a union. Finally, the UFW called the question. Being an honest man, Lersen accepted. A binding vote was arranged by impartial parties and Lersen lost 78 to 2.

The nearest thing to an election this time around happened before the strike began. Monsignor George Higgins, a consultant to the U.S. Bishops' Committee on Farm Labor, took twenty-five church and civic leaders into thirty-one fields and polled the workers. Their poll totaled UFW 795, Teamsters 80, no-union 78. If you are a Teamster or a grower, that adds up to a good reason not to vote.

Even without ballots, the Coachella Valley grape workers found ways of making their feelings known. One incident in the first week of the strike has become a farmworker legend. It began with a young woman member of the UFW and a bullhorn. She was with the picket line outside the Bobara Ranch, standing on top of a car. Behind her the sun hung like an egg yolk lobbed against a blue clapboard wall.

"Remember," she shouted to the workers in the field, "when we were under contract and we used to have fifteen-minute rest periods every four hours? I haven't seen anyone resting. Aren't there rest periods anymore?"

As she finished, the people in the vines began to break into bunches, sit down, and light cigarettes. When their break was over, the young woman started in again.

"Remember," she said, "under contract how we had water in the fields? Where is your water?"

The fieldworkers held up jugs and glass jars.

"Remember, too," she continued, "how our contract let us leave the fields to go to the bathroom anytime we wanted? I haven't seen anyone leave for the bathroom in two hours. Don't the Teamsters let you?"

Scattered workers began to walk to the portable toilets on the edge of the vineyard. When they returned, the bullhorn opened up again.

"Remember," the young woman said, "when we were all in the union and we used to shout, '*Viva Chavez*'? Is there anyone in the fields who still shouts '*Viva Chavez*'?"

The Teamster forewoman stood up over the vines. "*Abajo Chavez!*" she shouted. That's "Down with Chavez."

As soon as she finished, heads popped up and backs straightened all over the field. "*Viva Chavez!*" they yelled. "*Viva Chavez!*"

The Teamsters along the road ran back into the vines, stumbling along the rows and tripping on the crumbling furrows. "Shut up," they told the workers. "That's a rival union." With that, everyone except the forewoman walked out of the ranch and joined the UFW picket. The young woman got down from the car. "*Sí, se puede,*" she said. ("Yes, we can do it.")

The sun said nothing and only dripped along the young woman's back, leaving tracks on her shirt and toasting the dirt under her feet. On the other side of the avenue, the Teamster forewoman hunkered in the ounce of shade next to the vines, kicking at the heat with her new shoe.

[*Rolling Stone*, September 13, 1973]

Bitter Harvest

PART ONE:
[THE DESTRUCTION OF THE AMERICAN FARMER]

Things will be better for those farmers who can survive.
—James Earl Carter, Jr., at a meeting with farm leaders in 1978

O N JANUARY 20, 1977, the oath of office was administered to James Earl Carter, Jr., of Plains, Georgia, and he became the first farmer to assume the presidency since Thomas Jefferson of Shadwell, Virginia, did so on March 4, 1801. That distinction was the most prominent feature in the day's extensive press accounts of the new chief executive's life.

Ironically enough, as a young man, Jimmy Carter had not wanted any part of farming. When Carter abandoned Georgia for the United States Naval Academy, he had decided to leave turning red dirt to those whose dreams could fit inside the confines of the tiny village of Plains, Georgia (population 683). His could not. Carter figured that his younger brother, Billy, would be old enough to take over the family's farm and wholesale peanut shed whenever his father, James Earl, Sr., was no longer able to run the business. It took a family tragedy to get Jimmy Carter back from the navy and on the farm to live. In 1953, when brother Billy was still sixteen, James Earl, Sr., died suddenly of cancer and Jimmy cut his military career short to return to Plains, intent on saving his family's business from financial collapse.

In his first year back, the future president grossed around $90,000, and out of that he netted some $200.

Although the benefits did not show up in his 1953 ledgers, Jimmy Carter had returned in the middle of a transformation in the peanut industry. The first of these transformations was mechanization. Picking machinery, which let farmers multiply their acreage to more than six times their previous practical size, was introduced into Georgia during the fifties. Other technology proceeded to modernize quickly the drying, shelling, and sorting end of peanuts as well. Jimmy Carter followed the technological advance and bought his first peanut sheller late in the 1950s.

The Carters finally replaced that first sheller with the latest model during the year before Jimmy won the presidency, in 1976. The new machine is the size of half a city block, cost more than $1 million, shells 2,400 pounds of peanuts an hour, and has electric eyes that sort out the culls. The addition of the first sheller had let the Carter family business deal directly with such processors as Best Foods and Procter & Gamble, instead of selling through a middleman commercial sheller.

A stabilized market was the second development in the continuing transformation of the peanut industry, and the federal government is largely responsible for it. Government support for the peanut industry takes two basic forms. The first is the control of supply. The total tonnage of peanuts available to U.S. buyers is limited by both import restrictions and a federal program which requires that a farmer possess one of a limited number of government allotments in order to plant and harvest peanuts legally. The second form of governmental support is a system of federal purchases; peanuts not wanted by processors can be sold to the U.S. Department of Agriculture. The year Jimmy Carter began his run on the presidency, the USDA purchased 30 percent of the domestic peanut crop. During the month Carter accepted the Democratic party nomination, the government was paying $415 a ton for peanuts that were selling at $250 on the world market.

With that kind of help, wholesaling peanuts became a hard business in which to lose money. The Carters had done well by Plain's standards. In 1976, candidate Jimmy's net worth was estimated at $600,000. By then, the bulk of the Carter family business was concentrated in buying and selling peanuts, and the family simply grew seed peanuts on the side. The Carters' 227-acre peanut allotment was sharecropped by Leonard Wright, a black man who lived down the road.

Even so, it was as a farmer that Jimmy Carter became known to the rest of the nation. His projected image of farmer was a key element in his success. Although farmers make up only 3.8 percent of the nation's population and have relatively few votes, they are the living repositories of some of our central cultural myths and images. Since few urban voters know any farmers, the role has receded into a set of distant yet responsive chords in the electorate's mind, ideal material for advertising purposes. Farmers get up early, feed the chickens, eat well, practice traditional and patriotic virtues, and don't breathe smog. In noisy, nervous, and alienated urban and suburban America, a farmer seemed reliable, honest, and, above all, safe. Atlanta ad man Gerald Rafshoon's campaign commercials showed Jimmy Carter in jeans and work boots, striding through the red clods of Georgia toward a far line of pines. Jimmy's peanut became a symbol of virtue and the common person.

Jimmy Carter continued to seem the farmer on the day of his inauguration. Instead of riding in the president's armored limousine, the Carter family walked down Pennsylvania Avenue to the White House. The farmer's morning stroll was the lead on the evening news and was seized upon as a brilliant stroke of rural style, not to mention its being a goldmine of video opportunities.

At the time no one thought to consider this stroll an omen of things to come. In the middle of that winter, it was too much to imagine that one year later a crowd of more than ten thousand angry farmers would take the same route along Pennsylvania Avenue. They would call for a national agricultural strike and say nothing but bad things about the farmer who had preceded them the year before. Before the last wave of farmers finally left in April, they would stand outside the cast-iron White House fence, screaming that Jimmy Carter should never call himself a farmer again.

There are as many reasons for the farmers' political showdown as there are farms, but the farm that Jimmy Carter left behind had as cogent a collection as any other farm did. When Carter left for Washington, Leonard Wright was given full use of the Carter land without having to share the profits. Wright proceeded to plant corn and peanuts. That spring corn was selling at $2.50 a bushel. By June 1977 Georgia was in the worst drought since 1954. At harvesttime Wright's cornstalks came up only as high as his knee, and the peanut yield was poor. By then corn prices had fallen to $1.80 a bushel, far below Wright's cost of production. Wright would not say exactly how much money he had lost, but he would have to go back to the bank for refinancing in order to continue farming. By October 1977 Leonard Wright was considering applying for a federal disaster loan.

James Earl Carter, Jr,. of Plains, Georgia, the thirty-ninth president of the United States, had picked the right time to get out of farming. The bottom was rapidly falling out of the business.

Although the publicly buttressed and relatively tiny peanut industry had been slow to feel the effects of the worst farm depression in four decades, it had been brewing for three years when Jimmy Carter took office.

According to USDA statistics, the United States had some 2.7 million farms in the beginning of 1977. All together, they were the single biggest industry in the economy. Ninety-nine percent of those farms remain family operations, although their sizes vary greatly. Nineteen percent of them produce 78 percent of total U.S. agricultural output. By far the largest number of farms (1.4 million) grow wheat in the wide belt of prairies between southern Montana, northern Texas, eastern Colorado, and the Oklahoma-Arkansas border. Corn and soybeans are the next most common crops and are grown all over the Midwest and South. From a total national investment of $564 billion in 1976, agricultural producers netted only some $20 billion. At that rate of return, an average of one thousand farmers a week went out of business. After adjusting for the bloat in the dollar over the years, we find that 1976 was the worst year in real farm income since 1936. Within four months after Jimmy Carter's inauguration, it was clear that 1977 would be even worse and would approach 1934 in terms of total agricultural disaster. There was little relief in sight. In June 1977 *Fortune* magazine estimated that the total net farm income in 1978 could drop as low as $17 billion, a return to the depths of the 1929 depression in rural economies.

Rising production expenses were obviously eating agriculture alive. In five years, costs of fertilizers had risen by 253 percent. Diesel tractor fuel that cost seventeen cents a gallon in 1972 cost forty-three cents a gallon in 1977. One expensive 1972 tractor costing $16,000—unchanged in design except for a new door latch and a different seat—sold in its 1977 version for $32,000, a 100 percent increase in five years. During that same period, farmers' prices have traveled in the opposite direction. In 1949 one Kansas farmer sold his wheat at $1.90 a bushel. In 1977 a bushel of wheat sold for $1.64. It cost the average 1977 wheat farmer $3.55 to raise a bushel of grain. The price paid to farmers for that same bushel never rose above $2.80 and dropped as low as $2.03. Stated in simple terms, by the time Jimmy Carter became president, most of the nation's farmers had spent several years paying cash out of their pockets for the right to spend eighteen hours a day, six days a week, feeding the United States and a good portion of the rest of the world.

The only return that farmers were getting on their efforts took monetary form in the value of the land they farmed. Since 1972 the average worth of U.S. farmland has risen between 15 and 35 percent a year, while farm income has remained basically untouched and sagging. To gain access to that wealth, farmers either had to sell their land or had to borrow against it. The first option was anathema to most farmers. More than a business, farming was their culture. Plowing ground, raising crops, living in small towns, and going to church—this was the way they thought people ought to live, but it was an impossible proposition without their land. Taking their capital gains, moving to the suburbs for a job in a tractor plant, and becoming someone else was a transformation they pursued only when there was no other choice.

As a result, most farmers mortgaged their inflated equities in order to continue farming at a loss. Total farm debt between 1960 and 1977 increased 400 percent, and more than half of that increase has occurred in the last five years. Interest payments as a percentage of farmers' net income have risen from 20 to 40 percent in the same five years. By the time Jimmy Carter took his oath, the farmers were reaching the limits of their capacity to support this debt structure, and it had begun to totter.

ONE OF THE IRONIES OF THE increasingly disastrous economics of farming is that the family farm has always been pointed to as one of the greatest of American institutions, clear proof of the correctness of our "system." Although 144 of the United Nations' 150 member nations cannot feed themselves, this network of small family-farming businesses produces consistently bountiful portions of food at by far the lowest prices in the world. Attempts to replace family farms with corporate enterprise have, aside from accruing tax advantages, proved a failure. The secret to the system's acclaimed success is that, unlike wage workers or a nationalized proletariat, well-equipped people who work their own land will invest all their energies in it. They go out in bad weather and do not take holidays. Out of pride in themselves, they nurse food along, calling on the lessons learned by four and five generations.

Most of the present forces propelling farmers toward bankruptcy arose from the position of extreme structural disadvantage they occupy in relation to their suppliers on the one hand and their market on the other. By 1977 the nation's 2.7 million agricultural producers were caught in a vicious "free market" sandwich. In order to farm, they had to buy supplies from a set of agricultural service and manufacturing industries that have been described by a number of economists as "shared monopolies," an arrangement whereby a small number of companies effectively controls an industry and acts in unspoken agreement in order to mutually milk the market. Two corporations, Deere & Company and International Harvester, sell 57 percent of all farm machinery. Four firms supply 74 percent of all agricultural chemicals, and another four sell 67 percent of all farm petroleum products. More than half of all hybrid seed sold in the United States is sold by either the Dekalb or Pioneer seed companies. The huge size of these agribusiness suppliers gives them an overwhelming advantage over the farmers.

The same difficulties characterize the farmers' attempts to pass on to others their constantly rising costs in the marketplace. Grain farmers are typical. The grain farmer's customer and immediate link in the food chain is the commodity merchant. This merchant in turn sells the grain he purchases to an agricultural processor, who sells to a food manufacturer, who sells to food merchants, who in turn sell to grocers, who sell to the consumer. Since 90 percent of the world's exportable grain supply is produced in the United States, virtually all the trading of the world's commodity merchants is centered in either the Minneapolis, Chicago, or Kansas City Boards of Trade. The bidding on the floors of those boards sets the farmers' prices through a process so elaborate and instantaneous that few farmers a thousand miles away on their tractors can even keep steady track of it, much less participate in it. Thousands of merchants pass paper on the board, trying to buy low and sell high, but as usual, the giants dominate the pricing. Cargill, Inc., and Continental Grain Company alone control 50 percent of all international grain trade. As a result, grain prices have had a long history of reflecting the economics of commodity merchants rather than that of farmers.

The only potential weapons the farmers have for wresting control of their pricing structure is either withholding their product from the market or producing less. The first option is currently relatively useless, since only a minority of farmers have access to the necessary storage capacity for any longer than a year, and even fewer have cash flows enabling them to continue without harvest income sufficient for paying the prolonged storage charges involved in waiting out the Board of Trade.

Producing less, the second option, is the source of farming's biggest dilemma. Farming is one of the few occupations in which the success of the entire membership is a collective disaster. When things are going well in banking, each banker prospers. If all the nation's autoworkers are working at their maximum, successfully producing cars, each of them is obviously succeeding. However, if every farmer has a good harvest, every farmer goes broke. American agriculture is enormously productive, easily surpassing the appetites of the world's best and most cheaply fed people. In years when weather and pests fail to cut out large chunks of the world harvest, the Board of Trade is glutted and prices hit the basement. Only shortage will bring them up again. For example, when summer hailstorms sweep across a county whose farmland is rich in soybeans, the few farmers in the neighborhood whose plants have not been reduced to pulp stand to make a lot of money out of the community's misfortune. Pitted against each other as they are, farmers have a history of acting as separate individuals, and cooperative efforts to hold down production have traditionally failed miserably.

For fear of being among those whose harvest is destroyed by hail, most farmers prefer to plant as much as possible and are often swamped in the resulting glut. When evaluated according to its precision and reliability as a means of planning both our own and the world's food supply, the farming end of the food chain closely resembles the early World War I fighter plane whose pilot randomly fired his machine gun through the path of his own spinning propeller, hoping that he wouldn't hit a blade, disable the engine, and fall four thousand feet straight down, without a parachute.

Since World War I, military aviation has developed to the point where it has weaponry that can be aimed dead center on a target traveling twice the speed of sound and invisible to the pilot's eye. The only thing farm production planning has added during that same sixty-year period is the parachute. Ever since the great farm depression of 1924 culminated in the stock market crash of 1929, the federal government has played the role of breaking agriculture's fall. Franklin Roosevelt's administration, in its working analysis of the causes of depressions, gave agricultural failure a key role. The precipitating problem, it was argued, was that extremely low agricultural prices and income were out of sync with the rate of reward in the rest of the economy. The resulting massive farm failure was eventually catastrophic to the entire nation. Attempting to determine a level of subsidy that would bring rural and urban economies back into balance, Roosevelt's Agricultural Adjustment Administration eventually struck on the years 1910–14 as a model. That period of U.S. history had been characterized by a healthy balance of prosperity. Thus a mathematical formula was developed that would translate present prices into farmers' 1914 economic power. That model was called "parity," and all subsidies were set at a percentage of the "parity index." Percentages of parity were used as agricultural-subsidy yardsticks until 1973, when the subsidies were phased out by Earl Butz, Richard Nixon's secretary of agriculture.

Since then, the great bulk of government agricultural programs have relied on two thrusts: low-interest, nonrecourse USDA loans and a system of target prices set by Congress and adjusted at the discretion of the secretary of agriculture. In the first program money is lent with future crops placed as collateral. The loan is keyed to a "loan price" that theoretically sets a bottom on the various commodity markets. Whenever the market price falls below the loan rate, the farmers enrolled in the program can forfeit their crops to the USDA and their notes are fulfilled. The loan rate on wheat in 1977 was around $2.30 a bushel, $1.25 below the cost of production. The system of USDA target prices pays the enrolled farmers a direct subsidy that will make up for the difference between the market and target prices at the end of the year. In early 1977 the target price of wheat was $2.47 a bushel, $1.08 below farmers' costs. If 1977 prices were set at 100 percent of parity, wheat would have brought farmers $5.05 a bushel.

In the past farmers had obviously gotten a lot more from Congress, but these days the political numbers are running in the opposite direction. The total percentage of the population engaged in farming has dropped steadily for the last sixty years, sinking from 80 to 3.8 percent. With the exception of a few select products, this has meant a steady reduction of political influence for most farmers. At the same time, the American consumer movement came into maturity, and politicians were quick to pit one constituency against the other. Farm prices, it began being argued, should be kept down in order to help consumers. Richard Nixon gave *de facto* recognition to this new political pecking order in 1973, when he froze beef retail prices in response to a housewife boycott, knocking the bottom out of the cattle market in the process.

There are two primary ironies in the pitting of farmers against consumers. The first is that farmers are the biggest consumers of all. An enormous amount of America's domestic industrial production is consumed by agriculture. In 1977 farmers owned millions of trucks, tractors, combines, corn pickers, and assorted implements, valued at $72.3 billion. Their family cars alone cost more than $7 billion. Every farmer is serviced by ten merchants, and every agricultural dollar makes seven more before it is finished circulating in the economy.

The second irony is that shoppers' prices bear little relationship to farmers' income. Over the years the processing, not the production, of food has come to dominate the consumer price structure. When buying cornflakes, the consumer pays the grocer $37 a bushel for corn the commodity merchant bought for somewhere around $1.80 a bushel. If cotton farmers donated their crops to the shirtmaking industry, the cost of a $10 shirt would drop only thirty-five cents.

Ironic or not, this political opposition between the two extreme ends of the food chain has characterized American food policy throughout the 1970s. As a presidential candidate, James Earl Carter, Jr., the peanut farmer from Plains, Georgia, pledged himself to stand up for farmers in the conflict.

"I will," he promised during a harvesttime visit to the corn belt in 1976, "support prices equal to at least the cost of production. Like most of Carter's promises, it was clear and simple. The problem with the future president's pledge was that farmers remembered it, even after Jimmy Carter apparently considered it ancient history. Eventually, the widening gap between Carter's promise as a peanut farmer and his performance as chief executive was filled with an angry rush of men and tractors that splashed across the nation's front pages and TV screens under the heading of "The 1977 Farm Strike."

THE 1977 FARM STRIKE WAS basically a reaction to both the collapsing farm economy in general and the inadequacy of Jimmy Carter's 1977 farm bill in particular. When the bill was finally passed by Congress in August 1977, its biggest effect was that 1977 wheat-support prices were raised to $2.90 a bushel, which was still sixty cents a bushel under the cost of production. Agriculture secretary Bob Bergland, a former farmer and Minnesota congressman, said that the bill was full of new "benefits," but farmers, especially those in wheat, tended to disagree. If they were going to survive, they needed a lot more than Carter offered. By September 1977, the national press was full of reports about the president's sagging farm support. Bergland denied them.

"My own soundings vary," he told the *New York Times* on September 24, "but I don't see any farm revolt brewing at this point."

In fact, the agriculture secretary had just received strong indications to the contrary. On September 23, the day before Bergland's statement, he had attended a scheduled meeting with farmers in Pueblo, Colorado. Three thousand wheat and milo producers showed up from as far away as Oklahoma and Kansas, and they were all angry. A number had brought their tractors along. The huge machines were parked out front with signs on them urging farmers to stop production until they received a fair price for their product. Inside the Pueblo Memorial Hall, whenever Bergland tried to defend the Carter farm policy, he was shouted down. Most of the farmers in the audience were part of what they called the "American Agriculture Movement" (AAM). Bergland had never heard of the group before, but he would hear a lot more of it soon.

AAM had no elected officers and no formal organization to speak of, but all its members wore baseball caps that said STRIKE across the front, and they carried signs saying the same thing. One of the hand-lettered placards waved in Bergland's face that afternoon seemed to typify the movement's strategy.

YOU'LL REMEMBER THE FARMER, it read, WHEN YOU DON'T HAVE FOOD.

The American Agriculture Movement that organized the 1977 farm strike has never really been much of an organization as such. The group has always been officerless, preferring to operate in a direct partnership with each and every farmer involved, and its strike has never had anything approaching a modern, pyramid-shaped organizational chart. The movement congealed around a simple set of demands when talk of strike first surfaced during the week before Labor Day 1977, in the town of Springfield, Colorado (population 1,750).

Thirty years earlier, Springfield, the Baca County seat, was the "Broom Corn Capital of the World." Broom corn is the primary ingredient in the business end of a broom, and southeastern Colorado farmers once grew more of it than they did wheat. Ten years ago low-priced Mexican imports finally drove them out of the market. Many of them began farming sugar beets along with their grain. By 1977 only one sugar plant was still operating in Colorado, and it was rapidly going broke in a domestic market swamped with South American and Caribbean imports. Most of Baca County's farmers had now settled on trying to make a living from wheat and cattle and were not having much greater success. After the harvest of July 1977, it was clear to everyone around Springfield that they had the latest of many disasters on their hands.

The Baca County farms that raised cattle had first been clobbered in 1973, when Nixon froze the price of beef. For a while afterward it seemed as if those who survived might recoup all their losses with wheat: in 1972 a great deal of the rest of the world's grain crop was destroyed by bad weather. When the Russians eventually entered the Chicago wheat market with a handful of federal export subsidies and bought millions of bushels at $1.65 a bushel, the market took off and climbed as high as $6, staying near $4 until 1975. There was a lot of talk at the time about starvation, and the infant Ford administration urged farmers to plant "fence post to fence post." As the bumper 1975 crop approached harvest, Ford suddenly reversed himself in response to an AFL-CIO protest against wheat exports and the rising price of bread and invoked a presidential embargo on the Russian grain sales. The market took a nosedive to $2 a bushel, and Baca County lost money hand over fist. Two more bumper crops later, in September 1977 they were still sinking. One 1977 farmer had borrowed $170,000 to finance his crop, produced the best yield of either his or his father's lifetimes, and lost $28,000.

When he went back to the bank to get new financing, he saw all his neighbors there doing the same thing.

The American Agriculture Movement sprang out into the open for the first time when four of those eastern Colorado farmers—Jerry Wright, Alvin Jenkins, and Derral and Gene Schroder—met for coffee in early September. Derral Schroder, in his fifties, farms a total of eight thousand acres with his seventy-seven-year-old father and his grown sons, Gene and Billy. They raise wheat, milo, and corn, as well as cattle. All summer long, the Schroders had long discussions about going out of business. While they were talking over coffee that morning, the idea came up that farmers just ought to stop producing. Gene Schroder was the first one to speak up and use the word they would all soon begin marching under. He said they ought to have a strike.

Strike is a word that has always had a slightly foreign ring to it for farmers, and those four men were no exception. Their easy acceptance of the word *strike* that morning is testimony to how they all disliked the word *bankruptcy* even more. All four thought that striking was a good idea. Within a few days they had arranged a meeting of forty of the county's farmers with their banker on the ground floor of Springfield's First National Bank.

The Schroders and Jerry and Alvin told those at the meeting that agriculture was on the bottom of the pile and being treated badly. Skilled farmers, with good water, land, and crops, and favored by good weather, were losing money and being driven off the land. It was time that they all stood up for themselves and stopped being taken for granted. One farmer at the meeting walked out, but everyone else, including the banker, stayed all two and half hours and eventually agreed. On September 12 a countywide meeting was called, and six hundred farmers attended. Most already had their winter wheat planted, and all six hundred voted unanimously to call for a strike. They set December 14, 1977, as the day their strike would commence if their demands were not met.

The strikers' demands rapidly evolved into a five-point program that centered on guaranteed minimum agricultural prices set at 100 percent of parity. The strike pledge bound the strikers to boycotting new equipment purchases and to reducing their production by 50 percent. The first leaflet calling for an "agricultural strike" was distributed the next day at the state fair in Hutchinson, Kansas, five hundred miles away.

The AAM received its first public recognition in the September 15 edition of the local Pueblo, Colorado, newspaper, *The Chieftan*; the report was soon carried throughout the western wheat belt. The Baca County farmers announced their strike deadline and told the *Chieftan* that they were going to inform agriculture secretary Bob Bergland of it personally when he visited Pueblo on September 23. "We can't see anything [in Carter's farm policy]," Derral Schroder explained, "but a four-year program that guarantees farmers a loss on all major commodities." The response in farm country was immediate.

The meeting on September 23 at Pueblo Memorial Hall had originally been scheduled at the behest of Rep. Frank Evans (D–Colo.). Whatever the original intentions of the gathering, it became the embryonic strike movement's first show of force. Three thousand farmers rallied beforehand inside a giant ring of tractors at Rocky Ford, Colorado, and paraded in a tractor-led caravan for the remaining forty-seven miles to Pueblo. Bergland's appearance became a hearing for a long litany of grievances. The secretary of agriculture stood on Memorial Hall's stage in his shirtsleeves while farmers in work clothes addressed him from the floor mike. The secretary wanted to seem sympathetic but was not well received. "This is an extremely complicated situation," Bergland concluded, "and I want to talk to the president about it."

Few farmers had expected any other response. The AAM continued to organize frantically after Bergland returned to the District of Columbia. The striking western wheat farmers parked their machinery, called other farmers, set up meetings, and traveled to them to spread the word. Meetings and rallies blossomed throughout the West.

Thus 250 farmers showed up for the first rally, held in Umbarger, Texas. Another thousand paraded to a meeting at the Lexington,

Nebraska, fairgrounds, carrying barrels of manure labeled "Ag Profits." Strike offices opened in Pampa, Texas, and Soper, Oklahoma, and spread across the panhandles at the rate of two a day. The strike grew even faster in Kansas. Farmers in Goodland, Kansas, paraded their combines through town, and farmers in Cimarron, Kansas, organized to send back all the mail-order Christmas catalogues in the county with an American Agriculture Movement leaflet attached. Some five thousand farmers from all those states and more gathered for a rally in Amarillo, Texas, on October 14 and vowed to organize the whole nation before the December 14 strike deadline.

In a matter of weeks, the western wheat belt's fervor had spread to the agriculturally devastated areas of the American Southeast, Jimmy Carter's home turf.

The farm strike first made contact with Georgia on October 24 at the Plains High School auditorium in the president's hometown. The meeting was officially billed as an evening of cultural exchange between Plains, Georgia, and Plains, Kansas. Six farmers from Plains, Kansas, visited as part of a delegation of striking farmers from Kansas and Colorado; 120 Georgia farmers, most of them from the neighborhood served by the Carter peanut business, attended the meeting. The western wheat farmers received standing ovations when they blasted Jimmy Carter's farm policy.

"They put a little ole plastic elephant in a pack of corn toasties," Alvin Jenkins from Baca County, Colorado, charged, "and get more for it than you get from a year's work." The crowd roared. "They come up with this farm bill," Jenkins added, "and it's just as lousy as the last one." The crowd roared again.

The wheat farmers tried to make it clear they were not asking for a handout. A broke government borrowing more money to lend to broke farmers so that they can become even more broke made no sense to them. They wanted a marketplace price no lower than the parity price set by law. By law a farmer who wants to hire help can't pay less than $2.65 an hour minimum wage; so why not institute minimum-price laws to protect farmers?

The strike meeting received heavy coverage in the Georgia

press, and local television stations filmed the demonstration that followed in downtown Plains. The president's brother, Billy, had just announced the inaugurating of his own personal brand of beer. A sign had been erected downtown, urging people to buy Billy Beer and support the Georgia economy; so the visiting wheat farmers held an impromptu demonstration at Billy's sign with signs of their own saying NO BARLEY. NO BEER. The Macon, Georgia, television accounts of the incident reported that the president's brother had been upset to the point of allegedly threatening some of the striking farmers before they left.

One of the Georgia farmers who watched that television coverage was Tommy Kersey of Unadilla. The western farmers' demands had touched one of his raw nerves. Kersey, 38, farms six thouand acres with his father and two brothers. When the Billy Beer demonstration flashed on the evening news, Tommy had just finished filling out the papers for a Small Business Administration loan. The Kerseys are diversified farmers, growing corn, cotton, soybeans, peanuts, vegetables, and some small grains. They also keep one thousand breed cows and some six hundred brood sows. In 1976 they lost more than a half-million dollars. It was their third losing year in a row, and they were luckier than many of their neighbors.

Unadilla, Georgia (population 2,000), sits along the red-dirt border of Houston and Dooly Counties. Most local finances began crashing in 1973. When the Kerseys started farming that year, most of their land was almost paid off. By late 1977 they were mortgaged to the hilt again and figured that they had equity enough to finance one more losing year. Going on strike made sense to Tommy Kersey from the first time he considered doing so. The only name he could remember from the news reports was that of visiting Kansas farmer Gene Short, and Kersey spent the weekend calling Gene Shorts all over Kansas until he found the right one and arranged for two Kansans to come and address a meeting in Unadilla. When they arrived on November 10, more than seventeen hundred people attended; the others converged on fairgrounds a mile outside of Statesboro, Georgia, and paraded with an estimated three thousand tractors to the Bulloch County Courthouse square. Reporters on the scene noted signs saying THANKS TO THE GOVERNMENT, FARMERS ARE AN ENDANGERED SPECIES and THE HAND THAT FEEDS THE WORLD IS EMPTY. Speakers at the accompanying rally promised to get even bigger crowds when they paraded again in Plains, the day after Thanksgiving. "If the president comes home to eat turkey," the farmers announced, "he's going to have to talk it, too." The Carters decided to take their Thanksgiving at Camp David. Nevertheless, four thousand tractors and ten thousand farmers jammed the president's hometown on November 25. Tourist traffic was tied up for miles.

DESPITE HIS COST-OF-PRODUCTION price promise during the election, it was clear by then that James Earl Carter, Jr., was not about to give the farmers a new farm bill. He had enough problems with the one that Congress had already passed. The key to Carter's stated objections was the total cost. In the last year of the Ford administration, farm subsidies had run around $734 million. Under the 1977 farm bill, which the striking farmers called "inadequate," public costs were expected to increase to $3 billion. Under the new law, Congress set wheat target prices at $2.90 a bushel, sixty-five cents under the cost of production. Carter had tried to hold Congress in line at $2.65 a bushel by frequently threatening to block any program costing more than $2 billion. Apparently, a minimum-price law such as the striking farmers suggested was never considered. On October 1 the 1977 farm bill was finally signed by the president after weeks of rumors of impending veto.

Jimmy Carter gave the strike his first public sign of recognition almost two months later, when he invited four AAM members from the Maryland area to the White House. The former peanut farmer evinced sympathy with their goals but made it clear that he had signed the only farm bill he intended to. No one from AAM was surprised. Tommy Kersey and the others rightly assumed that the striking farmers would have to show the nation that they were dead serious before anything would happen. By now Unadilla was the Georgia state strike headquarters. The next step the Peach State had planned was the largest tractorcade in history.

The enormous parade took place on December 9, five days before the strike's December 14 deadline. Farmers from all over Georgia gathered at assembly points on the three major highways leading into Atlanta, the state capital. When the lead tractor from Tommy Kersey's starting point reached Atlanta, tractors were still leaving the assembly area forty-one miles to the south. Observers estimated that seventeen thousand tractors clogged the highways and streets around the Georgia capital. The AAM estimated the crowd at thirty thousand. The numbers were doubly impressive because a number of other tractorcades were forming throughout the state at the same time. Gloria Carter Spann, the president's sister, rode a tractor in the strike's Macon, Georgia, parade but issued no public statement.

On the next day striking farmers on tractors made their first appearance in Washington, D.C. Two twelve-block-long columns of slogan-clad tractors and trucks from Kansas, Colorado, Oklahoma, Maryland, and Virginia inched along Independence and Constitution Avenues, snarling traffic for more than an hour. WE'RE BROKE, one banner read, AND THAT'S NO JOKE.

Fifty of the Maryland tractors remained in Washington until the morning of December 14. To signal the official commencement of the 1977 Farm Strike, they rolled down Pennsylvania Avenue and circled the White House at 12:01 a.m. That signal was followed by a flurry of activity across the nation. Long, flag-draped caravans of tractors in Texas attempted to block deliveries of food and milk. Kansas, Nebraska, and the rest of the wheat belt were full of parades. The first instance of vandalism in strike activity was reported in Blackshear, Georgia, where two farmers cut the air hose on a feed truck. Back in Baca County, Colorado, where it all began, the strikers paraded through Springfield. Afterward, Gene Schroder disabled his giant wheat combine on a bridge ten miles south of town, and Highway 287 into Springfield remained cut for most of the afternoon.

The passing of the strike deadline invoked no sudden halt in work or production. Striking in December against an August crop meant little with snow on the ground or winter seed planted. It was only at harvesttime that the strike's impact could be measured. What the strike amounted to when it began in December, with six hundred strike offices in forty states, was a threat. The credibility of that threat could be estimated only by the farmers' midwinter show of force. And that demonstration, even doubters had to admit, was unlike anything that agriculture had ever seen before.

Twenty-four-hour picketing of food warehouses had commenced throughout Wyoming, and 140 tractors advanced on Chillicothe, Ohio. Seven hundred of the same machines cruised highways in Champaign County, Illinois, the largest corn-producing county in the world. A statewide rally was held in Salt Lake City, Utah, and Kentucky stockyards were closed by strikers. In no uncertain terms, the farm strike served public notice that at the very least farmers were prepared to make a nuisance of themselves all winter long. When questioned on December 14, Bob Bergland expressed doubts about the effectiveness of the strike, but he endorsed its withholding action on the grounds that the price-bolstering effect was consistent with the purposes of the Carter farm policy. "I say go to it," the secretary of agriculture remarked.

The farmers did.

Huron, South Dakota, held a three-mile tractorcade in the middle of a blizzard. Hays, Kansas, rallied eight thousand people and ten miles of tractors while Montana averaged six strike meetings a week. In Abilene, Texas, picketing farmers halted bread deliveries. In Portland, Oregon, they shut down a Cargill grain elevator for a day. In Lubbock, Texas, American Agriculture Movement members, incensed over a *Lubbock Avalanche-Journal* editorial accusing them of "union goon tactics," blockaded the newspaper and delayed the morning edition four hours. As usual, Georgia had one eye on the tractor throttle and the other on Plains.

Shortly after the giant Atlanta demonstration, the striking Georgians began to talk of getting twenty-five thousand tractors to Plains when the president came home for Christmas. Soon after the word had gotten around, the demonstration's organizers were approached by some of Carter's friends from Sumter County. The president's neighbors said that if they would not come in such numbers and kept it small, "maybe" Jimmy would address the crowd. The AAM reluctantly agreed, and plans for Plains were changed to make it a symbolic act rather than a show of force. No thought was even given to not going at all. The farmers had been trying to corner the president in his hometown for three months, and they knew that he would not stay north for Christmas. They set December 23 as the day for the action.

On December 21, Jimmy Carter and his family arrived in Plains for the holidays. On the morning of December 23, the members of the American Agriculture Movement arrived in Plains in exactly the manner they had promised the president's friends. The crowd that gathered downtown was modest by Georgia standards. Even so, it more than jammed Plains's one-block-long main thoroughfare facing the railroad tracks. The shops there sell Jimmy Carter ashtrays, Jimmy Carter penknives, Jimmy Carter fingernail clippers, and hairbrushes embossed with the presidential seal. Early in the day Jimmy Carter sent a message to Tommy Kersey and the rest of the AAM organizers that he could not address their meeting for "security reasons." If, however, the group selected twenty-five representatives, he would meet with them on December 24. By 4 p.m. that day, the size stipulated for the invited group had been reduced by Carter to four, and the president wanted all four to be from Georgia. The AAM accepted the reduction but refused to limit the group to Georgians. The meeting was set for 8 a.m. the next day.

"As long as farmers let the consumers know they have got a problem, that is good," Jimmy Carter told the press corps as the demonstration made its way out of town. "But if they ever turn the consumers against them," he warned, "they will be worse off than they were before." Observers noted that Carter's remark was a good deal testier than his earlier comments. None of the departing farmers stopped to buy Jimmy Carter tie tacks or postcards of brother Billy's garage.

At the appointed time on December 24, the president greeted Harold Israel of Plains, Tommy Kersey of Unadilla, Carl Hawkins of Lake Butler, Florida, and E. E. Money of Dothan, Alabama, at his front door. Jimmy Carter was dressed in a flannel shirt and jeans and was accompanied by his son Chip. He and the farmers gathered around the table in the Carter dining room for thirty-five minutes. Now that the farmers had the president cornered, they felt a little self-conscious. They refused an offer of coffee and for the first few minutes made quiet and polite country conversation. The president wanted them to know that he had met with them only because he was a farmer interested in agriculture and not because he had been pressured into the meeting. Then Carter asked if the farmers had really taken a "close" look at his farm bill. At that point, the politeness level dropped several notches. One of the participants responded to his question by saying a glance was enough. He personally would not use it even for toilet paper.

According to the participants, the president visibly stiffened at the remark. As one later put it, "Jimmy tucked them ole teeth up, and we didn't see 'em again for the rest of the thirty-five minutes."

Carter then became very serious and said that the world was going bankrupt and could not afford the high cost of food along with the rising costs of energy. The president went on to stress that if his farm bill was given time to work, it would turn things around before his term had ended. The farmers said that they had no time to wait. When the meeting was over, they left some of their AAM literature with the president and saw themselves out. The only promise Carter made was that he would have Bob Bergland meet with farm leaders from all fifty states in early January 1978. "I sympathize with them," the president told waiting reporters.

Twenty-four hours later, on Christmas Day, a visitor to the Carter household noticed the AAM leaflets left by the farmers the day before. They were stuffed in the dining-room wastebasket in one large bundle.

PART TWO:
[THE FARMERS STRIKE BACK]

The first farm strike in the nation's history extended into 1978, with no time to lose. Even though the striking farmers were bound by their strike pledge to grow only 50 percent of their normal production, they would have to return to their fields in four months and work the dirt if they were to grow anything at all. They would have little time to parade their tractors come April.

On Tuesday, January 3, South Dakota strikers turned back five truckloads of imported Canadian beef at the border. Early reports from Texas indicated that the town of Lubbock was completely surrounded by tractors. In Denver, Colorado, five hundred strikers in three hundred vehicles descended on a regional Safeway warehouse, and twenty-five police were dispatched to the scene. A farmer was arrested after he and others moved a tractor across the warehouse gate. In the ensuing scuffle several farmers were sprayed with Mace.

These local actions maintained the strike's visibility but had little other effect. If the American Agriculture Movement was going to win any relief for farmers before planting time, it would have to be won in Washington, D.C., against the stiff opposition of the first farmer to be elected president since 1801. On the face of it, the AAM was not well suited for the task.

The farmers were bona fide political amateurs, and they had little tolerance for greasing the wheels of power. When they heard the word *lobby*, most of them immediately thought of the movie-house foyer. To compensate for a lack of experience, the farm strike had to count on visibility and enthusiasm.

Throughout American history, the farmers have always been convinced that agriculture was democracy's taproot in Mother Earth. In addition to that sense of historical mission, farmers now felt an immediate urgency inspired by the bankruptcy breathing down their collective necks. As far as these farmers were concerned, their strike was a crusade for survival, and they had no qualms about acting in accordance with that realization.

It is not surprising that the world of federal agricultural policy had trouble understanding the farmers. In the halls of Congress and the USDA, agricultural policymaking is a well-worn towpath watched over by several key politicians and a host of economists. For their farm policy the reduction in the number of farmers was a natural and even desirable outcome of the advance of technology and its inevitable tendency to "concentrate" the farm industry into a smaller number of larger producers. Added to this legacy was the Carter administration's overriding concern with inflation and the federal budget. Neither higher market prices nor higher subsidies were acceptable.

The collision between these two viewpoints on agriculture was preordained. During the first four months of 1978, the conflict grew into a running political battle, which culminated in the farmers' making a massive assault on federal legislative bastions. When the dust cleared, James Earl Carter, Jr., of Plains, Georgia, had held the line on every front. Carter would claim to have marshaled a great "victory for consumers," and the farmers took to calling the former peanut farmer the Benedict Arnold of agriculture. Furthermore, part of the credit for the president's victory would go to another ex-farmer, Secretary of Agriculture Bob Bergland.

It was fitting that the strike, which had first announced itself at a 1977 meeting between Bergland and the farmers in Pueblo, Colorado, began its 1978 campaign on January 6 with a rematch in Omaha, Nebraska, the agricultural capital of the Midwest. The gathering was arranged by Nebraska governor J. J. Exon and was planned as a small meeting between the secretary of agriculture and selected AAM members. Exon called the meeting a "bargaining session" when he announced the arrangements. If it was, it resembled few of the backroom and closed-door powwows that "bargaining" usually evokes.

On the morning of January 6, starting from three different assembly points, mounted farmers paraded single file toward Ak-Sar-Ben Coliseum, the Omaha entertainment complex where the session was to be held. One of the converging tractor columns was more than four miles long. At the coliseum itself 300 AAM members were seated in the dining room along with 250 members of the press. Five hundred farmers who could not fit in the dining area listened to piped-in sound in the bleachers of the coliseum's ice rink. Still more waited in the parking lot with the tractors. All of the proceedings, including the "bargaining session" with Bergland, were broadcast live by Nebraska Public Television.

The secretary of agriculture arrived at the coliseum after the preliminaries. The "bargaining session" itself was held in a brightly lit room apart from the crowd and was shown on video monitors in the dining area and on home sets throughout the state. Secretary Bergland sat down with selected farmers and listened to their arguments. Throughout the meeting he maintained an air of neutrality and calm and said little. In fact, Bergland had heard everything before.

So had the farmers, but both sides played their roles as if mindful that all Nebraska was watching. Around the table farmers from South Dakota, Kansas, and Nebraska told stories of their losses. They argued that they deserved a rate of return equal to those available in the rest of the economy and that they would not get it until the prices reached 100 percent of parity. "If you allow the family farm to go down the drain," a Texas farmer warned, "the blood of this nation will be on your hands." When Gene Schroder's turn came, the Baca County, Colorado, farmer tried to concentrate on the question of inflation. Schroder had spoken similar words to hundreds of strike meetings in forty states since he and three others had first talked of a strike over coffee in September 1977. Agriculture, he argued, was the biggest source of real wealth in the nation. It started with nothing but dirt and seed, and it produced enormous quantities of mankind's most essential asset. Even at present prices, he explained, agricultural exports were the only thing keeping the U.S. balance of trade from dropping out of sight. If, by maintaining a cheap food policy, the United States refused to generate any income out of its primary source of wealth, of course the dollar would be worthless. It was a stupid policy, he concluded, not unlike a bunch of Indians selling Manhattan for $24. A well-paid agriculture industry would stabilize the economy, not disrupt it.

Bergland listened to it all, occasionally nodding and smiling. When the time was up, he made a brief statement. The secretary noted his sympathy with the farmer's goal of 100 percent parity. "Thanks again for being so direct with me," Bergland concluded. "I'll be discussing this with the president on Monday morning." With that, the "bargaining session" was officially over, and programming switched back to the main studio.

Before returning to Washington, Bergland stopped at the much friendlier convention of the Texas branch of the American Farm Bureau in Houston. The farm bureau is the nation's largest so-called farmers' organization and the only organization whose national officers came out in immediate and vehement public opposition to the strike. Bergland told the farm bureau that parity prices were unacceptable because of red tape and cost to the taxpayer. The secretary of agriculture made no mention of his previous promise to help the strikers achieve it and referred to the strike as "irresponsible."

No reporters were present at the secretary of agriculture's promised Monday discussion with the president to see how these seemingly contradictory positions were resolved, but whatever transpired there made no ripples on the surface of their farm policy.

SINCE DECEMBER THE AAM had been making plans for visiting Washington, D.C., and the encounter with Bergland in Omaha only spurred the group on. By consensus of the membership, January 18, 19, and 20 were finally set as the demonstration dates, and word was flashed to the nation's strike offices. In the meantime, the AAM worked to extend its base. After spreading throughout the western wheat belt and the devastated Southeast, the strike was now beginning to extend into the prime corn-belt land in the heart of the Midwest.

The very center of the corn belt is Bethany, in central Illinois. Central and southern Illinois are blessed with the richest farmland in the nation. The strike had reached Bethany and surrounding Moultrie County when Bill Rowe watched the December 30 evening news and heard an announcement that the AAM was planning a meeting at Taylorville Junior High School in Christian County, thirty-five miles away. Rowe was curious but, like most farmers in the area, far from desperate. Blessed with strong ground, Illinois farmers have some of the best economies in all of agriculture. Illinois alone produces 10 percent of the total world production of both corn and soybeans. Nevertheless, Bill Rowe and his wife, Carole, drove to Taylorville to find out more.

Bill, 29, and his father, Eugene, 58, farm 1,120 acres of corn and soybeans. All of the farmers in the neighborhood pride themselves on their farming skills and race to see who will get their crops in first when the cover of winter snow finally melts off the fields. Last year Bill and Eugene, thanks in no small part to their huge $50,000 four-wheel-drive Steiger tractor, were the first ones in and had all their corn planted by April 18. Their beans were down by the middle of May.

Moultrie County farmers like to get in early so that their plants will be strong enough to survive the vagaries of the Illinois summer. Last year temperatures rose to more than 100 degrees during the crucial time when most of the corn crop was pollinating, and much of the local farmers' production suffered. Thanks to an early start, the Rowes' corn was already pollinated and forming ears before the heat wave hit. The Rowes' crops also survived the June-to-August hail season, and Bill and Eugene were among the first to reach the elevators with their harvest. Even so, the price was too low, and Bill Rowe and his father decided to store their grain and wait for the price to rise. When Bill and his wife attended the Taylorville meeting, they had been waiting four months and the price had yet to respond. At that time, Bill had $136,000 in outstanding obligations on his crops above and beyond his land payments, and his stored grain was worth barely $90,000. Despite the losses staring him in the face, he was not worried about going out of business in 1978 or even 1979, but he did worry about what would happen if losses piled up.

Tom Kersey of Unadilla, Georgia, gave a speech that hit Bill Rowe's vague worry right on the head. The next day Rowe threw in with the strike and began organizing a meeting for January 6 in nearby Sullivan, where his father lived.

Although Bill Rowe had never enrolled in USDA programs because of the mountains of paperwork involved, he understood that the government's policies were the major ingredient in the failing economics of agriculture, and he had no doubts about the lameness of the 1977 farm bill. Under this act subsidy levels were set by a number of mathematical calculations. One of them was the USDA's estimate of farmer costs. Rowe knew from his own experience that these figures were so low as to be bogus.

The strike meeting that Bill organized in Sullivan attracted 130 farmers. Most were from the areas around Lovington, Bethany, and Dalton City; Bill's father was practically the only one from Sullivan itself. Sullivan was known as "Charles Shuman country," and farmers there were suspicious of talk about strikes. Charles Shuman, a Sullivan native, was a former national president of the American Farm Bureau, and the farm bureau leadership had from the beginning attacked the AAM and its parity demands.

Unlike the AAM, the farm bureau had an orderly organizational chart shaped roughly like a pyramid. The farm bureau's present membership size is largely a function of its Farm Services Division, which, among other things, sells cheap insurance. Out of the entire Illinois membership of 275,000, for example, only 145,000 were directly involved in agricultural production.

One of the strikers' favorite possessions was a wallet-sized card describing their attitude regarding the farm bureau. The short tract was entitled "I Have a Problem."

"I have two brothers," it read. "One is a farm bureau member. The other brother died in the electric chair for murder. My mother died from insanity when I was three. My two sisters and my father sell dope. Recently I met a girl who was just released from a reformatory. She served time for smothering her illegitimate child to death.

"My problem is," it concluded, "if I marry the girl, shall I tell her about the brother who is a member of the farm bureau?"

Strikers liked to pull the card out of their pockets and show it to anyone who cared to read it. The implications were obvious, and the farm bureau responded in kind. The bureau's national officers dismissed the strike as one comprising only a few young farmers who had made unsound investments and had managed their money badly. Bill Rowe resented the charge. He and his father farmed with the best in their neighborhood and still lost money. The market, Rowe was convinced, was the problem. He opened Moultrie County's strike office in the den of his house.

As with the rest of the nation, the Illinois strikers' attention shortly shifted to the District of Columbia. Farmers from across the country were preparing for their first pilgrimage there. Bill Rowe figured that things had not gone well enough in Moultrie County for him to leave yet, so he followed the demonstrations on the evening news.

All the commentators agreed that Washington had never seen such demonstrations before.

The first people in the nation's capital to encounter the farm strike were those who work there but live in nearby Virginia. During the rush hour on Wednesday morning, January 18, commuters on Route I-66 had slowed to a crawl behind eight giant green-and-yellow John Deere tractors from Georgia and Virginia. Each tractor was twice as wide and three times as tall as a car, and they were all proceeding along the interstate at 10 m.p.h. After traveling twelve miles, Virginia Police intercepted the convoy.

State trooper W. F. Eanes tried to flag down the tractor driven by Phillip D. Olinger from Bealeton, Virginia, but Olinger drove right by, knocking Eanes down in the process. Eanes got back in his car and resumed the chase until Olinger's tractor sideswiped and eventually disabled his car. Trooper R. J. Shaw tried the same tactics with the giant machine driven by James Loveless of Remington, Virginia. Shaw's patrol car was eventually pushed into a ditch. The state troopers had by now been reinforced by units from the Fairfax County Police. When the tractors reached the weigh station just past the Centreville turnoff, officer James Phillips blew out the back tires of Loveless's John Deere with a twelve-gauge shotgun, and the farmers finally pulled over and submitted to arrest. Traffic had been delayed for an hour and thirty-five minutes. Later that day in Fairfax County Court, Loveless explained that he and the others were "not trying to break any laws."

The rest of the estimated ten thousand farmers who had come to Washington heard of the battle on I-66 when they gathered across from the White House at 8 a.m. Some of the strikers shouted that they ought to go "get our people out of jail," but nothing much developed out of those comments. They were, however, a good indication of the mood of the crowd. The farmers were angry about having to be where they were. Most of them considered Washington a chairborne town full of pencil pushers and windbags, and they had little idea of the actual workings of the process from which they needed help. What they knew was that if wheat farmers' prices had gone up at the same rate as congressional salaries over the last sixty years, wheat would be selling at $6.90 a bushel instead of at $2.35. And they resented the equity.

The AAM had little detailed strategy for their legislative assault on Carter's farm policies and hit the halls of Congress with the precision and finesse of mud being slung at the door of a barn. Once again, the strikers were counting on their visibility to pull them through.

On Wednesday the farmers marched down two lanes of Pennsylvania Avenue from the White House to Capitol Hill, wearing red, blue, green, and gold baseball hats with WE SUPPORT AGRICULTURAL STRIKE patches sewn on. Many farmers wore matching windbreakers. Traffic snarled all along their path, and at several points there were brief incidents of farmers shoving the police who were trying to keep them from spreading across the entire avenue. All along the route of the march, enthusiastic strikers stuck WE SUPPORT AGRICULTURAL STRIKE bumper stickers on light poles and parked cars. After arriving at the Hill, they visited congressional offices in flocks ranging from five to fifty, kept their hats on, and told whomever would listen that they were going broke and that they didn't intend to stand back and let it happen.

The next morning the strikers returned through the cold rain to the Hill by way of Pennsylvania Avenue and continued articulating their case. Up there the USDA was quick to respond to their assault.

Citing Agricultural Department cost studies, a staff member of the Senate Agricultural Committee told the *Washington Post* on January 19 that 100 percent parity might cost as much as $40 billion. "What they [the farmers] don't understand," the staffer complained, "is the politics of the situation. One hundred percent parity is not in the cards. The cost would be staggering, and no one knows how to go about doing it."

The farmers disputed the figures. They didn't want any government money; they just wanted a law that said that no agricultural commodity could be sold at less than parity. Just as the government had already said that no one could hire labor at less than $2.65 an hour. At parity prices, the cost of wheat in a one-pound loaf of bread would only rise from three to five cents, which was still less than the expense of the plastic wrapper. The potatoes used in a twenty-cent bag of potato chips cost the manufacturer one-seventh of one cent; parity potato prices added another one-fourth of one cent. Why, the farmers argued, were they supposed to go out of business producing cheap food while everyone else in the food chain filled their pockets? It was not fair, to say the least.

The politicians to whom they addressed themselves either were not in or adopted a sympathetic but noncommittal position. At the last minute, both the House and Senate Agricultural Committees scheduled hearings for the next day.

While the majority of strikers continued to lobby on Thursday morning, a group of one thousand went down Independence Avenue toward the offices of the Department of Agriculture. Once there, they jammed the USDA's huge lobby and refused to leave. A smaller group of two hundred went upstairs and occupied Bob Bergland's office. They demanded a meeting with the secretary of agriculture, but his staff said that he was out of town. When the farmers finally left, it was with what the *Washington Post* described as a flurry of "barnyard epithets" directed at the deputy secretary of agriculture, John C. White. If Bergland didn't meet with them the next day, warned departing Alvin Jenkins of Campo, Colorado, "America might learn that farmers are not the God-fearing people they've always been."

On Friday, January 20, the AAM began the last day of its initial siege of Washington by walking up Pennsylvania Avenue, again behind a phalanx of farm equipment. While the farmers walked, agriculture secretary Bergland was addressing a hastily convened meeting of thirty-nine AAM representatives. He told them that the Carter administration would do everything it could to improve farm prices but that it would not raise subsidies or price supports.

Being political neophytes, more than a few of the strikers had expected to swamp their opposition in a forty-eight-hour rush, and by Friday they were disoriented by their considerable shortfall. While the AAM was in Washington, its only means of internal communication had been the CB radio system on the farmers' tractors, and the demonstration had eventually broken down into a series of independent guerrilla farm bands that ran back and forth at various levels of desperation between the places they thought made a difference.

At noon on Friday, two hundred such farmers descended on the USDA once again. They were carrying PARITY NOT CHARITY signs and refused to leave until the secretary of agriculture met with representatives of the AAM. The farmers were informed that Bergland had already done so three hours earlier. They milled around the lobby for a while, figuring out what to do next, and eventually they drifted back to the Hill, where the respective agricultural committees were holding their hearings.

Bergland testified before the Senate and said what the senators had all heard before. The House's hearings, like the Senate's, were packed with farmers. When Alvin Jenkins testified before Congress, his fellow farmers broke out in their biggest applause of the day. After blasting the 1977 farm bill, Jenkins warned that farmers back home who ignored the strike and tried to take advantage of their fellow farmers' sacrifice in order to make a killing "might be shot out of the cabs of their tractors."

That threat proved to be the last note struck by the farm strike in Washington that month. The farmers headed home that weekend but left behind them Washington, D.C.'s first AAM office. If nothing else, after three days in the capital, the strikers had learned that they would have to come back.

SEVERAL WEEKS AFTER THE strikers had returned to the countryside, President Carter scheduled a meeting in Washington with representatives of all the nation's farm organizations. Three AAM members were included. The president repeated his statement that no new farm bill would pass his desk. "Those who can survive," he reportedly told the group, "will be better off."

Those words sounded particularly hard and cruel coming from the mouth of someone who was a farmer himself and had promised to "support prices equal to at least the cost of production" when he had come to the farmers as a candidate, asking for votes. The strikers' resentment of Carter smoldered while they continued to organize in the farm belt.

And the president's point man in the countryside continued to be Bob Bergland. After the Washington demonstrations, his reception in the hinterlands became steadily less polite. On February 22 the secretary of agriculture was in Amarillo, Texas, delivering a speech in which he praised the 1977 farm bill and asked farmers to give it a chance. When Bergland left for the airport to catch a scheduled flight to Wichita, Kansas, he was greeted outside by a crowd of strikers who let loose with a barrage of snowballs and raw eggs. Bergland was rushed by police to a waiting squad car. Tom Sand, the secretary of agriculture's press aide, later told reporters that his boss had remained unruffled throughout the incident. "He wasn't too upset," Sand said. "Matter of fact, we were laughing all the way to Wichita."

The strikers, however, were not laughing at all. February was a hard month, with lots of waiting and little action. The strike's organizers began to worry about losing support, because they had not yet been able to deliver on their demands. Although the total number of strike offices had risen to eleven hundred, several of them had recently closed down. In late February a group of the movement's most active organizers met in Calera, Oklahoma, to discuss the situation. They were all convinced that something dramatic was needed to keep up the momentum. The group decided that agricultural imports was the question to focus on. One farmer wanted to form a modern Boston tea party by boarding a beef ship in the Gulf and throwing meat over the side. That suggestion was dismissed in favor of having a demonstration in Texas. The Lone Star State was strong strike country, and Mexican imports was a burning question there.

The Mexican farms had a double advantage. The first was labor costing $3 a day, instead of $3 an hour. The second was Mexico's public health standards. Pesticides, which are strictly controlled and in many cases banned for use inside the United States, are used in Mexico at will. At the same time, American growers, denied the stronger pesticides, must dust their crops five times as often as Mexican growers in order to maintain pest-killing efficiency, which increases production costs even more.

The spot the strikers picked to make their stand was the town of McAllen, Texas, which is connected by bridge to the Mexican state of Tamaulipas. March 1 was set by the AAM as the date when they would descend on McAllen and close the border. By the time the bulk of the farmers had shown up on Monday, February 28, several AAM representatives had negotiated a deal with McAllen's mayor. He had agreed to allow the farmers to stop trucks without police interference for five minutes, beginning at 11 a.m. the next day. The mayor assured them that there would be plenty of vegetable trucks for them to stop while a gaggle of reporters looked on. But when, at 11 a.m. on March 1, two hundred striking farmers from ten states assembled on the McAllen Bridge, the only truck that appeared was loaded with bricks. The farmers told the mayor that they would come back later when there were more trucks.

When the farmers returned, the whole scene had changed. By 1 p.m. the American side of the bridge was lined with police and sheriff's deputies. More than one thousand people gathered on both sides of the border to watch as two hundred farmers walked onto the span. The first truck that approached was loaded with watermelons. The strikers stopped it and talked to the Mexican driver. He became frightened, abandoned his truck, and ran back to the Mexican side of the border with his keys.

The rest of the demonstration consisted of two hundred farmers watching the police try to move the abandoned vehicle. The only wrecker that was available for unclogging the bridge weighed barely a ton and a half. It could not budge the farm truck and reared up on its back wheels amidst small clouds of burning rubber. The farmers laughed and shouted insults.

The cops became angrier and angrier. Finally, the police gave the order to clear the bridge. The farmers protested that they had a deal with the mayor, but that did not carry much weight. After a brief bullhorn warning, the police advanced with billies drawn. A sixty-two-year-old man from Kansas was knocked down by a policeman who ground his face into the asphalt with his foot. A forty-seven-year-old grandmother from Oklahoma was soundly beaten on the face and shoulders by a huge McAllen police officer in the skirmish line until the other cops restrained him. The farmers were quickly herded into a group and taken on buses to the Hidalgo County jail. Before the afternoon was over, the total population of the facility had been doubled.

Hidalgo County officials wanted each of the farmers to post a $500 bond before release, and most refused. While they waited in jail, word of the "McAllen Massacre" soon spread throughout the strike. Within two days a crowd of several thousand farmers, complete with tractors, was camped outside the county detention center. On Friday, March 3, the crowd drove a huge four-wheel-drive John Deere tractor up the steps of the jail and aimed the vehicle at the front door. They said that they would break the door in unless the 180 farmers inside were released. Later that afternoon, after agreeing to pay $28 in traffic citations, the arrested farmers were freed. This time the mayor agreed to let them block the bridge again if they would only leave town soon afterward.

On Saturday, March 4, the AAM successfully closed the McAllen Bridge for an hour without any incident. The second truck that they stopped was loaded with bagged onions, fresh from Mexico. The bags were labeled "Produced and Packaged in Hereford, Texas." Despite the absence of USDA inspection stations south of the border, all of the bags were reportedly already stamped with USDA inspection seals saying that the onions were fit for American consumption.

Word of the farmers' stand at McAllen spread rapidly. AAM partisans called the demonstration "another Alamo," and news of it seemed to stiffen the strikers' resolve.

BY MARCH 15, SOME THIRTY THOUSAND farmers were in Washington.

This time the AAM had come to Washington with a strategy. Two major emergency agriculture bills were circulating in the Senate Agricultural Committee. The first, authored by committee chairman Herman Talmadge (D–Ga.), would authorize payments to farmers for voluntarily holding land out of production. The other, sponsored by Robert Dole (R–Kans.), set up a sliding scale of production reduction and parity guarantees. Neither bill was what the farm strikers really had in mind, but most of them had decided to back Dole's measure as a stopgap until a good parity bill could be written.

Washington, for its part, had been speculating for weeks about what the farmers were going to do to the city this time. Office-building windows along Pennsylvania Avenue were crowded with spectators as the sea of strike hats and waving signs flowed toward Congress. Two Missouri strikers had stopped at the Pauper's Bluff Auction Barn on their way north and had bought eighty-two goats, which they turned loose along the avenue. Some of the animals walked along with the crowd, and others bolted down side streets. The Capitol police tried to chase down the scattering animals on their Honda motorbikes. When the procession reached the Capitol steps for a rally, the remaining goats were joined by more than one hundred chickens, several of which ended up wandering into congressional offices before the day was over. The farmers were obviously back in town.

Bill Rowe and most of the Illinois delegation went straight to a House hearing room for a meeting with several Illinois congressmen.

The farmers filled all the seats and lined up against the back wall. The major speaker was Senator Charles Percy (R–Ill.), who arrived after an hour of congressional talking and made his way through the people who jammed the aisles. The farmers were especially conscious of giving Percy a polite reception. Two days before, a farmer from Vermilion County, Illinois, who had arrived in town early had stomped up to the senator's office and thrown a raw egg in. The Illinois delegation wanted to make it clear that the farmers did respect the dignity of the Senate, whatever they thought of Percy personally.

The senator gracefully accepted their apologies and said that he was grateful that the egg had been fresh. A few farmers laughed. Percy was "concerned about the way agriculture is going" and went on to praise the American farmer profusely. He praised the strikers for their "great public-relations job," even though he didn't agree with them in every respect. After a few more words about the need to export, Percy closed his speech with an appeal that the nation return to "the days of Earl Butz, who had faith in the American farmer." The senator was late for another meeting and left without answering any questions.

One farmer sitting near Bill Rowe spoke up as Percy scuttled out the door. "Grease job," he drawled.

Similar scenes were enacted all over the Hill on Wednesday. Washington, D.C., is a slippery place, and, like anyone unfamiliar with the vagaries of government, the farmers had trouble getting a footing. By 6 p.m. the Illinois delegation had the feeling that it had learned much but accomplished relatively little. Back at their motel in Virginia, the farmers watched as the evening news spent two minutes describing their demonstration and four minutes telling the story of a dozen goats that had ended up at the district dog pound, where they were initially locked up with the dogs and fed kibble. The remainder of the eighty-two goats had apparently been absorbed into urban life.

As in the January demonstrations, the focus of Thursday's actions shifted to the USDA. While some farmers lobbied on the Hill, two thousand others showed up in a very angry mood at the USDA on March 16. The department, well aware that it was a target, had adopted a policy of refusing entrance to anyone who didn't have an appointment. Several small groups of farmers had been turned away on Wednesday. Thursday's crowd planned to rectify that condition. After the crowd had stood in the rain for a few minutes on the steps of the building, pushing closer and closer to the entrance, someone broke the glass door and the leaders of the crowd scampered into the lobby. Once they were inside, most of them had no idea what to do, and the police seemed to have things well in hand until a farmer lost control and punched a cop.

The farmer was wrestled to the ground, and shoving matches broke out between the vanguard of the crowd and the security force. Farmers farther back started to surge forward to get in on the action, and for a moment it looked as if two thousand farmers would sweep in the doorway and crush the assorted two dozen policemen. At this point, several of the most active strike organizers jumped to the front to restrain the crowd. Acting as intermediaries with the authorities, the organizers struck a bargain with Bergland's staff. They promised to get the crowd back outside if a group of representatives stayed inside.

As a result, thirty-seven farmers from seventeen states went upstairs and occupied conference room 5066. Bergland himself had been whisked out of the building to an undisclosed location. Early in the afternoon, word was sent to room 5066 that Bergland was unavailable. The farmers responded that they had promised the crowd that they would stay until they met with him, and they were serious about doing just that. Twenty-two farmers stayed in room 5066 until 9 a.m. Friday morning. When they finally left, their names had been added to the list of the AAM delegates that Bergland would meet with that day.

The Friday meetings were all very polite, and everyone sat down in private and said all the same things that the two sides had been saying to each other in public for six months. It was a sterile exercise, and the March demonstrations closed with scattered lobbying and newspaper interviews. Planting time was near, and the farmers had little to take home to show for their efforts and little more time to spend.

Bill Rowe and his father were back in Illinois by Saturday afternoon. On Sunday, Bill watched Bob Bergland's appearance on *Meet the Press*. "Those who are most actively engaged in this current discussion," the secretary of agriculture said in response to a question about the strike, "are . . . young people . . . in trouble because they overextended themselves . . . . They don't represent all of agriculture."

Rowe wanted to throw his shoe through the television screen.

CARTER AND BERGLAND FINALLY carried the field of legislative battle three weeks after the twenty thousand strikers left town. On Monday, April 10, the Senate passed an emergency agricultural bill that combined various portions of the Dole and Talmadge offerings by a vote of 49 to 41. The bill reached the House floor on Wednesday, April 12. Two thousand farmers who had returned to the capital for the occasion were crowded into the congressional gallery. Some of the bill's Republican sponsors had complained beforehand of Carter and Bergland's "heavy-handed pressure" and "scare tactics" in mustering opposition. Whatever the reasons, it was obvious that the farmers didn't have anything close to the number of votes they needed. The strike, majority leader Jim Wright of Texas observed, was "a cruel charade." The final tally was 154 for and 268 against. The defeat of the emergency bill was hailed as a "major legislative victory" for the president.

Jimmy Carter appeared before the White House press corps shortly after the vote and was clearly pleased. "This is good for our farm policy," he said, grinning. "It is good for holding down inflation, and it is a very encouraging sign of cooperation between the Congress and the White House in dealing with the nation's very important problems."

Meanwhile, the farmers leaving the House gallery spontaneously began to march down Pennsylvania Avenue toward the White House. Several farmers were openly in tears. When the crowd reached the White House, several farmers pressed against the iron fence and shouted in order to attract the president's attention. The Texan manning the bullhorn blared that Carter should "never call himself a farmer again."

The defeat not only denied the strikers legislation for immediate relief but also was a message that they should put up or shut up, one issued with confidence that the strike would not dent actual farm production. If the government is right, the strike will disappear as another flash in the political pan. On the other hand, if significant numbers of producers withhold 50 percent of their produce, as they pledged they would, the Board of Trade will begin to feel the pinch in October, and the November election may prove to be rough on farm-state Democrats.

In the meantime, farmers will continue to go out of business at the rate of more than one thousand a month, whether they are on strike or not. The only certain long-term consequence of this winter's battles is that most of those who still own strike hats will do everything in their power to defeat Jimmy Carter when he runs again in 1980.

Carter will not run as a farmer in that election. He will run as the president who makes hard decisions with the weight of the world on his neck.

The change of image won't surprise many people in strike country. Folks down at the elevator and out in the "north forty" stopped calling Jimmy Carter a farmer a long time ago. Their hostility shows when they hunker down in small groups and the president's name comes up. Most of them just call him a son of a bitch and let it go at that.

[*Penthouse*, September/October 1978]

Zone of War

A S THEY WALKED NORTH on Revolutión Street in Tijuana that chilly Saturday night, heading toward the United States border, there was nothing to indicate to either Efren Reyes or Benito Rincón that they were about to be plucked out of the pack and made into object lessons.

Reyes, 24, and Rincón, 22, were on their way to meet a Guatemalan friend of Reyes's, sixteen-year-old Rogelio Méndez-Díaz, at a prearranged spot along the chain-link fence where Mexico ends and the United States begins. It was March 17, 1979, and Reyes and Méndez-Díaz were planning to cross over into American territory to look for work. Like Rincón, both had lived and worked illegally in the United States several times before. Neither had the proper immigration documents for a legal return this time either.

Reyes was trying to persuade Rincón to come along with him and his friend to *Los Estados*. But Rincón would agree only to hang out with them as they waited at the international boundary line for a propitious moment before making a dash across into the United States. He agreed to that, and to helping them to lower the level of the half liter of tequila that Reyes had purchased to mark the occasion. But nothing more. Rincón's reluctance to cross over that night was understandable: he had been driven back into Mexico barely twelve hours earlier on a United States Border Patrol bus in the aftermath of his seventh straight unsuccessful entry that year.

At that hour, there was little to distinguish Efren Reyes and Benito Rincón from any of the millions of other Mexican citizens who attempt to enter the United States illegally every year. At any given moment, anywhere from four million to eight million undocumented aliens just like them work and reside north of the border in direct violation of the McCarran-Walter Act's restriction of Mexican immigration to twenty thousand entrants a year. Reyes was the more Indian-looking of the two, with higher cheekbones and a prominent nose; but neither of them would stand out in a Spanish-speaking crowd. Both were dark-haired and dark-complexioned, five feet, five inches tall and short on cash.

INCONSPICUOUS AS THE PARTICIPANTS in this northward tide may be individually, as a group they are part and parcel of what former CIA director William E. Colby has called the most serious problem facing the United States over the rest of this century. Amid mounting criticism of the Immigration and Naturalization Service (INS) following recent charges that mismanagement, sagging morale, internal corruption, brutality, and other wrongdoing were seriously hampering the agency, there is the likelihood of intensified scrutiny in Congress during the hearings on the agency's budget over the next few months.

But the challenge that the growing numbers of Spanish-speaking people pose for our nation's institutions—political, judicial, social— is as immense as the migration itself. It is common knowledge among today's border crossers that, if they are persistent, their chances of being prevented from working in the United States range from few to none, and they behave accordingly. Despite impressive-sounding arrest figures, hundreds of thousands of illegal immigrants enter the United States each year and manage to work and live here for protracted periods of time. They do not consider that what they are doing is wrong. Many Mexicans, including some at an official level, justify the influx of illegal migrants into the United States by saying that movement back and forth in border territory is a historical pattern that predates the United States itself. The Mexican government's attention to the question has been minimal. And although Mexico's president, José López Portillo, and President Carter have addressed themselves to the question during their recent meetings, those discussions have been fruitless.

Meanwhile, United States policy steadfastly continues to pursue the impossible—trying to enforce a law that is unenforceable. A recent congressional study, yet to be made public, concludes that the only feasible way to close America's southern border is to double the size of our military forces and to station all of the additional soldiery along that perimeter.

According to the United States Border Patrol—the arm of the INS that is charged with policing America's boundaries—illegal movement into the United States from Mexico is always heaviest at precisely the small stretch of border toward which Reyes and Rincón were headed that Saturday night last March. The eventual fate of the two Mexicans would become ample testimony to the distortion of American law that has resulted from the insistence on pursuing this impossible task.

Reyes and Rincón's immediate destination was located, in Border Patrol terminology, within the Chula Vista sector. One of nine sectors for the purposes of immigration-law enforcement along the 1,952-mile border with Mexico, Chula Vista is responsible for the last sixty-six miles of border that lead up to the Pacific Ocean. The most heavily violated sixteen miles are patrolled by no more than 35 Border Patrol officers at any one time. (The entire Chula Vista sector, which has only 430 agents spread over six stations and three shifts, regularly accounts for around 40 percent of the immigration arrests of illegal immigrants who are headed for the vast secondary labor markets of Southern and Central California. This is more than any other sector on the entire Mexican line.)

The Tijuana port of entry anchors that westernmost stretch of violated line. The landscape on either side of the sleazy border town—low but steep hills, covered with bushes, short trees, washes, and gullies—provides a perfect natural cover for those wishing to avoid detection.

The chain-link fence that had been erected in spots along this stretch to help slow down the persistent invaders had long since ceased to be much of an effective barrier by the time Efren Reyes and Benito Rincón approached it last March. The chain was torn all along the line. In some places, it lay flat on its back.

When Revolución Street finally dead-ended against the wire that marked the American line, Efren Reyes and Benito Rincón turned west on the street that runs next to the fence and kept walking parallel to the border. They had now entered what the agents of the Chula Vista Border Patrol sector call the "combat zone."

The image is apt. The Border Patrol is organized with a military chain of command, and the patrol agent in charge at Chula Vista compares his job to that of a brigadier general. To make the most of his limited troops, electronic sensors that were first developed for use on the Ho Chi Minh trail during the Vietnam War have been scattered in the arid landscape east of Otay Mesa. Infrared viewing devices introduced by Marine Corps snipers at Khe Sanh during that war have also been made standard equipment on the night shift.

Border Patrol field agents consider Chula Vista the worst assignment in the entire INS bureaucracy. The average agent only stays eighteen months before successfully transferring somewhere else. The generalized hostility—and the number of rocks and bottles thrown at agents from the other side of the fence—has increased dramatically over the last three years. So have the aliens' charges of police brutality. The lives that have been lost have all been Mexican. The Border Patrol has not taken a fatality in many years.

That there is little love lost between the United States Border Patrol and the poor Mexicans they have been charged with stopping is obvious in each side's nickname for the other. South of the border, the patrol officers arrayed beyond the fence are known as *la migra*, Mexican shorthand for *la inmigración*. (Whether describing one man or a hundred, it is always used in the singular.)

The *migra* in turn often refers to the aliens unofficially as "tonks," a name that, agents say, derives from the sound a flashlight makes when it contacts a Mexican's head.

AT 9 P.M., WHEN REYES AND RINCÓN finally met up with the Guatemalan, Méndez-Díaz, it looked like just one more border evening. As usual, "the canal" dominated the surrounding neighborhood's social life.

The canal is the Tijuana River Flood Control Channel, an international project designed to tame the disastrous flash flooding that has destroyed entire sections of Tijuana in the past. At the spot where the trio finally stopped to drink some of Reyes's tequila, the fifty-foot-deep canal bed measured some fifty yards across and was lined with long, sloping concrete sides. Each edge of the canal is a levee some ten feet to twenty feet higher than the surrounding elevations. Since the south level is also the only backyard of the tightly packed nearby neighborhood known as Colonia Zona Norte, crowds of Mexican nationals from that district commonly congregate on top of the levee to socialize, twenty yards inside the United States. Some are just hanging out, others are waiting for a ripe moment to sneak deeper into gringoland.

Efren Reyes, Benito Rincón, and Rogelio Méndez-Díaz slipped easily under the wire marking the international boundary, climbed the levee embankment, crossed over the road on top, and picked out a spot to sit. There were some three hundred other Mexican citizens in their immediate vicinity, all of them technically illegal immigrants. The word along the south levee that evening was that the *migra* had been around earlier but things had been calm for a while. They would stay that way for the next hour.

BENITO RINCÓN WAS ONE OF fourteen children of a *campesino* from the farming village of Miguel de Palma in the state of Querétaro, more than eight hundred miles south of the United States border at Tijuana. He received no formal schooling during his childhood, but he had taught himself to read and write Spanish. He first headed north toward the United States in 1973, at the age of sixteen.

Like the great majority of America's undocumented Mexican workers, Rincón left home for simple and traditional reasons: Mexico is a poor country, with a 50 percent unemployment rate and a per capita income of only $1,100 a year. Rincón knew very well that if he stayed in Querétaro he could never hope to have anything more than he already had, and there would always be more and more mouths with which to share it. He was determined to better himself. In the United States, he could get ahead. The English-speaking nation he was headed for had been on public record for the last hundred years asking to be given the poor, huddled masses, the tired and the hungry, and that description fit young Benito Rincón to a T.

If Rincón and the other Mexicans who enter the United States illegally were Swedes or Germans, there is little doubt that their influx would be viewed as much less threatening. Throughout its history, official American immigration policy has demonstrated a decided bent for peoples who look like those who were already here. That this latest tide emanates from a neighboring dark-skinned culture that has been dominated militarily and economically by America, and that it involves people for whom Americans have shown little respect in the past, makes the influx doubly disturbing. But this attitude impedes the northward flow not one whit. The vacuum of the huge southwestern secondary labor market lures poor people north in steady droves. Unlike most United States citizens, the illegal immigrants are content to work harder for less money, and they think they are getting rich while they do so. If all undocumented Mexican workers left Los Angeles tomorrow, the fast-food, garment, luggage, parking garage, landscaping, and janitorial service industries would be forced to shut down immediately, and a good portion of local manufacturing and Central California agriculture would go with them. And the effect on the four other states in America's southwest corner would be only slightly less dramatic. Benito Rincón and those like him are still one of the key forces in the rising prosperity of the American West and Southwest.

Like many Mexicans who immigrate illegally, Rincón infiltrated across the border easily on his first attempt. Soon he was working in a suitcase factory in Los Angeles for $2.32 an hour. During the two years of his first tenure in the United States, he regularly sent a $50 money order back to his family. In 1975, he returned to Querétaro on a visit and stayed on, helping his father farm, until 1977.

When Rincón crossed back over the border in 1977, he was surprised by a *migra* cruiser at a gas station in San Ysidro, California, just two hours after he left Tijuana. Along with the rest of that day's more than one thousand Chula Vista apprehensions, Rincón was held overnight in the sector's San Ysidro staging area. As part of the standard border routine, he and virtually all the others who were apprehended that day were never formally charged with illegal entry into the United States. That crime is technically a misdemeanor, punishable by formal deportation, and a return to the United States after such a deportation ranks as a felony.

However, there is no room in the American criminal-justice system for a million additional trials a year. So, an "administrative remedy" has evolved. Instead of being formally charged and deported, apprehended aliens are given the option of agreeing to a "voluntary departure," whereby they are bused back to a drop-off point in their homeland at the first light of the next day. Like everyone else who was caught that day in 1977, Rincón opted to return to Tijuana.

His next attempt, the following night, was no more successful. On his third attempt that year, the persistent Rincón made it all the way to Los Angeles, where a friend told him about a job in a factory manufacturing chlorine pellets. Soon he was promoted to full machine operator, with a jump in pay to $6.48 per hour. For a year, all was well, but then the factory owner sold all the machinery and Rincón was once again among the unemployed. After a while, he found a job three hundred miles farther north in a small farming community in the San Joaquin Valley. He did well enough to convince two of his brothers to come north and join him. The three Rincóns worked together in the fields around Modesto, California. In January 1979, he and his brothers were swept up with a crowd of other illegal immigrants in a surprise *migra* raid on their workplace. Within a week, he and his brothers had "voluntarily" been transported to Mexicali.

Back in Mexico, one of the brothers, Emilio, went to Tijuana, and Benito followed him there. By the time the two brothers were reunited, Emilio had found work for both of them in a Tijuana chrome shop, polishing wheels for 1,200 pesos ($50) a week. Benito stuck it out for close to a month, but some time in February, the lure of the infinitely greater rate of reward north of the line overcame him. During the next month Benito would amply prove that "revolving door" is the most apt description for America's policy for dealing with illegal immigration.

He made three subsequent illegal border-crossing attempts, and was caught and returned each time. On his fourth attempt, Rincón entered the United States through the hills between Tijuana and the ocean with a small Mexican group. Efren Reyes was among the border crossers that day, and the two became friendly before going their separate ways. The *migra* caught up with Rincón at a roadside spot check in Oceanside, California. His fifth attempt in two and a half weeks was terminated in the Los Angeles train station, where he was spotted by a railroad employee who informed on him to the Border Patrol.

During his sixth attempt—on the Ides of March—the twenty-two-year-old was flushed out of his hiding place under a San Ysidro bridge and manacled. While being processed at the by-now-all-too-familiar San Ysidro staging area, Rincón claims that he was pushed to the floor and kicked several times by an agent in a green uniform. The next morning, he was dumped back in Mexico, and the next evening he was snared once again in San Diego. After this seventh arrest in seven attempts, he was returned to Tijuana on the morning of March 17. Twelve hours later, he encountered Efren Reyes at the Pool Hall of the North, on the edge of downtown Tijuana.

After they exchanged greetings, Reyes told his friend that he was going to cross again that night. But first, he said, let's have a drink. When Benito declined because he had no money, Reyes turned both generous and effusive. "Don't worry about it, *compadre*," he said. "I've got some. We'll buy a bottle up the street and drink it out by the canal."

BORN AND RAISED IN THE CAPITAL of the state of San Luis Potosí, more than eight hundred miles from Tijuana, Efren Reyes was the first of the seven children that his father had by his second wife. The elder Reyes ran a small mechanic shop. Efren managed to finish the sixth grade before beginning a career of successive low-paying jobs. In December of 1976, at age twenty-one, he finally headed north to try and make some money. Once in the United States, he headed for the home of his half-sister, who had migrated illegally to Pasadena four years earlier and was working as a waitress. He, too, found work easily, as a handyman at a retirement hotel, where he stayed for the next year and a half, earning $2.90 an hour and mailing money orders home regularly. In December of 1978, Efren Reyes decided to return to Mexico for the Christmas holidays. His half-sister never heard from him again.

Much less is known about Rogelio Méndez-Díaz, Efren Reyes's teenage Guatemalan friend. Between attempts to enter the United States, Rogelio lived in the derelict hulk of a white 1966 Ford station wagon with blue fenders. It had long ago been abandoned near the fence some two hundred yards from the spot that Benito, Efren, and Rogelio chose as their outdoor café that Saturday night in March of 1979.

FOR ALMOST AN HOUR AFTER arriving at the inside lip of the canal, Efren Reyes, Benito Rincón, and Rogelio Méndez-Díaz stayed put. Their location as of approximately 10 p.m. that night in March was later officially determined to be some sixty feet into the territorial United States.

The three friends had picked this section of the levee to lounge in because it had a reputation for being a place that the *migra* did not often check. A scattering of other Mexicans were socializing along the fence and on the floor of the flood-control channel. Between 9:30 and 10 p.m. that Saturday evening, Reyes's bottle of tequila passed back and forth between him and his friends, but he apparently did most of the drinking.

Some ten hours later, the San Diego County Coroner's Office would test the alcohol level in Reyes's blood and come up with a reading of .16 percent, which, by State of California standards, made him legally intoxicated.

THE TRIO'S GATHERING SPOT was the enforcement responsibility of a twenty-person Border Patrol shift under the direction of Supervisory Border Patrol Agent Daniel Wesley Cole, a twenty-four-year patrol veteran. On March 19, 1979, Cole was working the 4 p.m. to midnight shift. He checked out Border Patrol vehicle No. 1507, a white-over-green four-wheel-drive Dodge Ramcharger with wire cages over the windows. Along the border, these *migra* trucks are known as "battle wagons." By the time of his fateful encounter with Reyes, Rincón, and Méndez-Díaz at precisely 10:17, Cole had already personally apprehended fifteen illegal immigrants, during which process his Ramcharger had been hit by a couple of dozen rocks that were launched from the Mexicans who were mingling along the broken-down fence.

Dan Cole was more than familiar with the immigrants' ways. He had started his Border Patrol career on the Mexican line at El Paso, Texas, in 1954. The next year, he moved along the line to Calexico, California, then, the year after that, north to the Canadian border, to Niagara Falls, New York. After forty-eight months in the New York State post, he did a tour of duty at Fort Myers, Florida. He was sent back to the Mexican border in 1962, and worked out of Tucson, Arizona, for the next twelve years. In 1974, he was promoted to the rating of Supervisory Border Patrol Agent, serving at the Casa Grande, Arizona, station. Three years later, he was made a Supervisory Agent at Chula Vista.

Since his assignment to that sector, the Border Patrol agents he worked with remembered him as a quiet, churchgoing man who struck them as being something of a milquetoast. But several of the Tijuana regulars who hung out along the south levee remember him as the *migra* who liked to use his nightstick when he arrested people.

During Cole's solo cruise (Border Patrol agents often operate singly) along the south levee, the Saturday-night rock throwers were out. As usual, identifiable individuals well known to border agents seemed to be agitating the anonymous crowds launching the missiles. It is the official contention of the Border Patrol that most of the barrage of thrown objects along the border is instigated by persons in the pay of the professional alien smugglers, who create diversions to distract the patrol agents while the smugglers move large batches of immigrants across open spots elsewhere. Cole later told San Diego Police Department investigators that he recognized one of the agitators, a fat Mexican male, from other incidents earlier in the week. As Cole's Ramcharger passed the fat Mexican agitator, the man ran over to the edge of the levee and threw an empty beer bottle. It shattered against the truck. Cole jumped out, pulling on his riot helmet, and pursued the bottle thrower. At the halfway point of the fat man's fifty-foot-long retreat back to Mexico, he turned toward the *migra* and threw a second bottle. This one was still partially full, and it sprayed Cole with beer as it flew over his head, and momentarily halted his hot pursuit. By the time Cole resumed his chase, his assailant had popped through a hole in the fence and was safely back in Mexico, out of Cole's jurisdiction. Once there, the fat Mexican picked up a large rock.

At that, Cole drew his Smith & Wesson .357 revolver and pointed it across the wire. The sight of the weapon froze the Mexican's throwing arm. "I think that if he had brought that rock any higher," Cole later told a team of San Diego Police Department investigators, "I would have shot him."

The Mexican backed off, and when things calmed down, Cole moved on to a spot called Dog Kennel Road, a thoroughfare known to be used by illegal immigrants. At around 10 p.m., Cole responded to a report that there was heavy foot traffic on the south embankment of the Flood Control Channel. As usual, he drove along the dirt roads with his lights off.

Despite Dan Cole's attempts to conceal his truck in the darkness, most of the Zona Norte crowd scattered down the embankment toward the fence at his approach. Among the few exceptions were the three men sitting together near the top of the canal's inside incline.

As soon as Cole spotted the trio hunched together, he brought the truck to a sudden stop with a small disturbance of dust and darkness. Cole expected the suspects to head south immediately, but the three men still did not seem to notice his presence.

Unlike everyone else on that stretch of levee, Efren Reyes, Benito Rincón, and Rogelio Méndez-Díaz never saw the *migra* coming until it was far too late to escape.

THE FIRST THE THREE IMMIGRANTS knew of Daniel Wesley Cole's arrival, the Border Patrol agent was standing over them and had seized Benito Rincón and Efren Reyes by their collars. According to both Rincón and Méndez-Díaz, the officer initially addressed them as *"cabrones,"* a Spanish curse, and told them that he was the *migra* and that they were under arrest.

Dan Cole's next move was to manacle the two largest, Reyes and Rincón, to each other—right arm to right arm. Cole controlled them by grasping the connecting chain between the handcuffs and pulling. He then grabbed the loose sixteen-year-old Guatemalan by the belt and impelled all three of them up the incline lip toward his Ramcharger.

When they were on the road topping the south levee, Reyes spoke up in Spanish. "Why take us, *migra*?" he whined. "We didn't do nothing. We're just sitting here."

Dan Cole made no response, other than pushing sixteen-year-old Rogelio Méndez-Díaz toward the Ramcharger and instructing him to climb into its caged rear. Rogelio complied immediately. Rincón continued to mouth off in Spanish. "This don't make no sense. Just let us walk back there," he pleaded with a motion of his head toward Mexico, fifty feet away. Cole's only response was to pull the handcuff again and tell Reyes and Rincón to get in with the other guy.

Reyes responded to Cole's continuing tugs with ones of his own, trying to move southward. Cole struggled with the handcuff chain in an attempt to maintain control. Most of the three hundred or so Mexican citizens in the immediate vicinity stayed put and watched. A few fled.

As later reconstructed by police interviews with the surviving parties and witnesses, the countervailing forces centered on the contested handcuff chain, propelling the men toward the south edge of the road and the twenty-foot embankment leading to Mexico. At the top of the slope, Cole tried to pull his nightstick to get the suspects back in line, but it dropped onto the ground out of his reach. Reyes was intent on getting back into Mexico and, with Rincón's assistance, was winning his tug-of-war with Cole. An investigation by the San Diego District Attorney's Office would later conclude that neither of the undocumented aliens made any moves to assault the *migra's* person.

Dan Cole told police investigators that, at that moment, he feared for his life.

The feeling only intensified, he said, when he heard the Ramcharger's tailgate rattle behind him and noticed a shadow moving to one side of the struggle. That shadow was Rogelio Méndez-Díaz. He had not been locked into the cage, and now he jumped out of the Border Patrol vehicle and ran past the struggling trio, down the embankment, and through the fence along the border. "At this point," Dan Cole later told the San Diego Police Department, "it became crystal clear to me that I was in trouble and had to do something fast. They were getting the upper hand on me."

What Cole did was pull out his revolver. As the .357 Smith & Wesson cleared leather, the two Mexicans were pointed downhill. Cole still held the chain between the two Mexicans with his left hand. His resistance had turned both the handcuffed men somewhat sideways, so that they partially faced each other. According to Cole, "I was so close, I was afraid I was going to shoot my own hand."

Supervisory Agent Cole fired. His first shot only singed Benito Rincón's hair as it went past him.

At almost the same time, the two Mexicans succeeded in pulling their handcuff chain from Cole's grip and headed for the border. The pair was no more than a step or two away from the safe haven when the explosion from Cole's first shot registered on their ears;

instinctively, they both squatted. After a second or two, Efren Reyes rose up out of his crouch and resumed tugging his compatriot south. By now, Dan Cole had brought his empty left hand up to steady his aim for the next shot. Both Mexicans were three steps away from him, turned somewhat sideways, with Reyes in the lead.

Cole's second shot entered Rincón's upper left chest at an angle that brought it out through the bicep of the Mexican's left arm. In the excitement of the moment, Rincón did not even realize that he had been hit.

"Don't worry," Efren Reyes shouted in Spanish, "they're just blanks." Those were the last words Efren Reyes ever said.

Dan Cole's third shot was fired from a range of no more than eight feet, sufficient to leave gunpowder traces around the entrance wound. As soon as it went off, Benito Rincón felt his friend Reyes go slack ahead of him, pulling both of them tumbling to the embankment.

The Border Patrol agent told the investigators that his immediate reaction when the Mexicans tumbled to the ground was to worry about being attacked by the surrounding crowd. He made a hasty retreat to his Ramcharger, fetched a light, and shone it at the fifty or more aliens who were still clustered in American territory, watching. In Cole's own words, "A few of them were making menacing moves, but none toward me."

Benito Rincón stayed where he had fallen, chained to the now dead Efren Reyes. It was not until ten minutes later, when he tried to push himself up to see what was going on, that he felt a searing pain and realized he had been wounded. Rincón was eventually unchained and taken to the Chula Vista hospital in an ambulance that arrived on the scene some twenty minutes after Cole's reinforcements.

Efren Reyes's corpse stayed on the embankment of the south levee, forty feet from Mexico, until San Diego Police homicide inspectors had finished examining the scene of his death early the next morning. Ten feet down the embankment, the dead Mexican's tennis shoe was lying where it had come off during the earlier tug of war. Five feet farther south was Cole's riot stick.

When Reyes's body was finally taken to the coroner's office, it was initially registered as John Doe, Mexican male. The cause of death was given as "massive hemorrhage, gunshot wound chest (right)." Daniel Wesley Cole's third .357-caliber Magnum round had bored a clean three-eighths-of-an-inch hole through Reyes's chest, lung, heart, and liver, before coming out the other side.

THE KILLING OF EFREN REYES raised few visible waves. Along the border, one more corpse devoid of proper immigration documents is back-page news at best. The San Diego–based Committee on Chicano Rights, which monitors such matters, issued a protest that received some initial media coverage, but only minimally, and there was virtually no follow-up.

The official response was twofold. The San Diego County District Attorney, exercising jurisdiction over all homicides within the stretch of United States territory where Efren Reyes died, announced the inception of a sixty-day investigation. The federal attorney for San Diego, pursuing the local responsibilities of the Justice Department, brought charges against the twenty-two-year-old Benito Rincón.

Life in the "combat zone" continued, routinely: On March 21, the Tijuana newspapers printed a front-page story about a young Mexican who had been wounded by a shotgun blast from a Border Patrol helicopter. On March 24, a Mexican corpse was discovered on the bed of the Flood Control Channel, and another was found floating facedown in the muck and scum of the Tijuana River itself.

When March 1979 was over, the Chula Vista sector announced that the monthly immigration arrests totaled 41,239 undocumented aliens, one of the busiest thirty-one-day Border Patrol periods that had ever been recorded. That mark would last all of two more months before being surpassed by the numbers for the following May.

May 1979 was also the month during which the names Efren Reyes, Benito Rincón, and Daniel Cole surfaced publicly again. The case against Benito Rincón was dismissed after his gunshot wound had healed and he had spent forty days in custody. Supervisory Agent Dan Cole was transferred to an undisclosed new Border Patrol assignment, and it was announced that he was scheduled to take retirement at the end of 1979 with a twenty-five-year pension. Finally, on May 17, the San Diego District Attorney's investigation was concluded.

On the basis of the evidence collected over two months, the San Diego County District Attorney's Office had gone as far as to type up formal copies of a criminal complaint charging Daniel Wesley Cole with manslaughter and assault. The papers were never presented to a judge, and the charges were never filed. Any county or state officer using lethal force on a "fleeing misdemeanant" would have been prosecuted, but in Cole's case, the state district attorney was stymied by his federal counterpart. There was, in District Attorney Edwin Miller's words, "an almost diametric opposition of state and federal law."

According to the district attorney, the United States attorney in San Diego, Michael Walsh, a former local Common Cause chairman, took the firm position that forced resistance to a federal officer during any federal arrest is, in and of itself, a felony and, therefore, sufficient grounds for gunfire under federal standards. Those same standards recognized Cole's fears for his own safety, accurate or not, as further justification for him to use deadly force. Walsh also ruled out prosecution under Title 18 of the Civil Rights Act because Section 242 specifically limited the law's protection to "inhabitants" of the territorial United States. No one's civil rights had been violated that night on the south levee because the law said no one out there had any, except Daniel Wesley Cole.

District Attorney Miller finally dropped the case, after noting his disagreement for the record. Given that any charges against an on-duty federal officer would be heard in federal court under federal rules, U.S. Attorney Walsh's position made "the prospect of obtaining a conviction . . . so diminished as to foreclose charging Agent Cole." With that, the case of Efren Reyes slipped between the floorboards of American justice and disappeared from public view.

IN PRACTICE, THE BORDER is a law unto itself.

On the evening of May 24, 1979, a rock-throwing incident enveloped the south levee. Before it was over, Guillermo Lozano, a nineteen-year-old Mexican national, had been shot in both legs and the stomach by a cruising *migra*. On May 29, Ismael Villa, 26, was shot while he and eighteen other illegal immigrants tried to elude the Border Patrol in a San Ysidro river bottom west of Dairy Mart Road. That same evening, eleven captured Mexicans escaped from the Chula Vista staging area when they removed a piece of sheet metal from the bathroom ceiling, punched a hole in the roof, and vanished in a northerly direction. With well over five thousand arrests, the previous four days in May had seen the largest concentration of alien apprehensions ever recorded in the Chula Vista sector.

After the end of that near-record month, construction on the sector's new border fence had begun. Framed with forged-steel posts and cable, the first three and a half feet are heavy-gauge steel mesh, and the next six and a half are chain link. Both posts and mesh are anchored in an eighteen-inch-deep concrete footing. When completed, the new barrier will run 5.6 miles from the Pacific Ocean, halting two hundred yards east of the Tijuana Port of Entry.

Like the dead Efren Reyes, it will make no difference. The section that runs through the hills west of Tijuana has recently been completed. The fence's top edge is already battered from the insistent wave of illegal immigrants that regularly passes over after dark. The people who live nearby are sure it will only get more so.

[*New York Times Magazine*, February 17, 1980]

The Vampires of Skid Row

*T*HERE'S A VAMPIRE DOWNTOWN. At least that's what the people on Los Angeles's Fifth Street say. As a matter of fact, Fifth Street has seen six of them. The monsters are storefronts bunched together on either side of the street between the tracks and the Greyhound bus station. They are not hard to spot. Most do not have windows, but you can identify them by their signs. The signs are small, up-front, and say BLOOD.

As it turns out, they are a thriving business. All it takes is $300, a doctor within a fifteen-minute drive who will swear that the help you hire knows a vein from an artery, and you've got a state license. Then you rent a storefront and buy the equipment. You need tables, stands, plastic bags, tubes, and needles to get the blood out at the crook of somebody's arm. Then you have to get a centrifuge and some technicians to make the blood into plasma. When you have gathered the blood, a pint at a time, you need enough ready cash to pay $5 to the guy who used to have it in his veins. All there is left to get after that is a connection. It is not hard. A lot of hospitals use a lot of blood these days and there is never quite enough to go around. When you get it ironed out, just send the pints on up each day in a cab. The hospitals will give you anywhere from $40 to $65 for each pint, depending on the market and the type. It is a good business. It has grown 10 percent each year of the last two and promises to do the same in 1973.

Of course, the folks with their cash tied up in the operation do not call themselves "vampires." They are a legitimate business licensed by the State of California. They call themselves things like Doctors' Blood Bank, California Transfusion Service, United Biologics, and Abbott Laboratories, Inc.

The people who do call them vampires are somebody else with a little less standing in greater Los Angeles, but they may still be right. After all, they ought to know. They live right next door.

These name-calling neighbors have a long record of being called a few names themselves. Over the years it has been "tramp," "wino," "deadbeat," "derelict," and "vagrant" until it comes out of their ears.

They do not call themselves any of those things. If you ask them, they will tell you they live on the Row, on Skid Row, down on Fifth Street. And it is an honest description of themselves. They are honest about themselves. It's a skid they know they're in: whipping around the surface of a spin, heading for the guardrail, the edge, and off into space. On this street corner there is a divorce in Cincinnati, and on the other there's a layoff in Gardena. They are not lucky people. They are ex-carpenters, ex–drill press operators, ex–cowboys and Indians. If you ask them what they are doing now, they'll tell you they're between things. At the moment, they have their hands full just being poor, hungry, cold, and miserable.

"It's not the misery we're yelling about," the "derelict" Bill Skahill says. "It's the people that come down here and live off it that's got us mad."

THE DAILY PAY OUTFITS ARE known on the Row as "the slave marts." The lines at their doors start forming under the streetlights at five in the morning. Right by the sign that says READY MEN. It is early, but not too cold. That is why these folks from the Row are in L.A. They're called "snowbirds." They fly in for the winter and leave when the crops come in up north. The lines have been harder this year because of the rain. It has made work slow too.

Hiring starts at six. Every outfit has its regulars, and they go first. The rest of the jobs are ladled out to whoever is first in line and sober. Work is anything from loading boxcars to putting labels on jars of mayonnaise. The company pays the slave mart, and the slave mart pays the minimum wage. No one is sure what the slave mart gets first, but the most common guess on the Row is three and a half.

If you miss at the slave mart, you can run down the block to the bill passers. They are door-to-door advertising companies who leaflet the suburbs. Six dollars for eight hours and a ride out and maybe back. Some have a habit of leaving men in Pasadena and not picking them up. When you hitchhike in, they give you your check. Sometimes. A few are known to say you did not distribute enough handbills and refuse to pay.

Working for the bill passers is risky business, and a lot avoid it. A good number, however, do not even have that option. They are too old to walk around Pasadena, and some are crippled. The only place for the back part of the line—the old men, the drunks, and the disabled—is the missions. And that is like having no place at all.

The missions are stuffed into every corner for twenty square blocks of the Row. They solicit contributions with a city permit and bring the burning word of Jesus to the downtrodden, the sinners, and the drunkards. To every poor son of a bitch who needs to come in from the cold. The biggest one has a neon sign forty feet across along its side. THE WAGES OF SIN IS DEATH, it says, BUT THE GIFT OF GOD IS ETERNAL LIFE.

Some of the missions give a bed. It is usually one night in, then ten nights out before they will give you another. If you take it, you are locked in until time for chores at 8:30. It is no way to find work, since the work splits by eight. The best deal is one of the pews in the chapel. That way you can roll out at five and make the slave mart in time for a chance.

All of the missions give a meal. A Bean Meal spelled with a capital B. Some serve their beans at eleven, some at one in the afternoon, and some top the day off with beans at 8:30. A couple give salads. One, the Union Rescue, has a health and dental clinic that is free on Saturday morning. It can handle twenty-five men. The missions are all sizes and tastes. The biggest has five hundred beds, the smallest has four and is open on Tuesdays and Thursdays. They come big and tall, fat and small, but the talk of the Row is Gravy Joe's. Everybody says it is because of the gravy, which is considered a luxury.

IF YOU GET TIRED OF GRAVY JOE'S and you cannot get on at Ready Men, the only remaining option is to find your nearest neighborhood vampire. If your blood passes the iron test, you are all right. After a while you get used to the routine and start shaping the whole mess into a life.

Richard Morgan has been visiting the vampires since he left the army eleven years ago. From New York to L.A., up to Portland for a while, then back down south again. Now he is on the staff of the Union Rescue Mission. He rolls the men out in the morning, sweeps up, and shows the new ones their bunks at night. He gets a room, board, and $4 a week. It is a good job. Still, to top it off with an extra ten bucks, he goes down to the plasma daily twice a week and works as a blood cow.

It is called "being on the program." The nurse takes a drop of your blood and drips it into a vial of light-green liquid. If it sinks, you are in. If it doesn't, you can go out, get a four-ounce glass of water, put five drops of iodine in it, drink it, and pass in an hour and a half. Everybody knows how to do it. It is part of the Fifth Street grammar.

When you are past the nurse and the forms, you lie on the table and get plugged in. The needle leads to a tube that leads to a plastic sack. When the first sack fills, a second is plugged in. The first pint of whole blood is taken back to the lab. This is all happening at fifty beds, one right after another, and the lab is covered with plastic sacks. One by one they are put on a centrifuge until the red blood cells sink and the plasma floats over them. Then the plasma is sucked out and the red blood cells taken back to the arm they came from. If the nurse switches sacks and gives you someone else's, it means a county grave or three months in the hospital at least. The first form you sign when you sell your blood is a waiver that frees the blood bank of any liability in case they fuck up. The whole process takes two hours, or an hour and forty minutes if you have good veins. Two pints of blood are extracted to get a pint of plasma. Twice a week is the legal maximum, but that is easy to beat if you need to. The blood banks only check between each other by putting a mark on the thumb with ultraviolet ink. It comes off with a short rubbing of battery acid or a mixture of lemon juice and bleach.

When you are done, you just go down the hall to the cashier's window. The nurse gives you a nickel to use in the coffee machine on the way. The cashier pays the five bucks. She will hand over eight if you let the nurse inject tetanus serum with the red blood cells when they drip them back in. The doctors are trying to find out what it does. It seems that nobody knows yet and they want someone on Fifth Street to be the first one to find out.

Rich Morgan will not. "I've got to take care of myself," Rich says. "I mean, who else is gonna if I don't? These goddamn blood banks won't, that's for sure."

"NONSENSE," IS THE WAY ONE of the doctors on Fifth Street responded. He did not want his name used, but he was short and sixty. "We treat them beautifully," he says. "I check them all for blood pressure. I have eight assistants and fifteen in the lab downtown. That's not the problem.

"The problem you see is the men down here. Some are nice, but the rest . . . They are driftwood. Just driftwood. Give them more money and they'll drink more. They have less intelligence than an insect or a spider. Because a spider has a plan and builds a home. It plans its life. These people don't. The have another fifty years to live. Have they got a plan for their lives? No. They're bums. They have no place to sleep. The solution to help these people is not to make trouble. The solution is to organize a kibbutz for the people."

When we talked, the doctor shouted at me over the constant scramble on the street. "The problem that you have to solve is what you call the drifters; this driftwood here." The doctor was standing in a doorway across the street from his bank and gestured at the passing wreckage. "You gotta organize it into something structural. Something that has positive value. Look at this one who stands here. Or this one there. Does he have a plan? I ask them. They talk back. 'Did *you* have a plan?' they say. I say yes. Since I was fourteen years old. I planned my life and I got it."

The doctor has five college degrees and a home on the other side of town. While we were talking, two men on a Coke truck were delivering next door. They overheard.

After the doctor left, the one on the top shouted down.

"Is he a for-real doctor?" he asked. "I see his white coat, but I mean is he for real?"

"He seems to be," I said.

"Good Jesus Christ," the man mumbled. "Ain't that a bitch."

The doctor is for real, no doubt, but there are still a lot of men on the Row who tell a different story. They could tell enough to keep you a month. Fortunately, there's a way to make sense out of all the claims. The commercial blood banks all over the United States have a track record and it seems to point in one direction. There are two parts to it.

The first one is a long way from the Row. It is in suburban hospitals all over the country. It is called serum hepatitis. It inflames the liver and causes extreme pain, itching, weakness, diarrhea, nausea, fever, and yellowing of the skin. You get it from transfusing dirty blood.

When the suburban doctors try to figure it out, they point at the commercial blood banks. Outfits like California Transfusion Service and Abbott Laboratories, Inc., are responsible for 47 percent of all the blood and plasma transfused in the country. The only regulations they operate under are those of the federal Division of Biological Standards. That code demands a certain extraction technique and freedom of the donor from infectious skin disease. If all you are is pregnant, syphilitic, feverish, infected with mononucleosis, tuburcular, or suffering from upper respiratory infection, cancer, kidney, or liver disease, then you can give. The bureau has checked five hundred of the seven thousand commercial blood banks this year. By June it will have checked a thousand. Violations are a misdemeanor under the Public Health Service Act. Since 1902, the government has taken action against a total of four blood banks. In Los Angeles, up until three years ago, the commercial banks pooled their plasma, mixing all the pints together. Until the practice was stopped, one out of every ten L.A. transfusions led to serum hepatitis.

A low estimate of the impact of the vampires is given by Dr. J. Garrott Allen of Stanford University, who has studied blood since 1945. He estimates 3,500 deaths and 50,000 illnesses a year. The Centers for Disease Control, in Atlanta, guesses higher. They put it at 35,000 deaths and 500,000 illnesses.

The second part of it is just as bad. It is all over the street corners and sleeping in the empty boxcars at night. The folks of Skid Row have wells in their arms. They live on Gravy Joe's chicken delight and get the protein sucked out of their veins twice a week. It has withered them, made them dizzy, given them heart attacks, and used them up. Every three hours, there is an ambulance on the Row. Now and then, a "vagrant" dies on the blood bank table. People who give blood should eat steak and orange juice. As it is, the last piece of raw meat to make it past the Greyhound station was a policeman's horse shot in an armed robbery.

Ray met one of the victims. He looked old and had pits in the crooks of both elbows. He had given plasma twice a week for three and a half years running. He was broke and none of the banks will take him anymore.

"They say I'm a health risk," he said.

"What do you do for money now?" Ray asked.

"I sleep out in the weeds. That's all," the old man said.

Ray felt like he was watching the leftovers from a sausage factory. They had just used this guy up and thrown him away. It made Ray mad. You haven't met Ray yet, but you can't really understand what's happening to the vampires now unless you understand Ray and Jeff and the place the men have come to call the hippie kitchen.

It does not call itself the hippie kitchen. But nobody down here seems to call anybody else by their right name. The kitchen calls itself the Ammon Hennacy House of Hospitality. It has been feeding on the Row for three years and has been on the corner of Sixth and Gladys since 1972. It is a kitchen. It feeds once a day, every day, from one o'clock until nobody comes, anywhere from two hundred to four hundred people a day. The hippie kitchen is the only one on the Row to give salad and fruit every day. It is the first feeding outfit to break away from beans to Spanish rice with little chunks of hamburger. It is also the only place to eat without having to sit through a service. They just feed and do not fuck with you when you're trying to eat.

Jeff Dietrich has been there since the start. He is short with a blond mustache and ponytail. He belongs to the Catholic Workers. His voice always has a smile attached and he means what he says.

"The missions have told these men that it's a sin to be poor. We think that the teachings of Christ have nothing to do with that. It's not a sin to be poor. It's not a sin to be a drunkard. It is a sin to be a member of that kind of corporate, capitalist rip-off that put these men here. It's an unchristian society that made the Row. It's not the men living here who are sinners, it's the men who own this place who sin."

About a year ago, Ray Corrieo heard about the kitchen and came in. It did not seem like much then, but it's meant a lot on the Row since. Ray Corrieo had been on one bombing tour already and he was sick of it. His officer came by and Ray stopped him. "I'm sick of killing people," Ray said. "I want out of the navy." His officer laughed. The next day Ray announced he was not working anymore. He was not going to eat either. Not until he got a discharge. After twenty days not eating in the brig, he was marched down the gangplank between a double row of marines. The marines spat on him every step of the way. After fifty-two days, Ray was down from 195 pounds to 125. He was in the hospital, and the doctors said two more days would kill him. At that point the navy gave in and he got his discharge. Three of the marines who spat on him came over to the hospital and apologized.

I probably don't need to tell you that Ray Corrieo is a brave son of a bitch with a good record of fighting when he thinks he's right. He hung around the Row and noticed the blood banks. That spurred his curiosity and he read every article printed about blood in the last five years. When he was done, he went in the kitchen and found Jeff.

"These guys are getting screwed," Ray said. "We got to call a meeting and figure out what to do about it."

They posted notices and had the meeting on the next Sunday afternoon. Jeff hoped for twelve guys to show. Ray was ready to settle for four. When the time came, the room had seventy people in it. They all knew they had been screwed. No doubt about it. That's all they talked about for the next two hours. Bill Skahill was there and so was Rich Morgan and Just Plain Bill. At the end, they decided to send a committee around to the banks with a list of grievances.

As everyone was leaving, a guy came up to Jeff. He handed him a folded paper and said it was a statement about the blood banks.

"What's your name?" Jeff asked.

"It's on the paper."

"Can we contact you?" Jeff asked again.

"I'll be back," the guy said.

The paper he left was short and simple. "I was lying on the table," it read, "and they'd just taken out the first pint of the two pints of blood for my plasma donation. I raised my head up on my fist and looked across the room at the guy on the table next to me. I saw the nurse unclamp the tube running out of his arm and kick a trash bucket underneath it. She was letting his blood run out into the trash bucket and starting to walk away. When she saw me looking at him, she reclamped the tube, but I know she would have let him die if I hadn't seen her." The statement was signed "Denny."

Jeff looked for Denny after that, but he was not to be found. Someone in the lunch line said he went back to Wyoming.

THE GRIEVANCE COMMITTEE GOT laughter at one bank and an "I'll refer it to our legal department" at another. That led to a second meeting, and that meeting led in turn to a union and a strike.

They call themselves the Blood Donors Union, and anybody who has given blood can join. It is simple: no dues and seven demands.

1. Respectful care and treatment.

2. The right to be advised. No experimentation on their blood without permission.

3. The right to informed consent. All processes must be explained by a doctor before they are done.

4. $15 a pint for whole blood, $9 a pint for plasma.

5. Abolition of the waivers of responsibility men have been forced to sign.

6. Their bodies are being drained of proteins by donation. The blood banks have an obligation to replace it. Fruit juices and vitamin supplements for each man who donates. In addition, the blood banks should put a quarter into a union fund for each pint extracted. The fund will be used to build and staff a free medical and dental clinic.

7. For the protection of the general public, they recommend the introduction of central records-keeping for all the banks so the men suffering from hepatitis may be located and treated.

With that they threw up a picket line. They chose the Doctors' Blood Bank. It is small and specializes in whole blood. That makes it especially vulnerable. Whole blood only keeps twenty-one days before it has to be thrown out. If the union cuts into their action, the Doctors' Bank cannot run on its reserves. The union wanted to leave the option for those needing money, so the union decided to take the banks one at a time. They hoped to break the Doctors' and then move on to the others. The last thing they did was set the rules: nonviolence in response to abuse, and no drunks on the line.

Then it was Tuesday morning, February 27, and every head on the Row snapped back. Pickets on Fifth Street? Nobody had ever heard of it before.

Just being there was as big a victory as had been won on the Row since the Japanese surrender. The men in front of the liquor stores and magazine shops cheered. Doctors' went from a daily average of 120 pints to 24. The bank hired an off-duty cop to watch the lobby, but even he dug it. He brought donuts, and a guy just in from St. Louis brought coffee.

On the third day, Hot Cross Bun approached Ray. He is called that because it describes his face. He had the misfortune of hitting Anzio, Palermo, and Cassino right in a row with the 45th Infantry Division. The doctors took a woman's rib and made him a nose with it.

"I'm due," he said, meaning his officially prescribed waiting period was up. "I'm as goddamn due as you can get, and have been for two weeks. But I'm not goin' in. No way am I goin' in." He laughed and went up the street.

People's spirits stayed high and they settled into their circle on the sidewalk eight hours a day, every day the bank was open. The only thing they had not counted on was Miss Louise. She turned out to be a spoiler.

Miss Louise is as close to being Queen of the Row as anybody will get. She is a black woman in her forties and has been down there for the last fifteen years. She runs the front counter at the Doctors' Bank. She knows everybody and everybody knows her. She works for the vampire, but she is not a hard or cruel woman. She buys men drinks out of her own pocket when they can't pass the iron test. Miss Louise tries to help them and has done just as many favors as pints of blood. She even brought plastic covers out for the pickets when it rained. Nobody in the union meant for her to, but she took the picket line personally.

Miss Louise does not own the blood bank. It is owned by six corporate directors. The only one of them anybody on the Row has seen is a white guy who drives a Porsche. Still Miss Louise thinks of the bank as her own.

"How much of that quarter a pint are you gonna skim," is what she started with. That did not work very well. Not many on the Row would buy it.

In the last few days, she has switched to, "You're just picketing me because I'm black." She stands in front of the door and says it to the brothers thinking about coming in. "Don't let a little race prejudice stop you, honey," she says. "Come on in and let Miss Louise help you out." It has hurt the strike. Not in numbers. Most everybody black, white, brown, and red is going someplace else if they have to go. It is the division by color that has gotten a little nasty.

Twice black men have threatened to stick some of the folks on the line. Miss Louise did not send them. They came because of their feelings for her, but she knew nothing about it. The second time it happened to Curly. He was on the line and a brother with a floppy hat approached.

"You're getting awful heavy on the sister's action," he said.

"It ain't on the sister," Curly said. "It's against the bank."

"If you don't quit," the man said, "it means trouble."

Curly lobbied for a meeting and got it. The meet was supposed to happen on Saturday, but the black guys never showed.

Out of frustration, Ray called Miss Louise.

"Well," she said on the phone, "just what is it you guys want?"

When you talk on the phone, one thing leads to another, and this phone call led to another meeting between the union and Miss Louise next Monday. She is not management, but she is an important woman to everybody concerned. If everything goes well, the union plans to move across the street to California Transfusion Service as a tribute to Miss Louise's willingness to talk.

IN THE MEANTIME, THE PICKETS stay right where they have been for the last two weeks. Rain or shine, every day from six in the morning until the banks close at two.

Miss Louise remains in place on her throne in Fifth Street, sending a cab full of the day's blood up to Huntington Memorial Hospital in Pasadena. If you are a regular there, I'd try to stay away for a while. At least until the union wins its cross-checking system. Doing otherwise could prove to be a disaster.

Old Henry's still down on the Row too. He comes every other day to lunch at the Hospitality House. Over the last fifteen years he has given 597 pints of blood and plasma. He thinks the strike is a great thing, but he is afraid to join the picket. Some men who have walked with signs have been turned away at the other banks, and he doesn't want to risk it. He only has three more pints to make 600. When he does, his regular lab has promised him a $30 bonus. Down on the Row that's big money.

[Originally published as "Skid Row Battle: Residents vs. the Blood Banks," *Rolling Stone*, April 12, 1973]

A Child of "The Land"

*B*Y 10 A.M. ON FRIDAY, JULY 15, 1977, Robyn Wesley, a midwife specializing in home births, and Kim Myers, a freelance carpenter, had reported to the Superior Court for the County of Santa Clara, State of California, the Honorable John R. Kennedy presiding. Later that day, Robyn and Kim's two-year-old daughter would begin dying, but on their way to court, the warm Friday morning bore no hint of approaching tragedy. The sun had already burned the dew off the mountains to the west, and by ten o'clock the peaks were hidden by the umbrella of smog rising off the interlacing housing tracts of the Santa Clara Valley.

Both Kim and Robyn were defendants in an eviction suit filed by one Alyce Lee Burns against Donald Eldridge, Mark Schneider, Robyn Wesley, and one to five hundred additional John Doe squatters residing at 32100 Page Mill Road, Palo Alto, California. This property comprised some 750 acres overlooking the suburban community of Palo Alto and neighboring Stanford University, three-quarters of the way up the eastern slope of the Santa Cruz Mountains that run down the spine of the San Francisco Peninsula. At the time of Wesley and Myers's court appearance, the acreage was occupied by fifty adults and ten children in twenty-seven dwellings. Like the first homesteaders to migrate to 32100 Page Mill in 1969, all of them felt they had found a place to be gentle, know each other, and get back to basics. The settlers had dubbed themselves, their homes, and the property "The Land." After eight years, this "counterculture" was now beginning its last act. Before 1978, The Land would be no more than the fifty people themselves, and they were scattered, and missing a child.

For the last three months, Robyn and Kim had been living apart. The couple's daughter, Sierra Laurel Wesley Myers, had been shared equally between Kim and Robyn since their breakup. At the age of two, Sierra walked everywhere by herself in the hillsides around her home and seemed totally unafraid. Sierra was an especially magical little girl. She had Rubens cheeks and intensely bright blue eyes. Many of her neighbors used to drop by her parents' cabin just to visit their little girl. During her parents' day in court, she went with one of her adult friends to the beach at San Gregorio. The eviction of Robyn and her neighbors had already been a long process when trial finally began on July 15. By early afternoon, the judge had recessed and scheduled another hearing for Wednesday, July 20, and adjourned court until then.

Kim Myers and Robyn Wesley had arranged that Kim would meet their daughter Sierra back at the Ranch House after court. He planned to bring her to the big house at Struggle Mountain, a mile down the road from The Land. As part of her midwife practice, Robyn had arranged to meet a couple at one of the Struggle Mountain cottages for a prenatal visit at 6 p.m. When her meeting was over, Robyn and Sierra would go back to their cabin by the walnut orchard on the 750-acre rolling watershed at 32100 Page Mill Road.

I

Sierra Myers met her daddy at the Ranch House around 4:30 Friday afternoon. Kim Myers remembers that Friday as a hot day. Father and daughter played for a bit and then went to Struggle Mountain. For the entire week, Kim had been having trouble starting his 1962 Rambler station wagon, and he planned to fix it while Sierra played.

Struggle Mountain is a cluster of four buildings on four and a half acres at 31570 Page Mill Road, and friends are welcome for short stays. That day Kim parked his Rambler near the side of the largest house, about thirty feet from the community's four-foot-deep circular swimming pool. Sierra began playing in the yard with Soul, the daughter of Struggle Mountain resident Joanne LeBright.

Kim popped the hood and opened the Rambler's carburetor. While he was working, Soul and her mother left, and Sierra went over to the swings near the pool. Kim got behind the Rambler's steering wheel to start the engine and test his work.

When he did, the carburetor backfired and exploded, momentarily engulfing the engine in flames. Sierra's father leaped out and began yelling, "Fire!" Iris Moore, Winter Sojourner, and Brigid McCaw came scrambling out of the big house, and Neil Reichline grabbed a fire extinguisher, but the fire was out before he reached the car. Soon, Robyn Wesley appeared on the scene to keep her prenatal appointment and to pick up Sierra. She spoke with Kim briefly about the fire and then joked about their daughter's day at the beach.

"Well," Robyn asked, "did SiSi drown herself today?"

Kim said no, that she'd had a good time, and he smiled behind his mustache. Despite their separation, he and Robyn were still close.

After a little more conversation, Robyn asked where Sierra was. Kim had last seen her right before the fire and did not exactly know where she was now. Neither did any of the other people still around the yard. Kim went to look on the downhill slope, and Robyn decided to check the cottages. Seconds later, Iris Moore screamed and the sound echoed in the marrow of Robyn's bones. Kim heard it too and bolted in Iris's direction.

Iris Moore had found Sierra floating facedown in the pool. The child's skin had a blue tinge and she was not breathing. Iris had just completed a course in emergency medicine.

"Work on her, Iris!" Kim yelled. "Work on her!"

At the top of her voice, Robyn Wesley begged God not to take her baby. While Iris applied mouth-to-mouth resuscitation, a car was brought up and Iris and Sierra got in the back seat. Kim sat in the front next to the driver and they charged down the hill toward the Stanford University hospital, twelve miles away on the flats. Robyn followed in a second car. Someone at Struggle Mountain called an ambulance and it met the caravan halfway down the grade. Sierra was transferred from the car and hooked to an oxygen apparatus immediately. Kim got in the following car with Robyn while the ambulance driver radioed ahead to the emergency room.

At around 6 p.m., Dr. Terrence Stull was notified that a Code 3 toddler was on the way to the Stanford University hospital. Stull was covering Stanford's Pediatrics ward that evening, and he and senior resident Keith Kimble decided they had better be in emergency to meet it. The toddler was brought in with an oxygen mask on her face. She was flaccid and had no heartbeat. Pure oxygen was being forced into her lungs by squeezing the inflatable bag on the side of the mask. The anesthesiologist on duty lifted the emergency rig off Sierra's face and ran a plastic tube down one nostril and into her trachea. It was attached to an oxygen bag that the anesthesiologist continued to squeeze rhythmically. Adrenaline was shot into the child's heart, and Stull performed external cardiac massage. Keith Kimble supervised the flow through the intravenous needles inserted in Sierra's arm.

In essence, drowning is a series of shocks sustained by the body. The heaviest of them is the effect of the absence of oxygen on the body tissues. As in all cases of shock, oxygen-starved tissues swell. Brain tissues, unlike most others, are tightly encased in bone. When the brain swells, it immediately begins pushing itself against the surrounding skull. To fight that cerebral swelling, a dosage of Decadron, a steroid, was administered through the tube in the toddler's arm. That was followed by dopamine to raise the blood pressure, calcium salts to stimulate the heart, phenobarbital to prevent seizures, and a form of sodium bicarbonate to reduce the acidity in the blood. Within ten minutes, a strengthening heartbeat returned, and within twenty, her blood pressure and pulse had stabilized somewhere close to normal. The child was still unconscious, and the bag still breathed for her.

As soon as Sierra stabilized somewhat, the doctors arranged to move her upstairs by elevator to the Intensive Care ward in Pediatrics. Once life functions have been restored or supported, the treatment for drowning consists of slowing down "body action" to reduce swelling. Upstairs, Sierra was laid on a thermal blanket that reduced her temperature to the middle 80s Fahrenheit. The cold induced shivering as a natural reaction, which in turn used up oxygen that would otherwise be used by the brain to heal itself. To suppress the shivers, the toddler was dosed with Pavulon, a derivative of curare, a poison used by South American Indians to paralyze game. A tiny tube was run in her arm, up the vein, and into her heart to measure her central venous pressure. It and a regular blood-pressure line were run into a button-covered blue box called the Tektronix 404, which emits a steady succession of electronic bleeps. Sierra's lung functions had not returned, and could not as long as she was paralyzed with Pavulon. A respirator did most of Sierra's breathing for the next eight days.

While all this transpired, the parents waited outside the emergency-room doors. Neither Kim nor Robyn thought it was helpful to bottle up their emotions, and their sobs and crying bothered the other people waiting to see the doctors. They moved outside by themselves, leaving inside a number of folks from Struggle Mountain who had raced down the hill and tried to offer comfort. As far as Robyn Wesley was concerned, nothing could have undercut her more than this tragedy. Her daughter had been the springboard for much of what now made up Robyn's life.

2

Robyn Wesley had been born in suburban Chicago to an upper-middle-class family that eventually migrated to Orlando, Florida. She married straight out of high school and moved with her husband to Savannah, Georgia, in 1969, where they both began selling advertising space for Time Inc. At first they were bent on success, working twelve hours a day, six days a week. Robyn and her husband brought in a good income, but after the first year, their enthusiasm for the routine began wearing thin. Her husband had grown his hair long but had to hide it under a wig whenever they went out of the house. They both enjoyed smoking marijuana, and they talked about moving west. Robyn and her husband finally left for California a few months into 1970.

They went their separate ways soon after reaching the West

Coast. Robyn ended up working in San Bernardino with mentally disabled children for a year and a half before moving north to Mountain View, California, to attend junior college. The ambiance of her neighborhood in Mountain View reinforced a lot of her strongest feelings at the time. Almost everyone she knew talked about depending less on the civilization of stucco and machinery around them and taking more responsibility for the basics of their lives. On her Mountain View block, three residents eventually moved to The Land. Robyn finally followed her friend Mary Konczyk there in 1973.

The dominant features of the property at 32100 Page Mill Road are two ridges running in roughly parallel lines across the land from the northwest to the southeast. The area contains the headwaters of the Stevens Creek and a five-acre cattail bog that is one of the Bay Area's few natural swamps. The tributaries are lined with heavy thickets of oak, madrone, and bay trees. Robyn, Kim, and the others lived mostly in these thickets. Their homes were made from recycled lumber and were sometimes referred to as "shacks" or "squatter dwellings" by the newspapers.

By the time of their 1976 court appearance, the community's buildings had in fact become relatively sturdy. Eventually, photographs of the structures were run in the local papers and were looked upon by some as a sort of folk art. Many buildings sported inlays of several shades of hardwood and had stained-glass windows created by the artisans of The Land.

The only structures on the property when Mrs. Burns first purchased it in the early 1950s were the original ranch house on Page Mill Road—built before the 1906 earthquake and surrounded by several outbuildings—and a large tin barn. By 1968, the growing university town of Palo Alto had extended its city borders and its utilities district to include the Burns property. At this time, the Burns family took steps to sell. The buyer was one Donald Eldridge, the first party listed in Burns's 1977 complaint.

Eldridge was a millionaire by virtue of his development of several key color video processes, and he supported a number of antiwar and community organizing projects through a San Francisco–based personal foundation. His liberal politics and cultural tolerance, combined with the beauty of the eastern Santa Cruz slope, attracted a late-sixties migration of young long-haired refugees from society at large. The vacant structures at 32100 Page Mill Road were occupied by an assortment of young people. Eldridge let them stay on as caretakers, and was later to say that he felt they didn't mar the natural setting and that their presence protected the place from four-wheel-drive vandals. By 1971, the overflow crowd from the ranch house had marched back on the remaining 750 acres, and groups had begun homesteading. The new residents did little to disturb the countryside. For the first year, they lived in tepees and tents until wooden structures were completed.

Over the years, The Land had become by far the largest grouping of its kind in a neighborhood full of such settlements. The last four miles of upper Page Mill Road east of the crest are populated with clusters of extended families that have names like Struggle Mountain, Rancho Diablo, and Earth Ranch. Electricity never spread farther than the Ranch House buildings, and water for the first backlanders had to be hand-carried from the spring. Later, cold water was brought to the buildings through a series of plastic pipes and hoses connecting a spring box with an outside tap. The new residents eventually named the shorter unnamed ridge behind the barn Sadhana Ridge, after a group called the Sadhana Foundation that came through in 1972. The name was taken from Sanskrit and refers to the path followed by Hindus in their quest for enlightenment.

Kim Myers, then 32, moved to The Land with the original backland settlers in 1971. Robyn Wesley, then 26, arrived in early 1973. Their daughter, Sierra, was born in one of the small cabins behind the Ranch House on the last day of April in 1975. For most of the more than three years they lived together at The Land, Robyn and Kim occupied a cabin below Sadhana Ridge, a mile southwest of the barn. It was next to a walnut orchard gone wild. Their nearest neighbors were across a steep gully and up the slope, but they saw them often. Everyone who lived on The Land knew everyone else and spent time together. In 1974, after The Land was found to be in violation of city building codes, the settlers prepared a booklet to explain themselves and to offer alternatives to enforcement of the code. In the preamble of the booklet, The Land was described as "a nonviolent, spiritually minded community . . . . While the society as a whole seems paralyzed by a deep loss of faith, the life on this land represents . . . a belief that trust, love and sharing are real forces in the world . . . . " Originally the internal politics of the community focused on conversation, making music, eating communally, and building houses. In recent years, as the community had to deal with outside political forces, gatherings known as "The Land meetings"— during which everyone had to reach a consensus in order for action to be taken—came into common use.

Robyn and Kim began living together a year after she first settled at The Land, and one of their first decisions was to have a baby. When Robyn became pregnant, she and Kim were sure about wanting to have their child at home, on The Land. Robyn Wesley considered birth to be both a natural and spiritual process. She wanted to experience it fully, and to do that she felt she had to have control over its setting. Robyn knew lots of women who had had negative hospital birth experiences and felt they had not gotten the support they had needed from the hospital environment. With the approval of her obstetrician, Robyn found a midwife who would help her deliver at home.

On the last day of April in 1975, Robyn Wesley spent most of twelve hours of labor walking around and standing up. Kim, the midwife, and five other friends were there loving her and cheering her on. When the last wave of contractions started, Robyn Wesley finally lay down on the bed, gave two quick pushes, and Sierra Laurel Wesley Myers was born.

Robyn said the whole experience felt like magic, and from that point on she devoted a great deal of energy to helping other women have the same kind of birth she had enjoyed. Robyn and two women from Struggle Mountain soon enrolled in a midwifery class in Palo Alto. After completing the three-month course, and backing up her teacher on a few training births, Robyn ran her first delivery. It was on a houseboat in the yacht habor of Redwood City, California.

Robyn built up a practice that took her to as many as five births a month. She charged $100 for each birth and $50 for the couple's prenatal meetings. Robyn always worked with both a backup midwife and a referring obstetrician. Sierra used to accompany her mother on a lot of the prenatal visits.

3

When Terry Stull found Kim and Robyn where they waited, both parents were in a state of agony and disbelief, but it did not prevent Robyn from recognizing him. Young Dr. Stull lived with seven other people in a house called La Cresta in Los Altos, and he had previously met Robyn when she delivered one of his housemate's children. Up until that moment, Dr. Stull had no idea who the toddler was.

"Is she alive?" Robyn begged.

"She's alive," he answered. Dr. Stull went on to explain that she was alive "for now." Robyn chewed her lip and tried to ignore the terror welling up in her.

Terry led the parents up to Pediatrics, where they established themselves on a couch in the waiting room. One entire wall of the room was papered with a photographic blowup of the Sierra Nevada range. Kim and Robyn waited in front of the mural for the next hour and a half while the Intensive Care nurses continued adjusting Sierra's equipment and further stabilizing her.

When Robyn and Kim finally saw Sierra in the Intensive Care ward on Friday night, she lay on her back on the cooling pad, covered by a blanket. One green towel had been wrapped around the back of her head and another was around the front to support the tubes running into her nose. The wrappings sat on the child's head like a turban. Robyn choked at the horror of the scene. This could not be happening. Not to her. Her mind battled to try and somehow deny what her eyes saw. That struggle would be the crux of Robyn's dilemma for the next eight days.

Robyn Wesley wanted to pick her baby up, but there were too many tubes, so she stroked her daughter's leg and talked to her.

Robyn tried to tell Sierra what had happened to her and that she would be all right. Sierra made no movement and gave no sign of recognition, but her mother was sure she was hearing inside there somewhere. The room and the hallway outside were full of the steady bleeping of the Tektronix 404. Robyn Wesley quickly understood that the rhythm of the bleeps was Sierra's body talking, and she constantly tracked the noise in the back of her mind. It was like a lifeline between the two of them.

4

Kim and Robyn never had to maintain their vigil with Sierra alone. Word about the accident had spread throughout The Land within an hour after the cars had screeched down the hill to meet the ambulance.

By Saturday afternoon, Stanford's Pediatrics waiting room had filled up with sleeping bags, backpacks, and bunches of wildflowers gathered off Lone Oak Hill. The crowd ebbed and flowed, but there were rarely less than twenty of Sierra's friends in the ward at any given time. People had come because they loved both Kim and Robyn and wanted to help, but mostly they came to see Sierra. She was thought by everyone to be an extraordinary child.

At least one nurse was always at Sierra's bedside, monitoring both the toddler and the Tektronix 404. The nurses turned Sierra over every half hour to minimize the damage done to her skin by the intense cold. Often they were assisted by one or another of Sierra's long-haired friends. Several of them were in the room most of the time. They told her stories and sang her favorite songs. There is no scientific evidence that people in deep comas receive communication, but no one from The Land had any doubts that Sierra did. The Land visitors believed Sierra Myers heard and felt the energy they sent her. The nurses shared The Land visitors' opinion and always made it a practice to talk to their unconscious patients.

Despite everyone's faith, it was at first difficult to believe that Sierra was really there inside the tubed and wired body on the bed. She was so still. But by Saturday, that had changed and everyone agreed that they now felt some of Sierra in her body and in the surrounding room. These feelings were interpreted as a hopeful sign and grasped at by some as the first signal of Sierra's resurgence. Robyn Wesley remained doubtful. That was not Robyn's Sierra lying there. She wanted to know where the rest of her daughter was.

Ignorance about the geography around the borders of death was widespread among the visitors to Pediatrics, and those in The Land vigil quickly took steps to correct it. Over the next few days, at virtually all hours of any day, someone was studying Dr. Elisabeth Kübler-Ross's *On Death and Dying*, or Dr. Raymond A. Moody, Jr.'s *Life After Life*. Both Drs. Kübler-Ross and Moody have examined death by studying the accounts of those who had been pronounced dead and who had then been revived. In those books, the people who "came back" reported that though it may be preceded by great pain, death is not in itself a painful process: it is a sensation of incredible and overwhelming peace. Some of those who had been revived reported being greeted in death by people whom they were close with, people who had died before them. Dr. Kübler-Ross does write of one two-year-old child of fundamentalist Christians who said he was met by Jesus while in a coma. Dr. Kübler-Ross is sure children are welcomed to death by an affirmative presence.

That knowledge soothed Robyn. After her first weekend in Pediatrics, Robyn was sure her daughter would be in a good place even if she did not come back, but that didn't make it any easier. Robyn did not want to live without Sierra. It was not right that her daughter should go off to death so fragile and small. Robyn both wanted and refused to accept the possibility of death, until she reached a state of total exhaustion Sunday morning. She and Kim finally curled up for their first sleep in the interns' room down the hall.

Robyn Wesley and Kim Myers awoke twenty minutes later when Maryann Konczyk shook Robyn's arm.

"Something's happening to Sierra," Maryann said.

Robyn and Kim were running down the hallway in an instant. The Tektronix 404's bleep had changed to ringing bells. Eight doctors and nurses were surrounding the bed and working furiously on the child's body. Sierra's heart had stopped.

Kim and Robyn took a space at the corner of the bed and beseeched the universe to let their daughter live. In a matter of seconds, the bells stopped ringing and the Tektronix 404's bleep returned, steady and strong. Deep down, Robyn knew the reprieve was just temporary.

She and Kim were sobbing and holding each other, there by Sierra's bed. "What if we're holding her back, Kimmer?" Robyn asked. "What if she needs to die and we're not letting her?"

When the crowd cleared out of the room as Sierra once again stabilized, Robyn Wesley told her daughter in a whispering voice close to her ear that it was all right if she had to die. Robyn said she would understand, but inside herself she knew her own acceptance was not altogether true.

For Kim Myers, the seizure marked a new level of reality. Before, he had been sure she would just wake up and be Sierra again, and everything would be all right. But now, SiSi was so close to being gone that Kim shivered. Over the next twenty-four hours, his mind kept spontaneously remembering bits and pieces of dreams he had had about dying throughout his life.

5

Kim Myers reached The Land via the United States Army. Drafted soon after graduating from California State University, Long Beach, with a B.A. in English in 1968, Myers spent '69 and '70 with the 24th Medical Battalion, first in Kansas and then in Germany. Myers hated the army. The only thing good that ever happened to him there was when a friend showed him one of the first copies of the *Whole Earth Catalog*. Its creed of simple living, peace, and reconciliation with nature was everything Private Myers wanted. After his discharge, he showed up on the San Francisco Peninsula looking for a place to live off his army unemployment benefits and grow a garden.

The place he found was a shack below the garage at Rancho Diablo, a cluster of buildings three miles from 32100 Page Mill

Road on Skyline Boulevard. The commune there was in the process of breaking up. Stewart Brand—who is now California governor Jerry Brown's appropriate-technology adviser—was at that time in the garage, finishing *The Last Whole Earth Catalog*. Kim eventually joined a fragment of Rancho Diablo's commune in looking for another place to live in the depths of Donald Eldridge's holdings at 32100 Page Mill Road.

In 1971, a group of approximately twenty settlers, with Kim Myers among them, moved back along the watershed and spread out in tepees under the trees. Kim began to feel a common mind growing among the settlers. Hooked into that shared feeling, Kim felt elevated. Everything seemed cleaner and more real. During the slow July days, he read *Autobiography of a Yogi* by Paramahansa Yogananda and learned carpentry.

The settlers lived poor and needed little cash to survive. What they had was shared. The Land community grew and shrank and stabilized during those first years. Kim Myers lived in both the back and the front of The Land, and he saw people come and go. He was at The Land when overcrowding fragmented the backlands settlers during the second summer and led to a second, deeper migration toward Black Mountain. He was still there the next summer, when the police helicopters began buzzing Sadhana Ridge to keep the squatters from lying out there in various stages of nakedness. The summer after that, Kim began living with Robyn.

From the first, it marked a new kind of commitment for Kim. He had decided to become a family man and took the responsibility seriously. He remodeled the middle cottage, in a row of three one-room buildings behind the old Ranch House, so Robyn could have the nicest possible pregnancy and birth. Kim and Robyn's move to the front portion of Eldridge's property proved to be an important event in the history of the squatter community. Until that time, the front settlers and the backlands folk had thought of themselves as two separate groupings. The presence of the backland couple behind the Ranch House who were expecting a baby gave those at the front of the land a new perspective and brought the community together. At about the same time, a settler named Mark Schneider began serving breakfasts for everyone in the Long Hall beyond the front cottages. This sealed the reunion and created a Land ritual at the same time.

The Long Hall had originally been constructed by one Louis O'Neal, who was the owner of 32100 Page Mill from the turn of the century until his death, in 1942. O'Neal was a leader in the Republican Party and had designed the building for rural caucuses and rallies. Legend had it that several California governors were first anointed there. Denizens of The Land used it as a general catchall gathering place. Breakfast was served regularly every morning to the thirty-five or so people who had to drive down the hill to work. On Sunday mornings, folks came for breakfast from The Land and also from up and down Page Hill Road. The institution of the Sunday breakfasts proved to be the final step in merging the groups on The Land into a single entity.

When Sierra was born, it seemed from the beginning that she was the special child of that convergence of energy. She and her parents stayed in the front cottage for her first year and then moved into the cabin by the walnut orchard.

Sierra thrived there and became the centerpiece of Kim Myers's life. He wanted to nurture her and was amazed at how much she nurtured him back. As only children can, she loved without reservation. Kim will always remember his daughter as she was when she would run up to him to ask what he was up to. "What doin', Daddy?" she used to ask. "What doin'?"

On Sunday, July 17, on her back in the Intensive Care ward, Sierra Laurel Wesley Myers asked nothing at all. She remained unconscious and the Tektronix 404 bleeped steadily through the night.

6

On Monday, July 18, the routine at the hospital changed. With the influx of regular weekly visitors, the ward staff shifted The Land's presence to make room. Several portable beds were set up on the patio outside Sierra's window, and the supplies and parcels in the waiting room were stowed under the couches. The changes were explained to the group at a morning briefing that became a daily feature for the rest of Sierra's hospital stay. The doctors in charge of relations with the patient's family and friends were Terry Stull and Frederick Lloyd.

Rick Lloyd was Sierra's personal physician. He and his wife had returned from vacation on Sunday to find a message that Sierra was in the hospital. He rushed over, and from then on he was a regular participant in her care. Lloyd was a pediatrician to a lot of The Land's babies. At the time he first encountered the mountain community, a number of local pediatricians refused to accept home-birth babies as patients because they had been the recipients of "less than optimal care." Lloyd disagreed with the rationale. Sierra began coming to him for all the standard childhood reasons and proved to be a remarkably healthy child.

At the first briefing, Stull and Lloyd tried to summarize the medical situation. There were three major factors that worked against Sierra's recovery. The first was that she had probably been immersed in the pool for longer than five minutes. Children's brains can sustain lack of oxygen longer than those of adults, but after five minutes, that advantage is lost. The second problem was that because she was not cooled until her arrival in the emergency room, the cerebral swelling had had a long time to develop. The last difficulty was that she had arrived at the hospital in a state of complete heart arrest.

Soon they would begin to take her off Pavulon and bring her temperature back to normal. At that point, they would measure the electrical activity in her brain with an electroencephalogram. The measurements would give them a broad picture of how much brain was still functioning inside her skull.

The Land community believed that Sierra had a spiritual consciousness, independent of her brain, that was fully operative. Aside from observing and cooperating with the routine in the ward, all their attempts to participate in her care were aimed at making contact with that spiritual consciousness. They engaged in common meditation to send their healing vibrations to Sierra. On the wall of the waiting room, drawings and words of encouragement were posted for the benefit of those who could only sit and wait. The vigil was exhausting for everyone. Neil Reichline left the hospital Monday afternoon to go home and try to rest after staying up all night talking with Robyn, but he could not sleep. The bird outside his window sounded like a Tektronix 404.

Robyn felt ravaged most of the time. She struggled to keep her feelings from shutting down. She wanted to experience whatever was going on as fully as she could. She had to work on herself to keep open, so she could try to understand and make sense of things. Robyn never went out of reach of the sound of Sierra's Tektronix 404, and she sometimes borrowed someone's child to hold, since she could not hold her own. Robyn desperately wanted her daughter to live, but she did not want to keep Sierra back from what Sierra needed to do, even if it was to die. She asked her friend Neil Reichline to counsel with her and they spent hours talking and trying to expose and understand the demons that danced in her mind.

The technique she and Neil used was called "co-counseling," a method that a good number of those on The Land had learned and regularly practiced. The premise of co-counseling is that people limit their clarity and creativity by shutting their emotions off and keeping a stiff upper lip. Co-counseling seeks to bring the emotions to the surface and allow them to discharge themselves. Crying, shaking, yawning, and laughing are all sought out as the natural physical mechanisms for emotional discharge. Neil and Robyn regularly holed up in the interns' sleeping room and went through them all.

By Monday night, Robyn felt as desperate as she had ever felt. Neil asked her if there was something more he could do, and Robyn said she wanted to talk to Baba Ram Dass. Although they had never met, Robyn considered Baba Ram Dass to be her teacher; she had read all his books. Ram Dass first won notoriety under the name Richard Alpert; he had been Timothy Leary's partner in his initial experiments with LSD at Harvard University. Alpert then went on to India in search of spiritual understanding, returned with the name Baba Ram Dass, and became a religious visionary and mystic.

With the help of mutual friends, Neil finally reached Baba Ram Dass at a house in Massachusetts at 2 a.m. Eastern Daylight Time. Ram Dass made no complaint of the hour and asked to talk with Robyn after Reichline explained the situation.

He told Robyn that she and Kim were "walking through the hottest fire." Robyn cried to him about how hard it was to be in Sierra's room, how helpless she felt. Ram Dass said she should go in the room and just look at what was really happening. She should not resist it and she should not want it to be different. She had to flow and float.

But what about her panic? Robyn demanded. It was driving her crazy.

Ram Dass said she should just experience it as well. When it felt holy, let it be holy, and when it felt scary, let it be scary. In recognizing that her panic existed, she would also recognize that parts of her that were not in panic also existed; that perspective would put the panic in its proper place. Robyn felt peace exuding from her teacher, even as they spoke on the phone. She finally slept again on Monday night, feeling more on top of things than she had in a while.

On the next day, Tuesday, July 19, her equanimity was destroyed by a twitch. The twitch was a tremor that ran down one of Sierra's legs. Robyn was sitting beside her daughter and saw it. It was the first movement the toddler had made in four days. The doctors were very cautious about its possible meaning. Even so, it made the little girl seem suddenly alive. Kim began telling Robyn stories about how they would all live in their cabin again, and make the best of whatever Sierra had left, but Robyn did not believe it. She had worked with damaged children and had seen parents pour out love and concern for children who could never even know the parents were there.

The chief topic for discussion around the waiting room Tuesday evening was what it would be like if Sierra lived. On the edges of that discussion, a few people talked about the case in court. The following morning, The Land was due back in front of the Honorable John R. Kennedy.

7

The forty-four defendants in Superior Court knew relatively little about Mrs. Alyce Lee Burns, the plaintiff. They had read in a local weekly that she was from Watsonville, California, and that her husband, Emmett Burns, had been suspended from the practice of law in the late fifties for comingling his clients' funds with his own, and that he had eventually been disbarred.

Mrs. Burns had reentered the picture in 1974, when she and Donald Eldridge disagreed over the terms of their payment contract; a series of lawsuits ensued, some of which are still undecided. In the meantime, Mrs. Burns held a foreclosure sale on the untitled holdings at 32100 Page Mill, bought them back, and began looking to sell the property again. In January of 1977, Mrs. Burns entered into a series of conversations with the Midpeninsula Regional Open Space District (MROSD). In March of 1977, negotiators for Mrs. Burns and the MROSD agreed to exchange 32100 Page Mill Road for $2.1 million. The vacant land would eventually become a cornerstone of the new Monte Bello Open Space Preserve. Eviction of the occupants was specified as a precondition to closing escrow.

On Wednesday morning, July 20, the defendants' first step was to explain to the judge why Robyn Wesley and Kim Myers were not present. He immediately severed them from the trial proceedings. Mark Schneider followed that explanation with a request that the entire trial be postponed at least until the following Monday, when the defendants would have a better idea of Sierra's outcome. Everyone, he explained, was tied closely to the fate of the young child; Schneider offered a letter from Drs. Stull and Lloyd attesting that the presence of the larger support group played an important part in sustaining both the patient and her parents. After hearing vehement objections from Burns's lawyers, Judge Kennedy denied the request and ordered the defense to proceed.

The Land's case revolved around three arguments. The first was that Mrs. Burns did not have a clear claim to title. The lawyers argued that her original deal with Eldridge had specified that, for every $3,000, Mrs. Burns would exchange title to one acre. Title to 151 acres had been transferred with Eldridge's down payment; the lawyers argued that Eldridge had finally stopped paying when Mrs. Burns refused to release any more titles, despite several years' worth of substantial payments. As long as the title was questionable, The Land community's lawyers argued, Mrs. Burns had no standing to evict.

The second argument was that Mrs. Burns came to court with "unclean hands." The Land settlers claimed that, in September 1976, members of the Burns family sabotaged The Land's water system, and that this violated the California law prohibiting turning off utilities to accomplish eviction. Lastly, Mrs. Burns had already entered into an agreement with the Midpeninsula Regional Open Space District. California law also provides that if a public agency causes the removal of people from their homes, that agency must relocate them in similar surroundings at its own expense.

Judge Kennedy listened to The Land's arguments and ruled that none of them was admissible in the trial. The defendants' lawyers would only be allowed to argue about whether the eviction notice was properly posted, and about how much damages ought to be. The defendants requested a trial by jury, but the judge pointed out that in civil jury trials the defendants must assume jury costs and post a bond ten days before trial. The defense then requested a pauper's jury, a legal provision in which indigent defendants' jury expenses are assumed by the county. The judge responded that he would rule on the request after each defendant filed an individual financial statement the following morning, and then he adjourned court for the day.

The next morning, the defense informed Judge Kennedy that only nine defendants had managed to get their financial forms filled out. Those nine, the judge ruled, would be severed from the case, along with Kim and Robyn, while he considered their applications. The other thirty-three would stand trial immediately after a recess for lunch. The suddenness of this ruling stunned the defense. The lawyers proceeded to do their best but could only make a case by trying to squeeze in information by lengthy and exhaustive cross-examination of Mrs. Burns's witnesses.

8

By Thursday evening, July 21, troublesome signs had also developed at the hospital. The respirator pressure had had to be increased. The initial chest X-rays, taken at the time of Sierra's admittance, showed what were called "fluffy infiltrates" in her lower lung. Those deposits of water were slowly causing a condition of chemical pneumonia. On the bed, covered with towels and tubes, Sierra looked to Robyn like she must be hurting intensely.

That vision of her daughter's suffering pitched Robyn Wesley into the worst anxiety of her life. She was seized with an absolute terror of her daughter's death that only deepened as Thursday night wore on. She felt cheated and misused, and she raged at God to show Himself and justify her pain. At the bottom of her descent, Robyn Wesley called Baba Ram Dass again.

"I can't find God anywhere, Ram Dass," she sobbed into the hospital's payphone.

Baba Ram Dass told her that there was nowhere to look. Before Robyn had a chance to respond, he asked her to breathe with him. Just let go for a moment, he said, and do no more than breathe. With each exhalation she should try to release a little fear; with each inhalation, ingest a little love. Robyn Wesley and her teacher breathed together for ten minutes over the static of their long-distance connection. The rhythm of the exercise let Robyn step away from her awful indecision and steady herself. After a while, Robyn felt lighter and able to float on the crest of her grief. She felt calm, and she felt a deeper sadness than she had ever known, a sadness that was so total it humbled her and made things seem clear. Whatever was meant to happen would happen. If mother and daughter were separated, it would be as part of a large wholeness that would connect them forever.

The next morning, Friday, July 22, started out looking like the answer to everyone's prayers. Early in the day, Sierra began making spontaneous efforts to breathe, independent of the respirator, while another series of tremors ran through her legs and feet. The toddler seemed to be coming alive, but the doctors cautioned that this was momentary. In several hours, they would have the EEG results and would know a lot more then.

Eventually, Drs. Terry Stull and Rick Lloyd asked the parents to come with them into the office. Robyn knew the request for privacy meant bad news. The EEG results were disastrous. They indicated a condition termed "diffuse slowing with several secondary runs of suppression" marked by a "preponderance of delta waves" in the brain. The presence of excessive delta waves meant that the brain was operating very poorly. Obviously there was extensive damage from lack of oxygen. The only part of the child's brain that the doctors were sure was still functioning was the stem of the brain itself. On the evolutionary ladder, a brain stem is the mental equipment of a salamander. Sierra Laurel Wesley Myers, as Kim and Robyn knew her, would never exist again.

Kim Myers and Robyn Wesley sobbed and talked more with the doctors. Stull and Lloyd had doubts whether Sierra would live at all, but it was clear to them that there was little chance she would survive without the constant support of the respirator. The doctors were crying too. They said Sierra seemed to be sinking, even with the equipment. Her vital signs were steadily weakening. It was finally decided between them that if Sierra Myers should go into arrest again, they would accept it as what was meant to be and make no attempt to revive her. When the news was passed on to the rest of The Land group, it produced what, for a moment, was an overwhelming tide of grief. A lot of people just sat and stared.

By Saturday morning, July 23, the Pediatrics ward felt unbearably claustrophobic to Kim and Robyn. They had to get outside. Tears were rolling down Kim's and Robyn's faces, and they headed for an oak tree in the middle of a large open field of dry grass behind the hospital. In back of the tree they could see the Santa Cruz Mountains lined up against the sky and they could see the brown folds of their home. Standing alone in the middle of the field they yelled and yelled. The sounds welled up from a bottomless pit of grief trapped inside them. They bellowed their anger at the universe for robbing them of what they had made themselves. They raged and threw fists of dirt scattering across the dust. Kim found an old rotted fence post and splintered it against the tree. Slowly the wave of rage passed and they sat in the shade sobbing. They said goodbye to their daughter over and over and over again. Finally, they felt cleansed and accepting. Robyn knew she was ready to let Sierra die. She and Kim walked back inside. They were still crying.

At the entrance plaza, the couple passed an old woman with gold coins arrayed on her breast. She noticed their tears.

"What's the matter?" she asked.

"Our little daughter is dying," Robyn answered.

"It's all right," the woman advised. "You are young and you will have many more daughters."

9

Through the rest of the day, Sierra continued to sink. By 10 p.m. Saturday, the only people left besides the staff were Kim, Robyn, Neil Reichline, Norma Shapiro, Kim's brother David, Diane Carter, Maryann Konczyk, and Mark Schneider. They were all squatting in the hallway, and Robyn had just finished telling the others the story of their encounter with the woman on the entrance plaza. Everyone there remembers feeling a common acceptance of Sierra's eventual passage into death. After battling through the turmoil of accepting the unacceptable, all of them felt a diffuse kind of joy that even brought an occasional smile. The gathering was interrupted by the woman resident on the evening shift. The resident said another crisis was coming and the group had better come in and say goodbye to Sierra. She did not have much time left. The resident was trembling.

Those in the hallway went into Intensive Care and made a circle around the toddler's bed with the two residents and two nurses. They held hands and spoke to the unconscious child in soft and gentle voices. The staff people were sobbing along with the others. Robyn wanted to pick Sierra up, but the tubes were still in place.

Inside her head, Robyn talked with Sierra and told her that she was going to be all right. Her mommy knew she would be. Sierra answered and told her mommy that she knew that Mommy and Daddy would be all right too.

For five minutes, Sierra's heart beat slower and slower but did not stop. Something seemed to be holding her in her body by the slimmest of threads.

"What is it, SiSi?" Robyn agonized. "What are you waiting for?"

Robyn thought it might be the window. Her daughter needed the window open. She turned to lift it, and when her eyes crossed Kim's, Robyn suddenly knew Sierra had died. Back on the table, the toddler's heart had finally given up. It was 10:33 p.m. and everyone was crying. Heart failure was the official cause of death, but to those present, it was simply a question of her time having come. Sierra Laurel Wesley Myers had finished what she had come among them to do. Finally, when they all left Intensive Care, Robyn went to the waiting room, held on to Norma Shapiro, and shook with sobs. The bleeping had stopped. The hallway seemed strangely empty without the sound of the Tektronix 404.

That night, Kim and Robyn stayed with friends who lived a mile from the hospital. Kōbun Otogawa, the priest at the nearby Los Altos Buddhist zendō, came and sat with them. The priest arranged to take Sierra's ashes after cremation and hold them for the traditional forty-day waiting period before Buddhist burial services.

10

On August 5, 1977, Judge Kennedy issued a memorandum decision on the case of the first thirty-three defendants in *Burns v. Eldridge, Schneider, Wesley, et al.* The judge found against them and they were assessed $1,400 in damages. In his decision, the judge announced that the other eleven defendants would only be allowed to speak to the issue of the level of damages, and nothing else, in their upcoming trial. The eleven recognized the inevitable, allowed their case to be subsumed under the first decision, and never went to court again. The Land's lawyers figured they could stall off the final eviction for a couple of months more and began filing for a series of technical restraining orders.

On the first day of September 1977, Sierra Laurel Wesley Myers was buried. The service was performed by the priest Kōbun on the side of Sadhana Ridge. Kōbun stood behind a low table topped with a charcoal brazier and an urn of ashes. The words he spoke were all in Japanese, a language no one at The Land understood, but the peace and vision of Kōbun were discernible in the sound of his voice alone. When he finished speaking, each person present filed by the table and dropped a pinch of incense on the hot charcoal. Kim Myers, Robyn Wesley, and the priest carried Sierra's ashes to her grave. Kim had dug the hole himself earlier in the day. It was on top of a little mound that poked up on the side of the ridge overlooking the walnut orchard and their house. After the urn was laid in the bottom, Kim and Robyn used their hands to fill the grave and sat staring for long moments before they packed down the final handfuls of earth.

On October 20, 1977, deputy sheriffs arrived at The Land and oversaw the final emptying of all the buildings. Throughout their ordeal, Kim and Robyn had tried to be very clear with each other that their mutual support during the death of their daughter did not mean that they would resume their relationship as it had been before. After the evacuation of 32100 Page Mill, they went their separate ways.

Robyn Wesley moved deeper south in the Santa Cruz Mountains, where she now lives with several other refugees from The Land. Her sense of herself has slowly rebuilt since the death. Some days she still feels SiSi is right there in the room with her, and some days she shivers uncontrollably at the fear Sierra's absence still inspires.

Kim Myers moved to a house in Mountain View but felt restless. Since the magic summer of 1974, when he had first moved in with Robyn and made Sierra, he had lost most of what was his life. Before the year was out, Kim Myers finally left, for a meditation center in northern New Mexico, where he hoped to get a better grip on the life ahead of him.

The rest of those on The Land spread in various directions, mostly out to the surrounding hills. Several groups found houses on the Santa Cruz crest. There, they now pay rent and dream of finding another place like the last one. During the remainder of October and November, a number of The Land's ex-residents occasionally visited their former homes. Slowly they began dismantling the structures in order to save the lumber for other attempts elsewhere. On the morning of December 1, the day before 32100 Page Mill's title passed to the Midpeninsula Regional Open Space District, approximately fifteen former residents were on the backlands, patiently stripping their former homes, when the inevitable final act in their drama played itself out.

Within the space of ten minutes, the Burnses, their lawyer, several members of the MROSD staff and board of directors, and eight Palo Alto police arrived on the scene. The district officials had brought two bulldozers with them. The caravan of once and future owners moved along the backlands, reducing the homemade houses to splinters one by one. The remnants of those on The Land walked along and watched without incident until the dozer reached a structure known as Murph's House. Murph's House was still being occupied by Daniel Steinhagen, Phyllis Keisler, and their young son Simon. Their cabin had never been served in the eviction, and the residents claimed it was in fact on the 151 acres to which Eldridge still had clear title. Burns's lawyer produced a map drawn by the MROSD staff that showed Murph's House on the district side of the line. No actual surveying of the boundary had been done in years. When Burns's lawyer ordered the bulldozer to proceed, Daniel got on the roof and refused to move. Burns's lawyer summoned the Palo Alto police, and three officers went up to get Steinhagen. Daniel went limp and the officers had to carry him off the roof and five hundred yards up the hill to their waiting squad car.

When the police returned to Murph's House, four more people— Edward Delatmne, David McConnell, William Wheatley, and Sarah Edgecome—had occupied the roof. Edgecome came down by herself, but the others had to be carried away while the bulldozer demolished Murph's House.

Before the day was out, the devastation was virtually complete. On the frontlands only a garage next to the Long Hall and the three vacant cottages had been saved. Everything else, including the barn, was leveled. The Open Space District planned to use the remaining buildings to store district equipment or to house a caretaker's office. In the backlands, only two structures were still standing. These were reprieved at the insistence of one Open Space District board member, who argued that the district ought to do a study of the feasibility of preserving them permanently as unoccupied architectural monuments to the "spirit" of The Land.

On Saturday, December 10, some time around 3:30 a.m., an unknown person or persons entered the Open Space District property at 32100 Page Mill Road and set fires in five of the six remaining buildings. All five buildings were destroyed. Santa Clara County fire marshals were unable to find any suspects in their subsequent investigation. The only remaining structure, one of the cottages behind the old ranch house, may be used to store equipment or may be demolished, but no one will ever live in it again. The only permanent resident of the new Monte Bello Open Space Preserve will always be Sierra Laurel Wesley Myers, there in the crust of Sadhana Ridge, looking over the walnut orchard toward the thicket where her mommy and daddy's house once stood.

[*New York Times Magazine*, June 11, 1978]

Michael Murphy and the True
Home-Field Advantage

NOTHING SINCE HAS APPROACHED the madness we reached
that season thirty years ago when Michael Murphy breached the
envelope of football reality and revealed both the unfathomed
dimensions of Mind and the dark powers of the True Home-Field
Advantage, which I now feel compelled to recount for the first time.

I am—given Murphy's dotage—the only remaining unimpaired
witness to those 1981 developments, and the responsibility for
keeping their secret has weighed more and more heavily as the
years have passed. I now fear that either Murphy's remarkable
manipulation of Newtonian reality will be lost to memory and a
definitive episode in the history of consciousness will disappear
without trace or that, dotage or not, Murphy will escape
accountability for what was, quite possibly, an unconscionable
breach of both sporting ethics and conventional morality and
something that, frankly, haunts me to this day. Either way, the need
for transparency has become overwhelming.

At the time, of course, we each knew that the other's primal,
even mystic relationship with the San Francisco Forty Niners far
transcended the shallow boosterism commonly attached to pursuit
of the ball with a point on both ends. Murphy's profound attachment
had been nurtured as a teenager at Kezar Stadium from the Niners'
Day One; I, born the same year as the team, gave myself to them in
Fresno, during a black-and-white television experience at age ten.
Both manias, however, were of a kind. And by late September 1981,
both of us were under a cloud. The team, then in Bill Walsh's third
year at the helm, was expected to end a long run of mediocrity, but

that expectation was looking extraordinarily misplaced. The Niners were barely 2–2 and lucky to be that.

Murphy finally raised the issue with me in a solemn voice. He could feel it in his bones, he said. We had won ten games and lost thirty-four over the last three years, and our mutual obsession's slide into football doom seemed about to begin once again.

"Unless," he added with a lift of his eyebrows, "you're willing to do something about it?"

That, I now know, was a fateful moment. I often wonder what would have happened had I just ignored his come-on, sloughing it off with a shrug, perhaps, or a chuckle. But I did not. "What do you mean?" I asked instead.

Murphy motioned me to sit down; it was a long story.

What he was about to tell me had grown out of the intersection of his Niner self with his then considerable meditation practice. He had been spending as much as six hours a day cross-legged on a cushion, eyes blank, chasing the transcendental, for months now. That search of his inner ether had been amplified with a series of techniques for remote viewing and telepathic communication taught to him by a trio of Kazakhs from the Central Soviet Bureau for the Study of Mind-bending, as well as the Hindu yogic trance inductions he had dabbled with as a young virgin on the ashram and his sports psychology research into performance enhancement and out-of-body visualization.

I nodded as though I had some grasp of what he was talking about.

Michael, now speaking with such urgency that flecks of spit flew off his lower lip, explained that it had come to him in a jolt, deep into one of his six-hour sessions exploring the void: The connection to the Niners we experienced as separate individuals was merely the surface ripple marking our linkage to a vast shared grid of psychic energy and elemental consciousness, obscured only by the shortcomings of our own understanding and the divergence of the grid's inherent physics from "normality." He called this grid "The Web." It was generated by the shared obsession of the Niner Faithful and occupied a dimension beyond the one with which we were familiar, yet was available for parapsychological exploitation—a force with enormous potential for influencing and even rearranging physical reality. This, he proclaimed, was "The True Home-Field Advantage," especially for the Niners, whose fans were just loopy enough to make the necessary steps to access other dimensions and wield this seemingly limitless tool. One had simply to connect to the Web and develop a transmission system to channel its energies to our team's purposes. And, he announced, he was now prepared to take that step into the unknown. He felt he had no choice.

He also needed an accomplice.

In his few experimental episodes out in the ether since stumbling over the Web, postulating ways to connect and manipulate it, he had found that channeling was impossible with only his efforts. He had called the Kazakhs in Moscow and they, though horribly drunk at the time, had told him before passing out that the key to mobilizing that Web energy was Triangulation. Adding a third pole to the interaction of Web and game would change all the psychic angles and supply the necessary leverage.

"That's where you come in," Murphy declared.

Me? "I have no idea what all this goo-goo shit is about," I told Michael—much less any faith in the drunken Kazakhs—but he would hear nothing of it.

"You won't have to navigate the void or make the Web connection," he explained. That was the hard part, and he would do that. "All you have to do is connect to me so we can channel energy from two different poles." That secondary connection would require only a little training in harmonic convergence, a meditation technique reportedly pioneered by the great Buddhist sage Milarepa himself and taught to Michael by an exiled Mongolian Ph.D. who had been experimenting with levitation down in Tierra del Fuego. Murphy could no longer remember the Mongolian's name—though he did remember the man had shown up at Esalen Institute driving a purple school bus—but his techniques were sound, he assured me with a cherubic smile. I could acquire sufficient skills for our purposes with a fifteen-minute introductory lesson.

Fifteen minutes later, I had managed to generate a little buzz in my extremities by staring as hard as I could at a point on the wall. Michael said that was great. He insisted we were now ready to get after it. "We don't know much about what we're about to do," he admitted in a further attempt to reassure me, "but we'll figure it out as we go along."

I found that small consolation at the time.

Nonetheless, I was ready for our experiment the following Sunday, when the Niners were playing on the road against the Redskins in D.C. Michael was stationed in front of his television in Mill Valley and I in front of mine in Menlo Park. The Niners jumped out to a 7–0 lead, but the Skins answered with a drive down to the Niners' twenty-two-yard line and looked like they were about to punch it in. At that point, my phone rang. It was Murphy.

"Let's take this baby out for a test drive," he said.

Lacking any other calibration, he told me he was just going to take as strong a hold onto the Web as he could. The rest was just a matter of transmission. Once he ascertained we were on the same wavelength, he instructed me to engage my harmonic convergence, lock onto the screen, and stay that way. He would take care of the rest. Then he hung up. I did as instructed.

And so, apparently, did he.

When the Redskins lined up for the next play, with me in a half-assed trance state staring at the television, a sudden onslaught of heat rushed out of my cortex and down to the soles of my feet. The air in the room instantly took on a purple haze, like after dropping Owsley acid in the old days, and then, to my considerable amazement, I rose about an inch off the couch and hovered there with a ferocious wind rushing through my eardrums. The Skins ran a sweep to their left and, through the haze, I saw Ronnie Lott come up from his cornerback spot like a heat-seeking missile. Just as Lott collided with the runner, the Niner cornerback dipped his helmet so it hit squarely on the ball, popping it out of the runner's grasp, straight up in the air, where Niner safety Dwight Hicks grabbed it and ran eighty yards the other way for another Niner touchdown.

I dropped back on the couch, feeling suddenly spent. The haze evaporated and the clamor in my ears receded. I called Murphy before the Niners lined up for the extra point.

"What the fuck was that?" I demanded.

"I think we're onto something," Murphy answered.

ALTHOUGH GRATEFUL FOR THE Niners' victory over the Redskins, I was seriously spooked by the display of power we seemed to have induced and I was cautionary when we spoke the next day, but that was not the case for Michael Murphy. He had no doubts about pursuing this further. He apologized for the "side effects" I had experienced and allowed that he had failed to adjust for the karmic winds that swirl over the surface of the Web. These winds were a significant element that had to be manipulated if we expected to direct the Web with any precision and, of course, he had a plan for that. The point was to generate positive karmic tailwinds for our team, adding to the force of their momentum, and that was best done in the lead-up to the game rather than on game day itself. Again Triangulation was key, but in this case we had to find a way to anchor our channeling to the team's preparations.

At three the following morning I thus found myself with Murphy in front of the Forty Niners' old headquarters in a residential Redwood City neighborhood next to a senior center about fifteen minutes from my house. Clouds covered the moon as we made our way over a chain-link fence to a corner of the practice field. Our mission was to bury a small plastic bag containing a toy football signed by legendary Niner Frankie Albert during Murphy's adolescence and a Forty Niner ornament that had been hanging on my Christmas trees since the early days in Fresno. These lifelong keepsakes would provide psychic ground to which we could automatically connect and through which we could generate the necessary karmic tailwinds as our team prepared. I had brought a shovel but soon discovered that Murphy's relationship to such a tool was only abstract. When I had finished the burying, he led us both in a short tune-in session for our harmonic convergence and then we fled. On the way home, Murphy spoke at length about how the Dallas game this weekend would give us a good yardstick. The

Cowboys were an NFL powerhouse and had beaten the Niners the year before, 59–14.

This year, however, was no contest. Niners 45, Cowboys 14.

After that, Murphy had the bit in his teeth and, I must confess, I increasingly submitted to being a lab rat in his experiment. When we deflected a field goal during the first game with the Rams, I ended up levitating halfway across the very purple room. The next time we played them, Murphy amped the Web up so high that it shattered my aquarium, leaving a puddle of seaweed and dying tropicals all over my family room rug. But the team kept winning. After holding off the Giants, I was left with scorch marks all over my television's plastic. Against Pittsburgh, Murphy directed our psychic beam at Joe Montana to buck him up, but it was a gigantic failure and Montana had his worst big game of the season. Finally, with the Niners clinging to a three-point lead with under a minute to go and the Steelers facing a fourth down in our territory, Murphy made a frantic phone call. "Peewee!" he screamed—meaning Dwaine "Peewee" Board, one of our defensive ends—"Lock on to Peewee!" I instantly switched my convergence to number 76, the ball was snapped, and Board sacked the Steeler quarterback to end the game. Our only outright failure was when Cleveland came to town, and, overconfident, we abandoned our triangle and went to the game together. Cleveland 15, San Francisco 12, during a rainstorm that flooded the Candlestick parking lot and required us to use a public bus shuttle to get from the city to the stadium. Afterward, a line of buses was waiting and the attendant at the door of the one I got on stopped Murphy from boarding after me, saying it was too full and to take the next one. My last view of Michael that day was of him standing in the torrent addressing my departing bus.

"Triangulation!" he shouted. "The Kazakhs were right! You have to triangulate!"

Otherwise, the results were plain to see. The Niners finished the regular season 13–3 and sailed through the first round of the playoffs with a victory over the New York Giants in ankle-deep mud at Candlestick.

By then I was feeling pretty much as though we had nothing left to prove, but not Michael. The Dallas Cowboys were coming to town to decide who would go to the Super Bowl, and Murphy was about to trump everything we had done with the True Home-Field Advantage thus far.

DALLAS IN THE PLAYOFFS WOULD be a game unlike any other, Michael explained that Tuesday as we got in my car for a five-minute drive from Menlo Park to East Palo Alto. Look at the early seventies, he insisted. Three times in a row the Niners had played the Cowboys on the verge of the Super Bowl, and three times in a row the Cowboys had come from behind to deny us. Clearly the karmic winds this week would be treacherous. Unwilling to risk disappointment, he felt the need for a secret weapon. And the Kazakhs had helped him find one, whom we were now about to visit.

After crossing the freeway overpass, we turned onto the frontage road and parked in front of an abandoned rib joint with a peeling sign declaring UNCLE PIG'S MEMPHIS STYLE tottering on the roof. Four-foot-high weeds were growing around the rib shack's foundation.

Michael finished briefing me before we got out of the car. The man we were about to see, Swami Loobootoolooboot, also went by the alias "Meatball Rinpoche." The Kazakhs had once used him to good effect in a stare-down along the Chinese border. The swami, a.k.a. Meatball Rinpoche, had remarkable meditative powers. And this week, the karmic winds would require the Web to generate far more energy than Michael's connection could muster on its own. The answer was to complement our reach into the Web with a push from the other side. The swami would lock onto the game and follow the signal back through his television, across the airwaves, and into the consciousnesses of all the Web's unknowing participants, amping up each of their energetic contributions and throwing the Web into hyperdrive.

That ramping up, however, would have a finite limit, perhaps a minute at most, and could only be invoked in the highest of emergencies. It also required me to play a special role. The swami had given up speaking forty-seven years ago and refused to even be near a telephone. He communicated by writing in Hindi on a notepad. To invoke his intervention, I would have to rush over the freeway to where he would be seated in front of a television and signal him by writing the word "Swarāj" on his pad.

I, true to my lab rat role, promised to carry out my task.

We then entered Uncle Pig's Memphis Style through the back door, to which Murphy had a key. The rib joint was a hollow shell inside except for the defunct counter. In the empty space where the ovens once stood, a man—perhaps four and half feet tall and dressed in a flowing white dhoti and with hair that had not been cut in more than four decades piled up behind him on the floor—was seated on a cushion in front of a television whose screen was black. Michael whispered that the game would be on the next time I saw the swami. Murphy exchanged Hindi notes with a.k.a. Meatball Rinpoche, the tiny man looked me over, and then we left. Outside, Michael handed me the keys to Uncle Pig's and repeated how critical my role was. The season was riding on it.

I was nervous on Sunday and secretly hoping my dash over the freeway would not be needed, but it was obvious by the end of the third quarter that it would be. Before the game was over, the Niners would have turned the ball over five times. We began the fourth quarter clinging to a one-point lead, but the longer the quarter lasted, the more the Cowboys seemed to be prevailing. Then we gave them the ball with a fumble at the fifty-yard line and they converted it into a touchdown. With 4:54 left in the game, we got the ball back on our own eleven-yard line, down 27–21.

As Montana walked the offense up to the line of scrimmage, my telephone rang. It was Murphy on a payphone at Candlestick. "Go to Meatball!" he shouted.

I rushed out to my car and headed across the freeway, only to find the frontage road blocked by an overturned big rig. I frantically detoured through the back streets of East Palo Alto, all the while following the game on the radio. The Niners were moving down the field, running the ball, then dinking passes, six yards here, nine yards there. At the two-minute warning, they had reached midfield. Under a minute, they were on Dallas's six, third down, with play stopped for a time out, and I burst in the back door at Uncle Pig's. The swami was in front of the television. The camera was focused on Montana consulting with Walsh along the sideline. I snatched the pad at the swami's side and wrote the code word.

The swami's eyes bulged a little at the message and then all hell broke loose. The room got purple instantly, and the hurricane roar I had previously experienced shook Uncle Pig's like a pit bull with a rat.

I, of course, was locked onto the swami's television and could only guess at what was happening around me.

By the time Montana lined the team up for play, wisps of smoke were coming out of the back of the TV and the swami was levitating over the floor with his face just inches from the screen. As the ball was snapped and Montana rolled to his right, the swami's enormous pile of hair broke into flames and the room was suffused with acrid smoke. The Cowboys chased the Niner quarterback toward the sidelines as he looked and looked for someone to throw to. Then he spied Dwight Clark along the back of the end zone and cut loose. It would later be a subject of much debate between Michael and me whether the Web had altered the trajectory of Montana's pass to make it catchable or had lifted Clark high enough to reach it, but either way it was a Niner touchdown. As Clark took two steps after the reception and held the ball up in triumph, however, the swami's TV exploded in a cloud of electronic debris.

The blowback sent a.k.a. Meatball Rinpoche flying across the room and knocked me on my butt. I started to scramble to the swami's assistance but he needed none. The explosion had doused his hair, and before I could get to him he picked himself up, brushed off his singed eyebrows, and returned to sitting on his cushion in front of the demolished television. Convinced everything was all right at Uncle Pig's, I ran for my car, turned on the radio, and headed back over the freeway.

I would later return to Uncle Pig's to check on the swami, but when I did, I found the back door open and no swami. The place had been cleaned out, television and all, and the only signs of what had happened were a few scorch marks and the vague odor of burnt hair. After that, whenever I would ask Murphy what had happened to Swami Loobootoolooboot, a.k.a. Meatball Rinpoche, and Uncle Pig's Memphis Style, he would always cryptically shrug that "the Kazakhs had taken care of everything."

In the meantime, I drove home with the blazing vision of Meatball Rinpoche fresh in my mind, listening to the Niner defense throttle Dallas's last-ditch attempt to drive for a field goal. Game over, Niners 28, Cowboys 27. The crowd at Candlestick was going berserk when I got back to the television waiting for me next to the counter where my fish tank had once sat. The phone was ringing.

It was Murphy on another stadium payphone. The crescendo of the primal wail around him made his voice barely audible, but he was obviously drunk on the moment. The wicked witch of Dallas was dead.

"Fuck the karmic winds!" he screamed into the receiver. "Fuck the fucking karmic winds!"

THE SUPER BOWL WAS AN ANTICLIMAX. We only had to invoke the Web at relatively low levels on two occasions in the third quarter, when the team went mysteriously dead in the water. It ended 26–21, and we had gone from the verge of collapse in October to World Champions in January.

I saw Michael several days later. Both of us were still in transports of ecstasy, glowing visibly, and understandably full of ourselves for what we had pulled off. Murphy could not stop smiling.

At my mention of the True Home-Field Advantage, he blushed sheepishly and arched his eyebrows like Michael Murphy does when he has something even more off the wall brewing in his inner ether.

"You know," he said, "we'll have to do this again sometime."

[From *An Actual Man: Michael Murphy and the Human Potential Movement*, 2010]

Nelson Rockefeller:
A Man of Many Talents

WHEN GERALD FORD CHOSE Nelson Rockefeller to be his vice president, he was quick to point out that his nominee would come in handy. Rockefeller, Ford assured the evening news, was a man of many talents. The president told no lies. Nelson Rockefeller comes in handy just about anywhere he's used.

Less than a month after his confirmation, the new vice president found a ready outlet for his skills. The Central Intelligence Agency was accused of spying stateside, and Rockefeller was called upon to head the Blue Ribbon Commission to Investigate the CIA. Ford was sure that Rockefeller was just the man to sort the charges out. A few folks have cried foul, pointing to the former New York governor's five-year stint on the committee that oversees the agency he is now to investigate. But Rockefeller views his appointment differently. His prior job was, he explained, all part of his "working knowledge of intelligence," and it was a central resource for a man conducting investigations such as the Blue Ribbon Commission's. That kind of working knowledge shouldn't be squandered.

If it weren't for his family's business, Nelson Rockefeller might not know nearly as much about intelligence as he does. The Rockefellers' business is money—its management and its accumulation. In three generations the family has bought control of $250 billion worth of corporations. It has also cornered one-half of the total of American private investments in Asia, Africa, and Latin America. Inevitably, the CIA and the family business crossed paths early in the agency's career.

Allen Dulles was appointed director of the CIA in 1953; he

came to government service straight from a job as a Rockefeller lawyer. That same year, the CIA, worried that the existing Iranian government might nationalize foreign investments, engineered a coup and replaced the premier with a former Nazi. Shortly thereafter, Standard Oil, the foundation of the Rockefellers' family business, began to tap Iranian oil reserves. In 1961, the same script was acted out in the Congo: Patrice Lumumba, that country's premier, was murdered by his own army and replaced by a soldier named Mobutu. In the aftermath of the Congolese revolution, David Rockefeller, chairman of Chase Manhattan Bank and Nelson's brother, led an expedition of businessmen into Mobutu-land to explore the "investment climate." It must have been good. Using Rockefeller financing, Pan Am acquired the local airline, AT&T built a subsidiary, Esso drilled for oil, and Standard of Indiana went into the copper business.

The next CIA director, John McCone, took over the reins of intelligence after working as a Standard Oil attorney. Following McCone's appointment, the familiar pattern of CIA intervention in foreign governments recurred. Salvador Allende, the first communist president in Chile's history, was overthrown by a CIA-financed coup in 1973. The year before, Allende had expropriated Anaconda Copper Company's copper mines in Chile, an important wing of the Rockefellers' family business. Henry Kissinger—chairman of the security council that approved, and may even have ordered, CIA intervention in Chile—is a longtime Rockefeller family employee. With a background like that, Nelson Rockefeller is establishing a whole new level of expertise in government service. He is also ensuring himself of a lot of work in the future. It will be nearly impossible to convene any more commissions without calling on Nelson Rockefeller's mass of "working knowledge."

The commission on high interest rates will certainly need the counsel of a man whose family controls 20 percent of the banks in the United States. It would be foolish to pass over his experience. And the commission on gas prices is a natural, too. The Rockefeller family has controlling interests in the Standard, Mobil, Amoco, ARCO, Esso, American, Citgo, Exxon, and Humble oil companies.

If Gerald Ford decides to take on the insurance companies, we can all rest easy knowing he has expert help. The Rockefellers have their hands on one-quarter of all the life insurance sold in this country.

After that we can look forward to the Blue Ribbon Commission on Consumer Prices. With Nelson Rockefeller in the administration, Gerald Ford has the inside track here as well. The vice president is one of the owners of Mazola Corn Oil, Karo Syrup, Kleenex, Nucoa Margarine, Kotex sanitary napkins, Skippy peanut butter, Best Foods mayonnaise, Orange Crush, and the American Sugar Company.

It's hard to imagine that the commission on corporate taxation would get far without the man whose company Standard Oil of Ohio earned $66 million last year and paid no taxes. Or that the commission on the distribution of wealth would be complete without the leadership of a man whose family's personal fortune is larger than the total worth of one hundred million Americans. And just think how useful the vice president could be to the commission on urban renewal and safer neighborhoods. The Rockefeller Pocantico Hills estate, which is staffed by five hundred servants and protected by thirty-five armed guards, covers five square miles and is surrounded by electric barbed wire. Living like that must have taught Nelson Rockefeller a lot. It's a shame not to put his knowledge to good use.

Gerald Ford made a shrewd appointment: whatever the subject, Nelson Rockefeller knows it like he owns it.

[Originally published as "To Own Them Is to Know Them: Nelson Rockefeller on the CIA," *Penthouse*, April 1975]

What Makes David Harris Run?

WHEN AMERICA VOTES ON NOVEMBER 2, 1976, I will have been running in California's 12th district for a year and a half. In those eighteen months, I will have recruited close to a thousand volunteers, raised more than $100,000, walked somewhere in the neighborhood of 750 miles, delivered at least eight hundred speeches, placed twenty-five hundred phone calls, and shaken enough hands to equip an army of octopuses.

There's at least a fifty-fifty chance I will lose.

If you are thinking about getting into politics, you should understand there are arguments on both sides of the question.

[TEN REASONS NOT TO RUN FOR CONGRESS]

1. *If you aren't rich you will be at a constant disadvantage.*

One of my problems has been that I make my living with a typewriter. Magazine journalism is one of the few professions where a person can rise to the top 10 percent of the business and still make less than a street sweeper. When I spend my time campaigning, I have no income. I campaign all the time. As a result, I'm much deeper in debt than when I started—which is only half of the disadvantage.

2. *Political campaigns are a bottomless pit.*

There are no limits to the work that must be accomplished. No one in a campaign ever does enough. The game demands that you do everything you can from the time you start until the whistle blows and everybody is told to go vote. A significant addiction to work comes in very handy, but it's not enough. The extra energy you need is best provided by a staff that treats you like meat, and an obsessive fear of losing and humiliation.

3. If you love someone, are married, or have children, you risk it all when you run for office.

Time has a lot to do with it. Relationships flourish because of the attention paid to them and based on the relationship's capacity to provide equally for all those involved. A candidate doesn't have time. Being single and trained in the priesthood is one of Jerry Brown's strongest suits as an office runner. It's not one of mine. I have a woman I'm in love with and a son by my first marriage who lives with me half the time. By virtue of a swarm of babysitters, an hour squeezed in between Kiwanis Club and junior college, and eighty minutes between precinct walking, my son still knows my name. It's even harder on a couple. Politics attacks the balance in relationships. My schedule defines our life together. If we go to a reception, I, the candidate, am spoken to. She, "the woman with the candidate," a very special person and widely known in her own right, is ignored. When I see her, the day's over and I have little interest left in talking. I want to unhitch my mind and she wants to relate. When you run for office, it hurts the people you're with more than you, especially if they don't seek or want the political rewards that tide you over.

4. You will become a product.

You're supposed to. It's the best technique to convince one hundred thousand people spread along twenty-five miles of freeway off-ramps. The candidate is packaged and sold. Three months after I started, I no longer needed to be convinced I was a commodity. I believe I'm a good product in a market where those are few and far between, but I *am* a product. I am also that product's chief salesman. In a six-day week of sixteen-hour days, that combination of roles begins to feel like an Arizona real estate transaction.

5. In your product-hood you will feel judged.

At times, the feeling is overwhelming. My name and someone else's will end up side by side with numbers next to them. The ego risks are potentially catastrophic. Election night in the primary was a gauntlet for me. My areas of strength on the north end of the district were counted last, and it was 2 a.m. before I edged up toward 60 percent, where I should have been. One TV station made a mistake off-stage, reversed vote totals, and signed off the air with me losing. "So much, Mr. Joan Baez," the commentator shrugged. United Press International woke me up at 7 a.m. for a comment on my "clear" victory.

6. You can never take a break from being the candidate.

I have no choice about running for Congress whenever I step out my front door. It's the sign of a good campaign. I am recognized and people want to talk to me. When I don't want to campaign, I stay home. Even at home I get a lot of phone calls since I'm listed in the book. My favorite is Mrs. Hill. She called the first time with a lot of questions about whether I was a communist. In successive calls we've discussed the care and breeding of Samoyed dogs and how she helped run the "reds" out of the Palo Alto Democratic Club. Twice she's called when she was drunk. She says she likes me.

7. You will ruin your body.

Politics is full of coffee, cigarettes, alcohol, tension, chocolate chip cookies, and very little sleep. As you make your way toward election day, your body will slowly unravel into a running set of aches, twinges, and occasional disorders. One of the strangest I've run into was a prolonged attack of gas. My digestion system went through a two-week collapse. While awaiting a cure, I concentrated on standing straight and clenching my buttocks while discussing the budget. It disappeared after I began swallowing whole cloves of garlic to balance my system.

8. *Politics is a shallow business.*

It's full of two-minute hypes, camera angles, and ten-second exposures. The majority of people going to the polls will remember six words about a name on the ballot. If you have a need for expression and recognition as a whole person, you won't find much of it running for office. I often feel unseen and unknown in the midst of waves of attention.

9. *Politics is full of treating people badly and being treated the same way in return.*

You will have to make a lot of decisions that disappoint or antagonize people you work with every day. Decisions are made according to the single criteria of what's good for the campaign. A lot of time is spent either maneuvering to keep catastrophe from breaking out or patching up after it has occurred. People have been known to hate each other in such situations, and friendships rise and fall like the stock market.

10. *It may not make any difference, even if you win.*

There is a lot of debate about whether a seat in Congress has much, if anything, to do with what goes on in America. Some have called the House of Representatives an institution with all the dimensions of a big-league Rotary International. Just enough power to be crooked and not enough votes to be honest. The House has a long history of being ruled by dinosaurs and shellfish. Change comes slowly. It's an easy swamp to disappear in and leave no trace.

[TEN REASONS WHY
YOU OUGHT TO RUN FOR CONGRESS]

1. *We need good government desperately.*

The future could very well have bad things in store for America. We represent 6 percent of the world's population and 60 percent of its wealth, and we consume 40 percent of its resources. That will change. As resources diminish, population spirals, cartels multiply, pollution compounds itself, and money changes hands over and over again, our margin of fat will shrink. The assumptions of national policy must change accordingly. We must get more out of what we have. Being the biggest, mightiest, and wealthiest got us this far but won't get us much further. We must become the most compassionate, the most efficient, the most farsighted, and the most genuine. It is necessary if we are going to survive. We're a nation drifting without a sense of ourselves and a common course to pursue. Our capacity to live in a new and scarcer world will be anchored in Washington, D.C. New leadership is essential. It is possible to make good and sensible policy, but not with leaders who have lost touch either with themselves or the people they represent. Like it or not, our future is at stake in the laws Congress approves and the budgets it initiates.

2. *You will grow as a person.*

Running for office is meeting strangers. The only way to do it well is to confront the limitations in yourself that get in the way. When I was fourteen, I had a paper route. Part of me was so shy I would be seized with fits of terror at the thought of approaching a stranger and asking for money. I paid more than a few monthly bills out of my own earnings to take myself off the hook. Now I spend most of my afternoons walking neighborhoods and approaching strange doors. I knock. A voter answers. "Hi," I say. "Hope I'm not bothering you, but I wanted to introduce myself. My name's David Harris. I'm the Democrat running for Congress in this district." For the past eighteen months I have been walking precincts, meeting groups of people in living rooms, leafleting the town dump, shaking hands at the county fair, speaking after dinners, eating hot dogs, and getting my picture in the paper. Your character develops as it responds to the challenges it faces.

3. *You will meet many kind and generous people if you're lucky.*

Without help from people who are willing to spend more time than they have, more money than they can afford, and more worry than makes sense, there would be no political campaigns. Folks who were once strangers will say yes when you ask them to help.

4. You will receive a huge amount of attention.

One of the nicest feelings I've had comes from people clapping after I say something. There is an overwhelming sense of satisfaction. I like talking and being listened to. It's a rare commodity in the world. Most people spend their lives in public anonymity, known only by their friends. Candidates are elevated to a very special plane and they become part of a much larger reality than themselves. That pays a lot of dividends in self-esteem.

5. You will do more than you imagined you could.

One of the essential parts of living is testing your limits. Politics is a big mountain to climb. It's a task that lets me throw myself into activity. The more ground covered, the more my sense of accomplishment grows. I'm proud to have started with nothing and built what a representative of the Democratic National Committee calls one of the best-organized campaigns in the country. I'm proud to walk into the campaign office and see all the phone lines lit, a crowd stuffing envelopes, and twenty staff members running about pursuing all brands of craziness.

6. You will become very good at standing.

I stand all day long. I've learned to relax and hold my weight so my feet don't begin to hurt until the sun goes down. In order to deal with all that vertical time, I've variously tried standing like a soldier, adopting a loose slouch, and pretending I'm a penguin. I picked a penguin because I couldn't imagine a penguin with sore feet. The penguin works best.

7. You will help other people come to grips with themselves.

Campaigns are a very genuine and quite rare form of human interaction. They give a lot of people looking for more meaning in their existence something to do and someone to share it with. Win or lose, that's a social service. You have a key role to play in making sure that it is done decently.

8. You will meet your neighbors and everyone else's.

America is an anonymous place where neighborhoods disappear and families break up. Isolation is a common affliction that candidates slide in and out of. During my campaign I've gotten a better sense of the San Francisco peninsula than I've had in all the thirteen years I've lived here. I know that most homes in Sunnyvale have their contents engraved with special markings to catch burglars, that there is a fee charged for putting up signs in Mountain View, and I know where all the housing tracts in Santa Clara join with each other like a stucco quilt. That knowledge makes me comfortable in my environment.

9. You will have a good reason to talk to people.

There is important information to deliver. Being a candidate is a good way to deliver it. A lot of people view an election as a reason to listen.

10. Strangers will go out of their way to be nice to you.

I remember walking a precinct one afternoon in Sunnyvale. It was August, better than 90 degrees, and I'd been walking for more than two hours. I was walking with Nick, my aide, and the rest of the advance team was up ahead and around the corner. We were walking past what used to be an orchard. Now it was just mounds of dirt connected by tractor prints. There was no sidewalk. We were in the gutter. Across the street, the new shopping center was swarming, selling a lot of Wonder Bread and high-octane electric knives. My knees felt like oatmeal. I was leaning forward trying to figure out how many more precincts I had to finish that month to cover all the Democratic ones as well as the swing vote. A new Ford turned the corner. The driver was almost leaning out his window and waving his fist. I'd never seen him before. "Go get em, David!"

he yelled. "Yahooo!" He sped off honking. I looked up toward the next tract and for a moment felt like it was all worth it.

[*Rolling Stone*, October 21, 1976]

Will the Real
Walter Mondale Stand Up?

*T*HE PLACE IS JACKSON, MISSISSIPPI, and former vice president
Walter F. Mondale is here to deliver a speech from the front steps
of the Mississippi Governor's Mansion. His performance is not
unlike those he has given in one hundred cities in twenty-six states
between January and June of this year. A sprinkling of national
press has come along to watch, and Mondale exhibits guarded ease.
He is fifty-five years old and has no illusions about the process he
must go through to win the presidency. The reporters have come to
examine his soft spots, and neither he nor they need to be told that
the last two decades of Democratic Party history have been littered
with the mistake-plagued wreckage of early front-runners.

On the other hand, not making mistakes is one of Walter
Mondale's strong suits.

Aside from the mistakes he does not make, his speech in Jackson
is most notable for all the things Walter Mondale does not say
about himself. It is typically well delivered and just as typically
unrevealing. He laments the collapse of the farm economy but tells
no stories about his father, the farming prairie preacher who lost
everything in the 1920 farm-price collapse. He warns about the
escalation of health care costs for the elderly but reveals nothing
about how his mother's insurance company dropped her coverage
when her cancer was discovered and then how her three sons bore
the costs of her prolonged treatment. As he stands on the front
porch of the mansion, his profile is dominated by the almost right
angle his nose makes after emerging from his face, but few people
in this football-playing state will learn that the shape of his nose is

a scar from the constant breakage it endured during his career as "Crazylegs" Mondale, the shifty iron-man halfback of the Elmore, Minnesota, high school varsity.

Walter Mondale is ashamed of none of those things, but he nonetheless does not bring them up on his own. He resists packaging his person, despite the potential political benefits, and his performance in Jackson reveals no sudden breaks in that resistance.

Mississippi is a state dominated by small towns, but Mondale gives only several phrases in passing to having grown up in Ceylon, Heron Lake, and Elmore, Minnesota, the largest of which had a population of 950. It strikes no one watching him that he is reportedly a direct descendant of a seventh-century Viking warlord. He mentions he is a "minister's kid" but does not mention, as he does in private, that "being a minister's kid was a free ticket for everyone to beat you up." Nor is there any indication that he was the kind of minister's kid who once organized his playmates to build a bridge using hymnals purloined from his father's church and is still possessed of a broad, if private, streak of mischief. And his manner does not suggest the kind of politician who once disguised himself as a farmworker to investigate conditions among migrant laborers.

All those parts of Walter Mondale are a vacuum in his public presence. He offers few clues to the facts that as a teenager he sang at weddings and sold vegetables door-to-door during the Great Depression. He promises the crowd in Jackson that if he is elected president, everyone's children will have the possibility of a college education, but he makes no mention of the heavy debt he assumed as a young man putting himself through college. That he is intelligent is apparent, but that he rereads the works of William Shakespeare every few years is not apparent at all.

He extols the virtues of family life and calls families "the basis of a strong nation," but even with his wife, Joan, standing behind him on the Mississippi mansion porch and smiling, he does not personalize the issue. That they mean a lot to each other and have been married twenty-seven years remains unsaid. That their three children are a former dirt-bike racer, an aspiring actress, and an undergraduate fluent enough in Spanish to translate on vice-presidential missions all goes unsaid as well. Choosing between their privacy and his image, Mondale has always chosen their privacy. Joan does their family grocery shopping through a neighborhood buying club and takes a regular trip to the Washington farmers market as part of the Mondales' membership, but consumers struggling with food prices will not learn that information from Walter Mondale.

This is an election in which Democrats will belabor "the rich," but Mondale does not point out that his own net personal worth when he left the vice presidency was a meager and palpably uncompromised $15,000. Similarly, he uses the words "strong" or "strengthen" seventeen times in twelve minutes but offers no descriptions of how, as a stand-in head of state, he faced down President Ferdinand E. Marcos in the Philippines, wrangled with Prime Minister John Vorster over South Africa, or softened up Prime Minister Menachem Begin at Camp David. He instinctively shies away from any talk that might sound too much like bragging on himself.

When Mondale finishes his speech in Jackson, the audience is impressed and the national press contingent agrees that he deserves his growing reputation as the best speechmaker of the Democratic pack, but his oratory, though enormously improved, is still a far cry from charisma. Few of the issues he addresses attach to his person. In imagemaker's terms, he lacks "projection."

The modern presidency is won with visceral characterizations and personified emotions, yet the absence of such images and associations from the presence of Walter Mondale is striking. There is indeed a person behind his candidacy, but Mondale resists revealing himself. That tendency in turn frames the ground where Walter Mondale's political and personal dilemmas overlap. By his own choice, he is at the same time a formidable enough commodity to be considered a political fixture, yet as a person so unknown as to be effectively indistinguishable from his circumstances.

At this writing, Walter Mondale leads the Democratic presidential race in national polls, money raised, and straw votes won. His campaign organization and strategy are commonly thought the most professional in the six-man field. His closest competitor, Senator John H. Glenn of Ohio, the former astronaut, is considered to be a serious threat to win the prize of the party's nomination.

Not surprisingly, then, the first question asked about Walter Mondale is whether he is really as boring as his coverage makes him seem.

THE ONLY ANSWER IS A character portrait that is much more complex than the stereotype "boring" implies.

Walter Mondale, to start with, is Norwegian. According to those around him, his often overlooked ethnicity is central to who he is and how he presents himself. Mondale is the Anglicization of Mundal, the village on the shores of Sognefjord, where his great-grandfather lived before immigrating to southern Minnesota in 1856. The winters are desolate and lonely in Ceylon, Heron Lake, and Elmore, and the broad prairie around them was consequently settled by a patchwork of Swedes, Danes, and Norwegians, whose culture is still among the nation's most distinct, if least visible, ethnic enclaves. Its orthodoxy is politically liberal and personally conservative, though "conservative" does not capture the scope of the Scandinavian emphasis on privacy, self-discipline, and emotional containment. "There is a restraint against feeling in general," one Minnesota writer observes. "There is a restraint against enthusiasm . . . there is restraint in grief, and always, always restraint in showing your feelings." The Minnesota subculture that nurtured Walter Mondale is very likely the most intense outpost of personal reticence left in modern America.

Mondale smiles as his press secretary, Maxine Isaacs, tells an illustrative Norwegian story. They, several staff people, and two reporters are flying in a chartered eight-seater to the Quad City Airport after a 7:30 speech in Dubuque, Iowa, on January 28. The story is about a Minnesota reception Vice President Mondale appeared at during the 1978 congressional campaign in one of the farm towns out on the prairie. Twenty people attended. When Mondale entered, the crowd issued several claps and then everyone stood where they were while Mondale patiently approached each and initiated conversation. No one approached him on their own or gave his inquiries more than a one-sentence answer. Meanwhile, the local Norwegian organizer of the event, obviously thrilled by the crowd response, approached Mondale's press secretary. "Quite a fanfare, isn't it?" he exulted in all seriousness. Mondale breaks into chuckles at the punchline.

Though by this point in his life Walter Mondale has evolved into a positively flashy figure by the standards of his native subculture, its expectations of reserve are ingrained in his personality.

During the question period at the Land O'Lakes co-op's annual meeting in the Minneapolis Civic Auditorium, Mondale is asked if he thinks he would be a good president. "I have trouble answering that," he confesses. "If my father had ever heard me tell him that I would make a good president, I would have been taken directly to the woodshed." The audience laughs, knowing exactly what he means.

"The whole idea of talking in terms of 'me' or 'I' is foreign to the culture," Mondale explains. It is March 26 and he is riding in a rented car, traveling from Portsmouth, New Hampshire, to the Boston airport. There, he will start a series of flights that will land him in Cedar Rapids, Iowa, for a 3 p.m. press conference. "Talking in terms of 'me' or 'I' just wasn't done," he continues. "In my family, the two things you were sure to get spanked for were lying or bragging about yourself. Both were equally unacceptable." He and a reporter are sharing the back seat, and Mondale answers most questions while staring ahead at the road. "Now, of course," he offers, looking the reporter in the face, "I have to talk about myself, and I do."

The answer is, not surprisingly, less than revelatory. According to his staff, Mondale still assumes, in an instinctively Norwegian way, that personal promotion is demeaning and that who he is will be apparent without being hyped. Both assumptions may prove crucial in an election that could be decided on television.

THE SECOND THREAD IN Walter Mondale that parallels his stereotype is his caution. It is a Norwegian character trait that has been buttressed by the unique mechanics of his twenty-three years in public life. Attorney general of Minnesota, United States senator, vice president, Mondale's career is extraordinary for the fact that he has never officially entered any political contest in which he was not either the front-runner or the incumbent. That unusual experience has entrenched his caution, and the most formative step in the process was the first. In 1960, when he was thirty-two years old, less than five years out of law school and already an experienced Democratic-Farmer-Labor Party operative, he was appointed by Governor Orville Freeman to fill the state attorney general's office, vacated by resignation. Out of nowhere, Mondale held the second-most powerful elective office in the state. His predecessor, Miles Lord, had been something of a controversial showboat, but Mondale went in the opposite direction.

"I am young and start with no base at all," he told a friend. He knew his best option was to play his role extremely close to the vest. "I'm not even going to smile," he explained. And he did not. He also never allowed himself to be photographed with a drink in his hand or to be seen talking to an "unattached woman." He went to work early and stayed late. Not surprisingly, he comfortably won "reelection."

Mondale's caution bred a style that is inoffensive, deferential, and thorough, and those virtues in turn made Walter Mondale a very successful, if relatively colorless, politician. In 1964, Governor Karl Rolvaag of Minnesota appointed him to the Senate seat vacated by Hubert H. Humphrey upon the latter's election to vice president, and Mondale won election on his own in 1966 and 1972.

In 1976, Jimmy Carter elevated Mondale to the vice presidency. "The thing that is most evident about Mondale," Humphrey once explained, "is that he's nonabrasive. He was not a polarizer. He coupled all this with what was obvious talent: He was young, he was articulate, he was intelligent and clean-cut. He kept filling the bill. It's most amazing." A less cautious man might not have been so acceptable to all concerned, and Mondale has made remarkably few enemies in twenty years of holding offices.

Thus far, Walter Mondale seems most cautious about the issue of Jimmy Carter. Carter's 1980 defeat is a disaster Mondale must distance himself from, yet he must do so without seeming to be disloyal or denying his own history. Indeed, Mondale wants his vice presidency remembered as much as he wants Jimmy Carter forgotten. It is a tricky balancing act. Questions about Mondale's attitude toward his former boss come up everywhere. At Mondale's March 7 press conference in Jackson, he gives his standard answer. He has recently been chided in several national columns for his remarks in an interview published under the headline MONDALE, NO MORE A LOYAL DEFENDER, TRYING TO ESTABLISH HIS INDEPENDENCE, and though Mondale considers the chiding unfair, he knows better than to whine to the press about the coverage he's getting. "I was proud to serve as Mr. Carter's vice president," he says instead. "There was much that we did that's going to look very good in American history. We had some problems, we had some bad breaks. That's the way it is. Now I'm running for president."

The answer is what one reporter calls "surefooted." Mondale's caution is, of course, "political wisdom" when the issue is how to avoid giving offense, but when the issue is "boring," it works against him. He provokes little heat either pro or con and consequently makes bland copy. It is one of the reasons analysts describe his support in the polls as "shallow." Having always run from the passive posture of either defending an office or defending a lead, he has never had to seize the public imagination and run with it, as most challengers must. Whether he can or not is, after twenty-three years, still an open question.

THE FINAL ELEMENT IN THE character behind Walter Mondale's stereotype is his inwardness. Though now one of the most charming elbow-rubbers and hand-shakers in the Democratic Party, when he first took the Minnesota attorney generalship he entered his office every day by a private door to avoid having to make small talk with the secretarial help. He is a private person and not instinctively convivial. He can entertain himself by staring out a window and is most at ease with just himself in the room. Though he talks little about his own psychology, Mondale admits that he has ritualized his need to drop everything and look inward in the form of regular fishing trips and that they are central to his inner workings. At an Iowa City Foreign Relations Council meeting he jokes about them. "I was once asked why I fished," he says, "and I said it was cheaper than a psychiatrist."

For the last twenty-five years, Mondale's partner in this emotional therapy has been Fran Befera, a Duluth television station owner. The two men angle for trout and walleyed pike in the Minnesota lakes reachable only by seaplane. In winter, they chop holes in the ice and do the same thing. Often Befera's sons come along, and the trips usually last five or six days. They stay in Befera's fishing shack, take along canned tuna in case nothing is biting, and what talking they do is just "camp talk." No issues, no campaigns, no public-opinion polls. Just understated male phrases about fish, the weather, and more fish. Most of the time, Mondale sits with his line in the water and says nothing. "Your system is driven by the sport to calm down," he explains. "That's what it's all about. After about the fourth day, I start to get my perspective back—the little irritations and anxieties disappear. I can think about the big picture again."

He finds sustenance and focus in being nobody with nothing much to say, and his therapy amounts to long, silent hours adrift, watching how the light lifts off the water and the ripples scatter toward the shore. Where others might be bored, Walter Mondale is rejuvenated.

But on the campaign trail, being interviewed in the back seat of his rented car, Mondale differs strongly with all the attention paid to his stereotype. "Maybe I am boring," he says. "I don't know. I read about it but I don't think my audiences are bored. You've seen them; are they bored?" The reporter allows that most of the people who come out to see Mondale seem to enjoy what he has to say. "Sure," Mondale continues, "I lay an egg once in a while just like anyone. But I think there's pack journalism operating here, too. If one of the bureaus writes a story that I'm boring, then all the rest do. What's really interesting is that for eighteen months I was on the road and none of the national press was there, but they were all writing stories about how boring I was. It always fascinated me how they knew."

DESERVED OR NOT, MONDALE'S stereotype has obscured some attractive attributes:

He is bright and, by politician standards, enormously literate. A friend, the historian Barbara Tuchman, supplies him with reading lists, and his favorite book is George Trevelyan's biography of Garibaldi. For fun, he hunts quotations in the Shakespeare concordance Joan gave him for Christmas. On the few occasions when he watches television, he sticks to old movies. His home life with Joan has an updated Ozzie and Harriet flavor. The Mondales live on Lowell Street in northwest Washington and, on his occasional days off, Mondale can be seen in chino pants, jogging shoes, and an old purple letterman's jacket, walking Digger, his daughter's dog, in Cleveland Park.

Joan campaigns, does volunteer work for the arts, and makes pots in her pottery studio. Mondale likes to sit up in the evenings and read. He is the son of a Methodist minister, she is the daughter of a Presbyterian minister, and today they are Presbyterians who do not get to church very often. He plays tennis and takes medication for what he describes as a "managed, controlled, modest" blood-pressure condition. Joan calls him Fritz and he calls her Joan.

Mondale's staff calls him Mondale or sir. He obliges everyone who recognizes him in airport lounges with conversations and says he enjoys doing so. Most of them call him Mr. Vice President or Mr. Mondale. He drinks one light scotch and water a day and chews three or four long, thick cigars. The cigars disgust Joan and she jokingly gripes about having to empty his ashtrays.

At home, they eat their dinners at the dining-room table and, following her lead, circulate on the culture circuit. They rarely entertain these days, but when they do it is mostly with senators and their wives, some of whom live in the neighborhood. Since the vice presidency, he has earned, according to him, a six-figure income as a Washington lawyer with Winston & Strawn, but the only signs of his new wealth are the car and driver provided by the campaign and the recently purchased home in Minnesota, where the Mondales plan to retire someday. "Decent" and "unpretentious" are two words all Mondale's friends use to describe him.

The most visible of Mondale's personal attributes is his sense of humor.

On the evening of January 28, he is speaking to a gathering of 125 Iowa Democrats in the Fleur de Lis Room of Dubuque's Julien Motor Inn. The room's glitter ceiling is lit with orange and yellow lights. Dubuque County has the second heaviest concentration of Democrats in the state, and doing well here is a key to carrying the caucuses next February. Ten minutes into his performance, he delivers one of the set jokes he salts throughout his standard Iowa stump speech. "This is a country where everybody can run for office," Mondale observes in his driest twang, "and, as you know, in the Democratic Party everybody does." The audience laughs. "Usually for president," Mondale adds. The audience laughs even harder.

Weeks later, he is at the solar-heated headquarters of the Society for the Protection of New Hampshire Forests in Concord. Senator Gary Hart of Colorado, a rival for the nomination, was here the week before, drawing an audience of fifty. Mondale draws eighty-five. In the question-and-answer period, Mondale makes a point about "the pursuit of happiness" as a national goal, using an off-the-cuff one-liner. "Did you ever see a picture of the politburo?" he asks rhetorically. "They all look like morticians who weren't paid for the last funeral."

At a Washington convention of the Community Action Program—the political arm of the United Automobile Workers— Mondale is one of the featured speakers. He is brought in to a standing ovation and introduced with effusive praise. The banner behind him reads: FORGING COALITIONS TO ADVANCE WORKERS GOALS. Mondale opens by recognizing most of the union's officers individually and then comes out with one of the standard lines he uses to josh his political friends. "I know how these UAW conventions work," Mondale begins, tongue-in-cheek. "You figure out who you'd really like to hear and then, when he turns you down, you ask old Walter Mondale if he has a new speech yet."

IF HE HOLDS THE LEAD, Walter Mondale will be the most quick-witted Democrat to head the ticket since John F. Kennedy. He will also be the most politically experienced since Lyndon B. Johnson. Walter Mondale held high public offices for twenty continuous years from 1960 to 1980. The twelve years spent in the Senate have left him completely familiar with the legislative process. His four as vice president are generally agreed to have included more direct and influential involvement in the daily workings of the executive branch than any vice president in history. The breadth of his experience is one point Mondale makes about himself with no reticence at all.

On the evening of March 7, Walter Mondale's tour of three Southern states has reached Chattanooga, Tennessee, where he addresses a reception sponsored by Chattanoogans for Mondale in the Sheraton Downtown Hotel. Some 250 Democrats attend, making heavy use of the cash bar. It is one of those audiences Mondale describes as "raw meat," and he works them determinedly. His face flushes and, as the words come out more and more rapidly, they shape themselves into a rhythmic cadence. The register of his voice rises and becomes increasingly nasal. "I am running for president," he declares. "I'm going to give it all I've got. I know state government, I know the Senate, I know the White House, I know the world. I know what I'm doing. And that's the final point: We need a president who knows what he's doing!"

The Chattanoogans applaud boisterously, and sweat trickles down the side of Walter Mondale's face.

When he is lathering up a crowd like the one in Chattanooga, Mondale sounds a lot like Humphrey, and the resemblance is no accident. Mondale refers to the late senator from Minnesota often, usually as "my old friend Hubert" or "my mentor, Hubert Humphrey," a "source of public inspiration and a deep, deep friend." Their relationship began as college student to United States senator, became aspiring politician to established power, and then, when Mondale came to the Senate and Humphrey assumed the vice presidency, junior public official to senior. It was while Humphrey was vice president that Mondale, at least partly out of loyalty to his mentor, supported Johnson's Vietnam policy, a stance he now calls "the worst mistake of my public life." When Humphrey left office in January 1969, Mondale came out against the war.

Despite their long association, it was not until 1971, when Humphrey returned to Washington as the junior Minnesota senator to Mondale's senior, that what one of Humphrey's aides would later call a "special communication" developed between the two men. As Humphrey's health ebbed, he increasingly saw Mondale as the political heir who might succeed in attaining the presidency where Humphrey himself had failed. According to Mondale, by 1978, when Humphrey lay in the hospital dying, their friendship "had blossomed into something very, very deep." The last time the two men saw each other, Humphrey talked at length about how much Mondale's career meant to him. "Keep it up," Humphrey said. A friend of both men described Mondale as "anguished" over Humphrey's death.

Ironically, it was Humphrey who first raised the doubts about Walter Mondale's staying power that have plagued Mondale's presidential aspirations for the last ten years. In a newspaper interview in 1973, Humphrey wondered pointedly whether Mondale had "the fire in the belly" it takes to become president. The question has been asked about Mondale ever since. Humphrey's remark was made in the course of the stillborn 1974 exception to Mondale's pattern of front-running, a sequence remembered now as "the last time Walter Mondale ran for president." Humphrey set the process in motion on election night in November 1972.

Mondale had just easily carried his second Senate reelection in the face of a Republican sweep, and Humphrey, ebullient, dragged him in front of the national television cameras and proclaimed him presidential material. When Mondale was slow to take advantage of the opening, Humphrey uttered his "fire in the belly" remark. In January 1974, Mondale finally announced that he was "actively exploring the possibility of running" and spent the next year on the Democratic rubber-chicken hustings. At the end of that year, Mondale stood at 3 percent in the polls.

"I was two points behind Don't Know and wanted to challenge him to a debate," he now jokes, "but Don't Know wouldn't debate me." In November 1974, Mondale called Humphrey. "Humphrey," he said, "I'm getting out of this thing."

On November 21, 1974, Mondale announced that he would not be a candidate for president in 1976. Until he called his press conference, both Joan and his staff expected he would run. Instead, Mondale joked to the press that he did not want to spend the rest of his life in Holiday Inns, and then he issued a brutal assessment of himself. "I do not have the overwhelming desire to be president which is essential for the kind of campaign that is required," he announced. "I admire those with the determination to do what is required to seek the presidency, but I have found that I am not among them."

Now, eight and a half years later, Mondale is talking about 1974 on his way to the Boston airport. He has spent the previous night in the Portsmouth, New Hampshire, Holiday Inn, the latest of dozens of such Holiday Inns he has stayed in since 1974. By now, Mondale is used to being asked if he is sufficiently driven to be president. He is chewing on a cigar when the subject comes up. "In 1974," Mondale explains, "I tried to run on a part-time basis for a year, and it became obvious that you have to run full-time. I was a senator, I loved being one, and I didn't want to give up being one. Deep down, I wasn't ready and I knew it. The more I thought about it, the more I asked myself, 'O.K., Mondale, what do you really want to do? What is it that you think makes all of this so important to the country?' I couldn't answer it. Now, with the experience of the White House, without the conflict of two jobs, I feel ready. I'm convinced I can run that government. I've got a clear vision. I believe I can be a very good president."

When he finishes, the cigar is out of Walter Mondale's mouth and he is looking off toward the countryside. The persistence of doubts about Mondale's drivenness is, among other things, a reflection of how little he is truly known. His considerable political skills are, to a great extent, the result of the diligent long-term exercise of his will to improve, and he has, through determined effort, elevated himself from running behind Don't Know in 1974 to running ahead of everybody in 1983. (At this writing, Gallup and Harris polls of Democrats show him ahead of the other candidates for the nomination.) Both developments bespeak the activity of someone who wants something very much.

HIS SCHEDULE LOOKS DRIVEN as well. In the 1982 elections, Mondale campaigned on behalf of ninety-five House, fifteen Senate, and eighteen gubernatorial candidates. Thus far in 1983, he has been on the road three weeks out of every four, working twelve- and eighteen-hour days. He exhibits little ambivalence about his task. Perhaps the more relevant question is not whether Walter Mondale is driven but what is doing the driving. As one of his aides has pointed out, he is not "the kind of guy who wakes up in the morning with 'Hail to the Chief' ringing in his ears."

The human being most responsible for the shape and intensity of Mondale's motivation was his father, Theodore. If will were a matter of genetic inheritance, there would be no question about Walter Mondale's.

Theodore, a stutterer, made himself into a preacher with a six-month course at Minnesota's Red Wing Seminary. After contracting lockjaw in a kitchen-table tonsillectomy during the early 1920s, Theodore regained the full use of his mouth by spending a year jamming a piece of wood between his jaws and slowly prying them open. He was fifty-two years old when his son Walter was born. Theodore had lost the last of his farms by then, and the Mondales were living on the meager proceeds of rural Minnesota ministerial postings in the likes of Jeffers, St. James, Ceylon, Heron Lake, and Elmore. Walter was the second son of Theodore Mondale's second family. Theodore's first wife had died after eighteen years of marriage, and their children were grown when he married Walter's mother, Claribel Cowan. (There are six children altogether from the two marriages.) Claribel gave music lessons and led the choir in each of Theodore's succeeding parishes. She and Walter were close, but, by all accounts, the dominant presence in Walter Mondale's childhood was his father, the minister.

"Being a minister's child is similar to being a public official's child," Joan Mondale explains. She is sitting in the Mondales' living room on Lowell Street. The house has two stories and is tastefully decorated. The neighborhood outside is leafy and upper-middle-class. Her husband, home for five days after several weeks of travel, is walking the dog. She is winding up the interview before rushing to a hairdresser's appointment. "As a minister's child," she continues, "what you say and do will be remembered. You have to be careful. What you say will be repeated. You aren't necessarily welcome when you move into a community. You have to think again about what you say and you have to prove yourself—prove that you're one of the gang—over and over. Fritz grew up with that."

The minister's son must prove himself to his father "over and over" as well. Theodore Mondale was a no-nonsense disciplinarian who administered the switch to Walter on more than one occasion, but they were deeply bonded. Theodore had high standards, and young Walter apparently lived up to them. He was a passable student, a school leader, and a local athletic hero. Theodore Mondale's passions were politics and Minnesota's homegrown Farmer-Labor party, and these, too, he inculcated in Walter. "Dad was basically the politician of the family," Mondale explains. "He was a devout Christian, a believer in the social gospel, a Farmer-Laborite. He believed Christ taught a sense of social mission, and this was heavily given to me throughout my childhood. He came out of the progressive Scandinavian tradition. We always discussed politics. My dad stuttered and wasn't a man of letters, never really more than a farm kid all his life. Often, I'd hear people ridicule him. He wasn't as smooth as he was supposed to be, I guess. But he had a lot to do with me going into political life. I wanted to fight for the things my father believed in."

The Minnesota Farmer-Labor Party Theodore Mondale taught his son to admire was a powerful force in the early 1930s but then waned until merging with Minnesota's Democratic Party into the modem DFL in 1944. A number of future national politicians rose out of that merger, all of them led by Hubert Humphrey, the exciting young mayor of Minneapolis. When Walter Mondale, twenty years old and a Macalester College undergraduate, enlisted in the ranks of Humphrey's 1948 Senate campaign, it was the kind of thing he had been raised to do. Reportedly, Mondale's proudest moment of that campaign was when he introduced Humphrey to his seventy-two-year-old father. Theodore Mondale's approval continued to mean a lot to Walter, and Theodore approved of Humphrey enormously. Theodore died six weeks after Humphrey won his 1948 Senate election. To this day, his father's expectations seem to be strung quite tightly inside Walter Mondale. He remains, at his core, a minister's kid who, having proved himself again and again, still has something left to prove.

"PROOF" THIS EARLY IN THE campaign has centered on joint appearances by all the candidates that Mondale calls the Democratic Party Traveling Gong Show. The first was in California in January. Each candidate addressed a party convention, and Mondale drew raves from press and delegates as "the most impressive." The second was in Massachusetts in February, and Mondale received the most enthusiastic reception.

On March 8, the Democratic Party Gong Show comes to Atlanta's World Congress Center to play in front of the Georgia state party's Jefferson–Jackson Day Dinner. Twenty-five hundred Democrats from all over Georgia attend in black ties and evening gowns. The music is provided by Dean Hudson and his orchestra. Dancing is planned for after the speeches. Dinner costs $150 a person, and the party will net a quarter of a million dollars. There is a dais, but no head table, just enough individual twelve-seat arrangements to cover the floor of a cavernous convention center decorated to resemble an upscale dinner club. Dozens of reporters and cameramen mill around near the podium and at the bar. Bert Lance, former Carter administration Director of the Office of Management and Budget, who was forced to resign and now is the state party chairman, is the evening's master of ceremonies.

Lance solves the only backstage controversy of the evening by arranging a group photo when all the candidates come to the dais. Mondale missed the group photo in California "for scheduling reasons" and did the same thing for the same reason in Massachusetts. Some national press photographers wonder if Mondale is ducking, and his press secretary has been assuring them all week that he will pose. He does. Smiling. Afterward, the candidates go at it in alphabetical order. In California and Massachusetts, Mondale spoke first for "scheduling reasons." Tonight, he speaks last. As each speaker is at the rostrum, the rest sit behind a long table. All of them stare into a spotlight whose glare obscures everything except the first row of press photographers two feet away.

Reubin O. Askew of Florida has a gray suit and a nervous tic in his right eyelid. Senator Dale Bumpers of Arkansas also wears gray and will be out of the race in less than a month. Alan Cranston of California has sent his son as a stand-in, effectively ceding the evening but paying his respects. Senator John Glenn tells a Walter Mondale joke: "Fritz Mondale spent the week listing his differences with the president," says Glenn, pausing for effect. "Fortunately, President Carter didn't take it personally." The line draws laughs, Glenn is applauded, but the applauders stay in their seats. Next, Senator Gary Hart proclaims himself the dark horse in a relatively dark and wooden way, and then Senator Ernest F. Hollings of South Carolina drawls through the longest speech of the night. Mondale listens with alternating airs of indifference, bemusement, and distraction. He does not seem nervous, yet it is apparent that he is just waiting his turn.

When he reaches the podium, last in line, Mondale starts slowly.

He mentions all the party notables present, tells a funny story about "old Hubert," and reminds the audience that Walter Mondale "helped elect the first Southern president in one hundred twenty years." Mondale does not, however, mention Jimmy Carter by name and will be the only one of the candidates not to do so. Mondale next talks about how the values at one end of the Mississippi River are the same as at the other. "I learned to believe in God, to obey the law, to tell the truth, to work hard, and to do my duty," he says. From that point on, Mondale steadily quickens the tempo. He is the only candidate who senses the raw meat in the audience and plays to it. They want stimulation, and his voice rises and the words pile out in bursts. He evokes "the values of the family" and says Democrats are "the party of caring." It is a performance one of the more cynical of the reporters present describes as "Walter Mondale sings Hubert Humphrey's Greatest Hits."

For the last two minutes, Mondale's chest is thrust against the podium while he speaks in a half shout and thumps the air with his arms. The Georgians love it and give him a standing ovation. He receives the applause with an abashed smile. He is genuinely thrilled that all those people could be clapping for him.

Mondale leaves the World Congress Center through a backstage entrance, accompanied by Joan, several staff members, and several national reporters. "Hell," one of the reporters joshes Mondale, "if you're gonna be that good, they'll make you talk last every time."

There is only the faint hint of a chuckle in Mondale's voice as he answers. "That was somethin', wasn't it!" he exclaims.

ALL CANDIDATES MUST CONTEND against not only their opponents but also themselves. In this second race, matched against his own limitations, Walter Mondale has yet to stamp his identity firmly on the lead he holds, and doing so is essential. He must also answer at least two significant outstanding doubts about himself.

The first is whether he can come across on television. "I'm not good on TV," Mondale admits. "It's just not a natural medium for me." Part of the reason is pure cosmetics. A reasonably trim man,

Mondale's face invariably looks heavier than the rest of him, and television cameras seem to heighten that jowliness. His eyes are dark blue and set in deep, permanently smudged sockets. In the esthetics of television, the lack of contrast translates into two distant dead spots in the middle of his face. The way his voice rises and goes nasal when making a point is a drawback as well. More central to his video difficulties, however, is Walter Mondale's own uneasiness with the medium. He is uncomfortable assuming the star quality it demands and has difficulty with the idea of presenting himself unselfconsciously to a box with lights on it. He has thus far resisted advice to seek coaching. Mondale for President will soon hire the Austin, Texas, advertising firm of thirty-three-year-old Roy Spence to handle its media. Spence did similar work for Governor Mark White's election in Texas but is a newcomer to national campaigns. He will have his hands full.

The second doubt about Walter Mondale is whether he can keep from being perceived as no more than the prisoner of his friends. Mondale was the only presidential candidate invited to the retirement dinner given by the United Automobile Workers for their president, Douglas A. Fraser, in Detroit's Cobo Arena. Autograph hunters swarmed around Mondale's place at the head table. "Fritz fits into our plans," an officer of Lansing's Local 652 explains. "He's a president of the people. It's people programs that make us go." Mondale receives a standing ovation when he is introduced to speak. "I want to thank you for making me feel at home," he says. At the end of the program, Mondale stands and joins hands with the rest of those at the head table in singing "Solidarity Forever."

On January 30, Mondale is the featured speaker at a black-tie fundraiser for the United Jewish Appeal at the exclusive Jimmy's Restaurant in Beverly Hills, California. More than $5 million will be raised from the sixty couples on the guest list, half designated for local projects, half for projects in the state of Israel. Mondale is introduced as someone who "shares completely the commitments that bring us together tonight." In the course of Mondale's speech, the return of territory by Israel as part of the Camp David agreements is likened to "an American President coming back and saying, 'I got peace with the Russians and all I had to give up was everything west of the Mississippi.'"

A month later, Mondale meets with a group of thirty-five farmers in the Hawkinsville, Georgia, public library in rural Pulaski County. The farmers have all been brought together by a local banker, and all of them are deep in debt. "I will be the best pro-farm president America has ever had," Mondale promises.

On March 25, Mondale stops at Boston's Harriet Tubman House, a federally funded community center, and meets with a dozen activists from the Hispanic community. Mondale takes his coat off and speaks with his hands on his hips. "I would appoint Hispanic Americans to positions of real power," he declares flatly. "I want to be the president who breaks the ice for Hispanic Americans."

Mondale's strategy is both orthodox and risky. He intends, quite simply, to reunite the fractious Democratic coalition by running as the candidate of each of its separate pieces, all at the same time.

The issues he emphasizes are appropriately "mainstream" in the spectrum of Democratic Party activists. Hart and Cranston are perceived as slightly to Mondale's left, with Askew, Glenn, and Hollings to his right. Mondale regularly opens his stump litany with unemployment, a condition he blames on high interest rates, weak trade policies, and the Reagan administration's enormous deficits. He also regularly attacks the imbalance of America's international trade posture, the threat of nuclear war, the "mishandling" of Central America, acid rain, James Watt, and the disintegration of the quality of American education. To deal with these national problems, he supports "domestic content" legislation as a necessary sign of "toughness" in our trade posture and proposes a series of international negotiations to establish trade "reciprocity." He also calls for new international monetary agreements in which the net result will be the devaluation of the American dollar, thereby making American exports more competitive and foreign imports less so. He has promised to repeal the scheduled tax cuts for people with incomes over $60,000 a year, to repeal income-tax indexing, and to "put a lid on hospital costs." He has endorsed a "verifiable nuclear freeze" and advocates "scaling the defense budget to reality." In the Middle East, he is pledged to continuing "the Camp David process," and in Central America he has proposed hemisphere-wide negotiations to stabilize the region. In response to the recent highly critical report of the National Commission on Excellence in Education, Mondale has proposed a new program of $11 billion in federal aid to local school districts. He also supports even tougher enforcement of the Voting Rights and Environmental Protection Acts.

The first risk in Mondale's "mainstream strategy" is that not all the pieces of the Democratic puzzle get along easily with one another, and the possibility of getting caught in a political crossfire is large. The second risk is that pleasing all of those constituencies sufficiently to win the Democratic nomination might well leave Mondale looking overpromised when the electoral base widens in the general election.

Mondale dismisses the second of those risks. "I want everybody to repair to my cause," he says. "The labor movement, minorities, the Jewish community, farmers, students, everybody. I'm trying to get all the support I can get. I don't think there's anything tawdry or sinister about it. There's a new theory I hear that the only way I can justify my position is to spend the next year offending people who would like to support me. That's a theory of politics I don't intend to participate in."

THE FIRST OF THOSE RISKS, however, has already ceased being speculation and has become a prominent early chapter in Mondale-for-President history. The place is Chicago and the date March 27, Palm Sunday. Mondale is here campaigning with the black Democratic mayoral candidate Harold Washington. In the primary election, Mondale backed Richard M. Daley, one of Washington's white opponents, and when Mondale first called to offer his help in the general election, Washington took eight days to return the call. Their campaign staffs eventually arranged today's half-day of joint appearances.

Everything goes as planned until Mondale and Washington's 11:30 a.m. drop-in at the Palm Sunday services of St. Pascal's, on the city's largely Polish northwest side. It is the kind of white working-class neighborhood where Mondale is thought to be strong and Washington is known to be worse than weak. When their campaign caravan stops one hundred yards up the street from St. Pascal's, 150 demonstrators favoring Bernard Epton, a millionaire lawyer and businessman, and carrying EPTON posters are waiting on the church's front steps. The next fifteen minutes provide the raw material for a fifteen-second film clip that will run over and over again during the following week as the Chicago election becomes a lead story on the evening news. All of it features Walter Mondale, trapped in a political no-man's-land between two warring factions, both of whose votes he hopes to corner.

The clip begins with Mondale and Washington making their way between angry demonstrators in the company of the parish priest. Shouts of "baby killers" and "not in our church" are drowned on the soundtrack by chants of "Epton, Epton, Epton." In St. Pascal's outer lobby, Mondale and Washington are shown huddling while their campaign aides decide whether to go inside—thereby disrupting the service—or simply backtrack to their cars and leave. Off camera, a teenage girl ten feet from Mondale is shouting at him. She has run in from the church's Easter pageant rehearsal and is dressed in a fluffy pink head-to-toe bunny costume, complete with floppy pink ears. "This is a church!" she screams. "This is a church!" The final sequence in the next week's film clip is shot from the front and shows Mondale and Washington, having decided to leave, descending the church steps with the taunting crowd massed on all sides. As he has throughout, Mondale appears contained, jowly, tired, and dignified.

After the camera is off, Washington and Mondale walk on opposite sides of the cars. Most of the hubbub follows Washington. For a moment, Mondale is by himself on the edge of the crowd and he is approached by a middle-aged man identifying himself as "a Norwegian." The Norwegian is furious. "I'm ashamed of you, Mondale!" he shouts. "What'd Washington's people ever do for us?"

Mondale ignores the comment. Several seconds later, two younger men step up and address him as "Mr. Vice President." They want to shake his hand, and Mondale obliges before driving off between two lines of bobbing Epton posters.

An hour later, Mondale is at O'Hare Airport, headed for a week's rest back on Lowell Street and then a push in Massachusetts for the state party convention straw poll there on April 9. Mondale will win in Massachusetts by a fat margin, and on April 12 Harold Washington will win by a slim one in Chicago. By then, a dilemma similar to Chicago is brewing in Philadelphia, where a black man, W. Wilson Goode, is running against a white man, former mayor Frank L. Rizzo, in the Democratic mayoral primary, which Goode later wins. This time, Mondale made no endorsement. According to several published reports, his heart was with Goode, but his two principal Philadelphia fundraisers were backing Rizzo.

It is hard to please all of your friends at once and, leaving Chicago on March 27, Mondale seems relieved to be rid of the obligation for at least the moment. He is glad to be offstage and headed home. In the airport, a reporter he knows approaches him, looking for a quote about what happened at St. Pascal's. "What'd you think?" the reporter asks, motioning vaguely back in the direction of the city.

Mondale shakes his head as he answers. "That was somethin'," he says, "wasn't it?"

His response is the same as after the adulation of Atlanta nineteen days earlier, only this time there is no hint of self-satisfaction in his voice. Chicago has been an object lesson and, despite his folksy nonchalance, Walter Mondale takes such lessons very seriously. He hears the footsteps behind him, even if it is too early in the race to tell if they are his own or someone else's.

[Originally published as "Understanding Mondale,"
New York Times Magazine, June 19, 1983]

São Paulo:
Megacity Metamorphosis

I
[THE ANTHILL]

The future of the planet straddles the Tropic of Capricorn, perched atop the Brazilian coastal escarpment at an elevation of 2,700 feet, sixty miles from the Atlantic Ocean. It is called Greater São Paulo, home to an estimated eighteen million people and still growing.

Megacities like São Paulo are the way much of our species will soon live. The world's population has almost tripled in the last thirty years, and half of all humans now live in cities. In 1900, only one human in forty did. In 1960, New York was the only city in the world with more than ten million inhabitants and was dubbed a "megacity" by demographers. Tokyo, now the world's largest megacity, joined it ten years later. São Paulo, now the second largest, joined in the decade after that. By 2015, there will be thirty-three megacities, mostly in the Third World, and unprecedented density will be the rule.

It has already been that way for a while in São Paulo. Here, sprawled across the Upper Tietê River Basin, immediately west of the mountains of the Serra do Mar and east of the broad *planalto* of the South American interior, there are virtually no trees, and the urban core is sometimes 50 degrees warmer than the remnants of forest on its outskirts. The horizon is always nearby, and entering this place from the airport feels a bit like being swallowed whole. The road in runs along the River Tietê, a slow-moving sludge of turds, laundry detergent, and battery acid.

"Some city you got here," I said to my taxi driver.

He answered in Portuguese, and I fumbled around for my dictionary. "Welcome to the anthill," is what I think he said.

2
[LOOKING DOWN ON THE MEGACITY]

All the world's megacities are different from one another: Only São Paulo, Beijing, and Mexico City are not seaports. All megacities are economic centers, but New York and Tokyo are far wealthier than São Paulo, which is better off than Buenos Aires, Argentina. São Paulo cannot match the squalor of Calcutta, India, but it comes close, and while it is better built than Jakarta, Indonesia; Cairo, Egypt; and Manila, Philippines, it has none of the civic nobility of Paris or even Los Angeles. Like most megacities, São Paulo's air is often foul, but that of Mexico City and Shanghai, China, is even worse. São Paulo is growing at more than twice the rate of nearby Rio de Janeiro, but far more slowly than either Karachi, Pakistan, or Lagos, Nigeria. São Paulo is a megacity easily described as either the best of the worst or the worst of the best.

And it does not reveal itself easily at ground level, where it mostly makes a noise like a buzz saw and stinks like a hot engine block. I never quite got what the place was about until I looked down on it.

The helicopter I hired took off in the afternoon, while an unseasonal rain blew off to the northwest. We flew to the city edge, then wheeled and made a run back from the outside in. First, the tatters of the Mata Atlântica forest give way to a sudden baldness full of four- and six-story housing projects flanked by two-room houses built out of cinder block. Squatter colonies living on red dirt and under tin sheets dot the watercourses that weave among the twelve-story stucco rectangles painted to resemble fast-food cartons. Then the sixteen- and twenty-four-story bare concrete towers appear, with tiny porches and metal window frames, many of which drip tongues of rust down the walls toward the asphalt. All of it lays out like a train wreck, each fragment at an obscure angle to the next, an arrangement of random eruptions rather than the footprint of a choreographed advance. Above Greater São Paulo's core, over Paulista Avenue, where much of Brazil plugs into the global economy, in every direction I looked the city was all bristling stalagmites.

And it was suddenly obvious that, like all anthills, the five thousand square miles of habitat below me acted like one enormous organism rather than eighteen million tiny ones.

3
[THIS IS BRAZIL]

Greater São Paulo is marked most by how quickly it has grown. Thirty years ago, it was a quarter of its current size. The city's engorgement was triggered when a revolution in Brazilian agriculture replaced small tenant farms with mechanized agribusiness, forcing the rural peasantry, still a majority of Brazil's population in the early 1960s, off the land and into an enormous exodus. Today, Brazil is 90 percent urban. Much of that transformation happened in a stampede out of Brazil's impoverished northeast and into São Paulo, where an influx of foreign capital was building the mightiest financial engine on the continent and the economy was growing at 9 percent a year. São Paulo's population grew 5 percent a year for the better part of two decades before shrinking to its current rate of about 2 percent. It soon became a joke among Paulistas that the only two things that never stop growing are cancer and their hometown.

São Paulo's inflation into a megacity was a land rush. The desperate, the poor, the unemployed, and the ambitious descended on the city in droves, carrying their lives in bundles or ancient suitcases on cross-country buses, unloading at the Terminal Rodoviário do Tietê or one of four other stations. At times, Greater São Paulo added a new population the size of Seattle to its rolls every year. People found places to live wherever they could. Settlement was relentless, spreading outward from the municipality of São Paulo into the thirty-eight surrounding municipalities that make up the "greater" area with such speed that neighborhoods were sometimes overpopulated before they were even named. The farther from downtown these locations were, the larger the likelihood that their residents were either poor or newcomers or both.

São Paulo had a master plan, zoning regulations, and a planning commission, but none of this seemed to make much difference against such a tide. Now, Domingos Theodoro de Azevedo Netto, director of the municipality of São Paulo's planning secretariat, estimates that at least two-thirds of all the construction done during São Paulo's thirty-year boom was completed without official permission. If forced to, the builders dealt with permits after the fact but, most often, they did it not at all. There were even instances of developers erecting apartment buildings, selling the apartments, and then disappearing without ever holding legal title to the land upon which the apartment buildings stood. Connection to city services was rare or haphazard. It was common for structures to be erected with indoor plumbing that emptied sewage onto a nearby hillside. Vacant land in the patchwork of São Paulo's growth—mostly the lowlands along the river basin's creek banks, flood plains, or public watersheds—was invaded by the impoverished, who erected illegal squatter towns known as *favelas* in Portuguese, most of which used open latrines or the watercourse itself to handle the sewage. By the early 1970s, only 1 percent of São Paulo's population lived in such squalor. Now there are almost two thousand *favelas*, housing some 8 percent of the population.

De Azevedo Netto provided me with that summary of Greater São Paulo's metamorphosis in his downtown office. He was dressed for the Brazilian winter in a sweater and tweeds. Mostly he spoke Portuguese to my interpreter, but sometimes he switched to English and spoke directly to me. When he said that two-thirds of São Paulo had been built outside of any planning structure whatsoever, my eyebrows lifted. I pointed out that this is an exceptional statistic by all the standards that prevail in the United States.

He compressed his lips and turned his palms toward the ceiling. When he spoke, it was in English. "This is not the United States," he said. "This is Brazil."

4
[MEGACITY FROM TOP TO BOTTOM]

Like all megacities, and like the rest of Brazil, São Paulo has a small top and a large bottom. Almost two million of the city's eighteen million people live in First World circumstances. They are cardholders in the global economy that stations twelve hundred branch banks and the outposts of major multinational corporations in office towers on either side of the eight-lane Avenida Paulista. They work on laptops, fly in jets, talk on cellular phones, attend universities, watch cable television, and shop at Benneton. They may patronize one of Greater São Paulo's eighty or so McDonald's franchises, where a Big Mac costs the equivalent of $5.10, or one of its more than two thousand pizza parlors, including a spate of Pizza Huts. They like to shop in American-style shopping malls, some featuring elaborate indoor amusement parks. On Saturday afternoons at the larger malls they find parking spaces with difficulty, often cruising the lot for as long as a half hour. They live near the city's hub, where the commute is short, and reside mostly in high-rise apartments featuring security perimeters. They think in dollars rather than cents.

For Greater São Paulo's remaining sixteen million, life is decidedly Third World. There are more poor people here than reside in either Haiti or Somalia. Most of them walk to work when they have it, sometimes taking as long as three hours to get there. The upper reaches of this Third World have found jobs in the factories where automobiles are built for Fiat, Volkswagen, and General Motors. Theirs is a small-change economy, largely unskilled. The staples of life are still often at issue for them, but thanks to television, they have learned to aspire to the consumption promoted by advertising agencies and credit-card companies. This world's bottom feeders camp in the garbage dumps, sniff glue late at night among the lesser side streets downtown, or have no homes at all, sleeping under freeway bridges and in doorways.

I met several of these people at a Sunday-morning outdoor prayer service under a freeway overpass, at which the sermon was delivered in Portuguese by a Korean Methodist minister. Then everyone who sat or stood through it was given a chit that could be redeemed for a cup of café au lait and a white-bread roll the size of a small mango. One of those in line spoke English. He said he had gone to a university in Lisbon, Portugal, lived in New York at one time, and confessed to having been headed downhill for a while.

"I tell ya," he said, "this place is a motherfucker to be on the bottom of."

The next two rungs up Greater São Paulo's ladder are only a little better. These are the *favelas* and the *cortiços*. *Cortiço* literally means "beehive" and is the name given to Greater São Paulo's tenements, home to some two million Paulistas. Many *cortiços* are aging grand houses or apartment buildings that have been divided into the tiniest marketable spaces and rented. Some landlords even rent a space—one with barely enough room for one person to lie down—to three different people, who occupy it in eight-hour shifts. More typically, a family of four or more occupies a six-by-ten space, the size of a maximum-security cell in one of America's older penitentiaries. In the *favelas*, the best of the dwellings has rudimentary cinder-block corner posts supporting a tin roof with a rough concrete slab for flooring. Though they have no legal standing, few of these squatter settlements are ever destroyed. The most notorious such eviction occurred at a settlement of some ten thousand residents, where the "official" order was supplied by resident gangsters. Over the years, an air of permanency has settled on the *favelas*, though at least a third of the homes in them are smaller than thirty square feet.

In Morumbi, one of São Paulo's richest districts, luxury high-rises share a hill with a *favela* that is home to some six hundred families. From squatter level at the bottom of the slope, you can see a high-rise condo farther up that features swimming pools built into the balconies. One morning, my driver took a shortcut on the dirt road that ran along one edge of that Morumbi slum on our way to see the building with the stacked layers of swimming pools. For a moment, we were halted by two residents of the squatter town who were digging a trench to the city's water line to make an illegal connection. While one of the men moved their tools out of our path, the other made conversation.

He wanted to know where we were going, and my driver said we were headed up to get a look at the building with all the swimming pools.

"Oh," the *favela* man said with a grin, "the birdbath."

5
[WILL THIS PLACE LAST? AND IF SO, HOW?]

Another morning, I interviewed Pedro Roberto Jacobi, a social scientist at the Centro de Estudos de Cultura Contemporânea, who had recently published a study under the auspices of the Stockholm Institute that surveyed the way Paulistas live and their impact on the environment. Jacobi is a regular visitor to New York and, like most Paulistas, expressed a considerable attachment to his hometown.

"Will São Paulo survive its own growth?" I asked.

"São Paulo will most certainly survive," he answered. "We just may end up wishing it hadn't."

Indeed: The ratio of open green space to residents in Greater São Paulo is less than a third of the World Health Organization's recommended minimum. Half the megacity's residents' water supply is rationed and available only once every two or three days. Until just a year ago, its poorest neighborhoods received water only once every eight days. During June, July, and August, the dry months of the Southern Hemisphere's winter, atmospheric inversions over São Paulo's core trap enough ozone and carbon monoxide west of the Serra do Mar to make the air unfit to breathe. The eighteen million people with little choice but to breathe it anyway also produce some twenty thousand tons of domestic and industrial garbage for daily interment in dozens of official and unofficial landfills. The unmeasured remainder of São Paulo's trash is mostly thrown in the Tietê or one of its dozens of tributaries. The same is true for excrement: 40 percent of Greater São Paulo's sewage is deposited out in the open, 65 percent is collected in the public sewers, less than 26 percent is actually treated, and all of it ends up back in the Tietê, sooner or later. Of the river's normal turgid flow, some 40 percent is raw human effluent laced with factory sludge, industrial chemicals, and heavy metals. The River Tietê is already dead before it is halfway through town, devoid of sufficient dissolved oxygen to support even the most rudimentary forms of aquatic life. It stays that way for at least a hundred miles downstream.

Judging by São Paulo, the megacity is a species for which the most dangerous predator is itself.

6

[WHAT MAKES A MEGACITY
CAN UNMAKE IT AS WELL]

When Brazil set off to join the global economy in a major way, it pursued an American model. The national transportation infrastructure was built for automobiles, most of which would be manufactured in Greater São Paulo. Now the city exports buses and heavy trucks to North America and Europe, and sedans to all over South America.

And Greater São Paulo itself is a town on wheels. Its automobile population is now some six million and rising, at a rate of perhaps one thousand a day. At least 420 cars a day must be added to account for those stolen during the same period.

Not surprisingly, traffic dominates São Paulo's daily life. During 1992, the daily average total rush-hour backup was 23 miles; during 1993, 33 miles; during 1994, 58. Once, traffic backed up for 17 miles at a single tollbooth. A Friday evening with three simultaneous accidents at three separate points in traffic flow raised the backup record to 110 miles, until an accident involving four big rigs on a main artery stacked up 153 miles of automobiles stalled end to end, belching exhaust to be recycled throughout the metropolis as part of the air that Greater São Paulo breathes.

As megacities go, São Paulo's air pollution is hardly the worst. In Mexico City the smog includes dried fecal dust as well as the usual chemicals, and in Shanghai it is often impossible to see the street from a fourth-story window. In São Paulo, the horizon shortens to several blocks away during much of smog season, and everyone coughs a lot. Vehicles driven by internal combustion engines excrete some five thousand tons a day of carbon monoxide into the surrounding atmosphere, some nine hundred tons a day of hydrocarbons, and slightly less than that of nitrogen oxides. In dry, colder months, when there are no rainstorms passing over the Serra do Mar on winds out of the south or southeast, and the calm is marked by heavy cold air sitting atop the city's own heat in a classic inversion, the exhaust lingers and lingers, making for at least a month's worth of very bad air days every winter and close to the same every fall.

One obvious alternative is, of course, to use railed mass transit, but the city has been remarkably inept at it. São Paulo launched its metropolitan train system in 1968. So far it has constructed barely twenty-seven miles of track. Montreal, which has completed its Metro, has laid far more track and at a cost of $48.3 million a mile. São Paulo's has cost $322 million a mile.

I first heard that price comparison from three executives at Logos Engenharia S.A., an engineering company that is a major player in the city's infrastructure construction and management.

"How do you account for that enormous discrepancy?" I asked.

The firm's vice president, Ladi Beizus, lifted his palms and shrugged his shoulders. "This is Brazil," he said.

7
[THE DOWNSIDE OF PROSPERITY]

Greater São Paulo is one of the Third World's success stories, a place where there was once never enough to go around, and where now there is that much, plus a lot left over to throw away. Not surprisingly, the issue that haunts São Paulo is where to throw it.

Some 80 percent of Greater São Paulo's estimated fourteen

thousand daily tons of municipal solid waste and sixty-five hundred tons of industrial solid waste are collected by a public system, with the municipality of São Paulo collecting the most. Most of the area's potentially toxic medical waste is disposed of by being burned in one of two aging incinerators, both of which have become so inefficient that they are major sources of airborne dioxins. The rest of the city's solid-waste collection is driven to landfills for burial.

Like New York, São Paulo is running out of such burial plots. The current Brazilian statutes require municipalities to inter their garbage inside the municipality's own borders, and the municipality of São Paulo has run out of potential landfill sites. Faced with the same problem for its twenty-two thousand tons a day, Tokyo has begun building islands out of its garbage at various locations in Tokyo Bay. In São Paulo, the city government has finally committed itself to replacing the landfills and current incinerators with a garbage-separation program that will produce commercial compost from organic waste, as well as two new, huge, state-of-the-art incinerators that can burn the remaining garbage and generate electricity to add to the city's power grid. The plan's detractors point out that the North Americans have put a hold on such incinerators, citing air-pollution risks, and it hardly seems appropriate for São Paulo to add even more bad air to its mix. At this point, the separation program has begun, but it is handling only 7 percent of the daily garbage and has found no stable market for its raw compost, and the contracts to build the incinerators have not yet even been bid.

Meanwhile, of course, the landfills continue to grow. Last year, São Paulo authorities were investigating the possibility that one of them had even started to shift at its base, where the refuse had decomposed into a viscous jelly and threatened to slide onto the nearby neighborhood. Bandeirantes, the city's largest landfill, is literally a mountain of garbage, and though it is well engineered, like all landfills it produces methane gas and something called leachate. Leachate is the liquid that is continually generated when rainfall is absorbed into the landfill and filtered through the accumulated layers of decomposing garbage. It is collected and dumped into the sewer system. At night, the methane is often flared off, producing spears of flame that can be seen for miles.

8

[WHAT WILL THE MEGACITY DRINK?]

Water supply is a critical issue for São Paulo, as it is for most megacities. That such is the case here, however, is particularly telling. The watersheds surrounding São Paulo receive an average of eighty-seven inches of rain a year, comparable in volume to some of the rain forests of the United States' Pacific Northwest.

The foundation of this modern megacity's increasingly inadequate water system was laid in the early decades of the twentieth century, when the British company that held the license to develop the water resources designed the city's waterworks. Its principal features were two reservoirs. The first and larger of the two, Billings, was named for the designing engineer and is formed by a dam across the Rio Pinheiros, one of the Tietê's tributaries. It goes on for miles in four major fingers, covering what were once valleys under the green blanket of the Mata Atlântica. Built to generate hydroelectric power primarily for industrial development, Billings ensured that Greater São Paulo was the only site in Brazil equipped for twentieth-century development when it came. The second reservoir Billings built is called Guarapiranga, after the river that feeds it. Guarapiranga has always been reserved for the public water supply.

This water system now includes some twenty-six thousand miles of pipe, roughly enough to circle the earth at the equator, and about 45 percent of the daily shipment is lost to either leakage or theft. Leakage is so bad that at least a half dozen sources volunteered independently of one another that the wells in the downtown area draw chlorinated water straight out of the ground. Even as rattletrap as it is, however, the delivery system is far from the most significant threat to Greater São Paulo's water supply. That designation belongs back up the line at the water's source and, of course, in the surrounding sprawl of Greater São Paulo itself.

To begin with, a full half of the megacity's supply is now brought in from the nearby city of Campinas, which is growing steadily, demanding that water for itself, which it may indeed prove to have rights to under Brazilian law. A relatively remote part of Billings is currently tapped to supply water to the industrial suburbs housing the auto industry. Large parts of Billings are too foul to be usable—thanks to a program ended in the late 1980s in which water from the Pinheiros, near its intersection with the Tietê, was pumped back up to the reservoir to add to the flow over the escarpment. A plant on the Tietê upstream from the metropolis accounts for 20 percent of the supply, and the rest is pumped out of Guarapiranga, the system's senior source. And Guarapiranga is threatened as well. Now, there are *favelas* and less-than-legal housing established on or near perhaps half of its total shoreline, many of them unconnected to any sewage system at all, making the entire metropolis's grip on its necessities even more vulnerable.

Water shortages are forecast for Greater São Paulo in the twenty-first century.

9
[THE RIVER TIETÊ]

In the perverse ecology of megacities, water pumped into São Paulo's pipes every second is balanced by the raw sewage that is dumped back into the myriad brooks, streams, trickles, and canals that feed the River Tietê. That translates into some 800 tons a day of domestic sewage, 370 tons a day of industrial sewage, and 5 tons a day of industrial inorganic waste, chemicals, and heavy metals.

In 1977, São Paulo began construction on a sewage plant that would be the first step in a ten-year campaign to clean up the Tietê. In fact, it took more than ten years just to complete that plant, and it brought the amount of sewage being treated up to only 11 percent. In 1991, the surrounding state of São Paulo, which has jurisdiction over the river, announced another program to clean the Tietê in its entirety, this time by 1994. The first stage of that campaign involved construction of a plant that would increase the amount of treated sewage to 18 percent. That plant is now scheduled to be finished by 1998. There is a second stage of the plan that will raise the treatment to 30 percent. Antonio Marsiglia Netto, a vice president at Sabesp, the state water and sewage monopoly, told me stage 2 would be finished sometime early in the next century if, of course, everything stayed on schedule in a way I already knew full well it never yet had.

"What takes so long?" I asked.

He shrugged. "This is Brazil," he said.

By then, the explanation was familiar, if frustrating. And it was hardly the last time I would hear it.

The actual last time was in an interview with Professor Ladislau Dowbor, an adviser to a former mayor who was seeking office again. Dowbor, now on the faculty at the Universidade Católica de São Paulo, was describing the ongoing failure of the city to provide infrastructure to service all its growth. "This is Brazil," he said, lifting his palms toward the ceiling.

"Just what do you mean by that?" I pressed.

"I mean, this is Brazil," he repeated. "We want to stop being poor before we have to clean up after ourselves, so we have done little. And what we do manage to do is trapped in a kind of collusion of interests among the state companies, the contractors, the developers, and the political parties. All that is done is done in their interests or usually not at all. It doesn't matter if it's a megacity. That's just part of the way this place works."

"Or doesn't work," I commented.

"Or doesn't work," he agreed.

It is perhaps São Paulo's crowning irony that, while on the verge of shortage and unable to guarantee continuous water service to more than half its residents, it spends four months of the year with more water than it can hope to handle. During the Southern Hemisphere's spring and summer, the Upper Tietê Basin is pelted with torrential storms. Some longtime residents think the region's rains used to be considerably less fierce, and some even argue that the megacity, by providing both the updraft of heat and the high atmospheric particle count necessary to milk rain out of the clouds blowing in off the South Atlantic, is in effect making its own weather. In any case, there is no disputing how hard it rains. One storm in 1991 dropped at the rate of almost five inches an hour, leaving behind 150 million tons of water in a twelve-hour period.

When it rains, sheets of water splatter onto the asphalt, and in moments, gutters are awash and puddles expanding. The runoff rushes down the slopes, along the asphalt and concrete, into the storm drains, and over the road shoulders. During the first half hour of a new storm, more pollution is washed off the city's surface and into the River Tietê than is carried by an entire day's worth of sewage. Not enough water drains into the earth, so it heads downhill and into a manmade drainage web whose strands are usually clogged with garbage, silt, and sewage. The overflow floods land that is either occupied by squatters or impermeable because it is covered by concrete or asphalt. When the wall of runoff reaches the Tietê, this sow of a river is clotted with foam and sometime overflows its own canalized banks. Throughout the city, some 436 different locations have been identified as subject to chronic flooding. The São Paulo evening news has run footage of pedestrians, hip deep in water, holding on to power poles to keep from being carried off their feet, and of automobiles being swept broadside down São Paulo's major avenues. Rumors abound that people have been sucked into open manholes, but no such fates have been substantiated. Perhaps the greatest danger is from disease spread either by sewage inundation or by rodents flushed from their usual haunts. The newspapers advise people caught out in a flood in their car and unable to get to high ground to pull onto a side street, climb onto the car's roof, and wait for help to come.

10
[THE END OF THE WORLD]

One morning, I accompanied photographer Sebastião Salgado and his assistant Carlos out to a small municipal garbage dump in São Vicente.

We parked off the dirt track leading into the place and advanced on foot, walking into the sunrise. Vultures flapped away at our approach, and pigeons exploded off the ground in a host of wingbeats. Several horses were grazing on the garbage piles, pawing through the packaging to unearth the castoff tomato slop and orange peels. Beyond them, the piles of garbage were smoldering, and an acrid smoke drifted everywhere. Trucks soon began arriving with their morning loads, and the proprietor fired up his tractor while a dozen garbage pickers mauled through the fresher mounds, each working with a three-foot steel rod that had a short right angle bent into the end, pushing aside the slop and extracting plastic soda bottles and aluminum cans. They worked at a constant pace, stooped, prodding, eyeballing everything. One man wearing a hat with a McDonald's logo found something interesting while I watched, chewed on it for a bit, and then threw it back in the pile. Most of the pickers live here, in a cluster of huts made from discards and located off to one edge of the dump.

Carlos and I went over to the hut belonging to a man who had built off by himself, away from the rest, in the main body of the garbage field. He had erected a structure out of a couple of old doors, a discarded piece of fiberboard, a couch, a car seat, several other sticks, and two or three abandoned tarps. He kept his pet blackbird in someone's old woven basket with a cardboard lid. When we approached, he quite eagerly produced a number of the treasures he'd extracted from the dump. Among them were a flashlight, which also made a siren sound when you threw one of its switches, and a tube of toothpaste.

When Carlos and I walked back through the wafting stink, the vultures were perched on a nearby transmission tower. Carlos stopped next to me and took in the panorama. He made an expansive gesture with his arms, embracing it all and shaking his head.

"Fin del mundo!" he exclaimed. The end of the world.

Without waiting for a translation, I knew exactly what he meant.

[*Rolling Stone*, January 9, 1997]

The Agony of the Kurds

SURROUNDED BY THE FROZEN RIDGES of the Zagros Mountains in northern Iraq, eighteen Kurdish families live in what was once a summer home of Saddam Hussein. Saddam fled the Zagros six years ago, during the Kurdish uprising at the end of the Persian Gulf War, and his palace—once an opulent edifice of stone and mosaics—has been reduced to a roofed hulk, gutted by the insurgent Kurds, picked over, and abandoned. The tilework has long since been shattered, and the leaded glass windows smashed. The driveway is strewn with ceramic shards. The almost two hundred impoverished Kurds who squat here now were driven from their homes, in nearby Ashawa, when Iraqi troops obliterated their village during the first weeks of the uprising.

Rasa Hassan, 40, a short man with a push-broom mustache, lives here with his wife and nine children. He invites me in out of the cold to have a glass of chai, the tea that Kurds serve in small glasses with a layer of sugar dumped into the bottom. Rasa wears the traditional baggy pants, called şalvar, bound with a waist sash, and a head wrap called a sarbend. The space that Rasa's family occupies was once Saddam's parlor. It is so large that they use only one corner, sitting on rugs spread around a stove fashioned from a twenty-gallon drum and fed with scraps of wood. The stovepipe runs out a hole pickaxed through the concrete wall, and the empty window frames are covered with blankets to trap the warmth. We leave our boots at the edge of the rug and gather around the stove, on pillows. In the dim light, we sit immersed in the smells of wood smoke and Rasa's pungent yellow tobacco. Like most Kurds, he is proud, sometimes to the point of self-absorption. He talks freely and is quick to laugh, playful, and a good host.

Rasa was an Iraqi conscript while this palace was being built, during the ten-year war with Iran, in the 1980s, but he deserted and became a guerrilla with the Kurdish Democratic Party. Before the 1991 uprising, Rasa's flocks of sheep were thriving, and he had saved enough money to build a two-room stone hut. Then the Ashawa Kurds rebelled and Saddam struck back, forcing Rasa and his family to flee. "Saddam attacked Ashawa with tanks and helicopters and foot soldiers," Rasa says, speaking through an interpreter. "We ran to Turkey. The snow was deep, and it took us twelve days. My father was too old, and he lay down and couldn't get up again; so he died. When we got to Turkey, we lived under plastic tarps and slept on the ground. We had nothing."

After several months in a United Nations refugee camp, Rasa learned that the United States had forced Saddam's troops to evacuate Northern Iraq, so he and his family returned home. They found Ashawa leveled. "The Iraqis took everything before they left," Rasa says. "Every blanket, every sheep; then they used tractors to destroy my house and everybody else's. I am a poor man now. Sometimes I find enough work to feed my children, but that is all I have until Allah smiles on me again."

After our second chai, Rasa guides me around the palace to meet his neighbors. On the second floor, in one of Saddam's huge guest rooms, a young man lives with his two older brothers. This man lost an arm fleeing to Turkey, and then he lost his foot last year when he stepped on an Iraqi land mine. No prostheses are available, so he has fashioned a kind of shoe to cover the stump on the end of his leg. He clumps along behind as Rasa and I finish our tour.

"Living here is neither life nor death," Rasa says, standing on the palace's marble steps. "Living here is some kind of other place, somewhere in between. According to the radio, things will get better, but we don't know. Right now it is bad, but we are Kurds, and this is just the way things have been for us."

THERE ARE AT LEAST TWENTY-FIVE MILLION Kurds in the world today. Most of them are living in an area roughly the size of New York and California combined that is divided among the modern nations of Turkey, Iran, Iraq, and Syria. There are more Kurds in this region than Greeks in Greece, Jews in Israel, or Czechs in the Czech Republic. Yet the Kurds are a persecuted minority in all the countries that comprise their war-torn homeland, and during the last thirty years, hundreds of thousands of them have been killed, and millions more have become refugees. In fact, the closest the modern Kurds have come to their own nation is a triangular area at the northernmost tip of Iraq; it touches Syria and is bordered by Turkey on one side, Iran on another, the third cutting across Iraq at the 36th parallel. These roughly twenty thousand square miles are known informally as the Protected Zone, a piece of Iraq from which Saddam's forces have been either entirely or partially excluded, under the verbal threat of American retaliation, since the last days of the Persian Gulf War, in 1991. At the moment, the zone is home to some four million Kurds and controlled in equal portions by two competing political parties, the Kurdish Democratic Party and the Patriotic Union of Kurdistan. The KDP represents the more traditional, rural northern reaches of the Iraqi Zagros; the PUK is affiliated with the urban and intellectual southern areas. The two parties are further divided by clan loyalties, historical grievances, and financial disputes. The zone's three largest cities are Duhok, the commercial capital of the provinces along the Turkish border; Erbil, in the southern part of the zone and one of the oldest cities in history; and Sulaymaniyah, the commercial capital along the Iranian border. Duhok is controlled by the KDP, Sulaymaniyah by the PUK, and Erbil has changed hands three times since the zone was established. It is currently in KDP hands.

The road to Duhok is dotted with aging Volkswagens, which are serviced by men selling gasoline out of jerrycans on their shoulders. The highway carries a steady traffic of oil trucks moving crude from the Iraqi lines outside Erbil to the Turkish border, and around the international trade embargo. Smuggling has always been a Kurdish craft. Commerce flourishes inside Duhok. The smell of fresh bread fills the streets at first light, and the bazaar is jammed with shops. Many residents are poor, but few are destitute; begging is rare, and the markets are full of fruits and walnuts. Even though there has been no fighting in the city for six years, the war is not easy to forget.

In the late 1980s, Iraqi military leaders—who had long chased down, tortured, and killed individual rebels—adopted a policy of executing Kurds en masse, which was called the Anfal campaign. Many of these Kurds came from the Duhok region. From February to August 1988, Kurdish villagers were flushed out onto roads by chemical-weapons attacks. They were rounded up and taken to transit centers, where men aged fifteen to seventy were separated from the women, children, and elderly. The men taken from Duhok have never been seen again. In some areas, thousands of women and children were also killed. According to Human Rights Watch, the Iraqi military murdered more than one hundred thousand Kurds in 1988 alone.

THE TRANSIT CENTER IN DUHOK was Nizarkeh Fort. The Iraqis hauled captive Kurds to Nizarkeh from the mountains in military trucks and unloaded them in the fort's barren courtyard. Among the tortures described by Kurds who survived was the forced ingestion of gasoline, scalding with boiling water, and simple bludgeoning, using sticks, clubs, and tire irons. The fort lay vacant after the 1991 uprising, until 1995, when a relief organization turned it into housing for a dozen families of Kurdish refugees.

Asya Brahim, a forty-three-year-old widow wearing a long skirt and a hand-me-down sweater that she received from a Western relief agency, lives in a second-floor cell that held more than one hundred women during the terror of 1988. Asya shares the room with her two daughters, her son, and her daughter-in-law. They sit the way Kurds do in any room, arranged around its edge, with their backs to the walls. "My husband died when we were young and just getting started," Asya says. "He was *peshmerga* [a volunteer soldier; literally, "ready to die"]. The Iraqis executed him when my son,

Sulliaman, was barely born. Now Sulliaman is *peshmerga* himself."
Her son sits against the opposite wall, his Kalashnikov leaning
in the corner. He is on duty at the front for fifteen days with his
Kurdish Democratic Party unit, and then off fifteen days here at
home with his family. During the September 1996 fighting with the
Patriotic Union of Kurdistan, he saw action in the mountains near
Erbil. Now, he is often stationed on the plain, facing the Iraqi army,
ten miles southeast of town. He earns $12 worth of Iraqi dinars
a month, which is his family's only cash income. They survive on
wheat, lentils, and oil provided by the U.N. World Food Programme.

I ask what it is like living amid so many past horrors. "A boy
downstairs went crazy when he learned about what the Iraqis did
in this place," Sulliaman answers. "The boy thought the wheat his
mother cooked was worms. He thought the water from the faucet
was blood." Like most Kurds, Bhajat, the forty-year-old *peshmerga*
who drives us from Duhok through the mountains to Erbil, calls
the nation they do not have Kurdistan. Bhajat's leg was savaged
by shrapnel ten years ago, when he was an Iraqi conscript in the
war with Iran. He steers high in the seat of his ten-year-old Toyota
Land Cruiser, using his stiff leg on the accelerator. At a truck stop
along the way, Bhajat scoops yogurt and fried egg off his plate with
a piece of doughy, flat bread called *naan* and watches a television
tuned to an Iraqi channel. After a few minutes, he dismisses the TV
with a wave of his *naan* and a diatribe in Kurdish. Our translator,
Raschid, is reluctant to translate. He does so only after cautioning
me that Bhajat is a crude man. "He said," Raschid stammers, "that
all these fucking camel jockeys have countries and the Kurds still
don't have shit."

EXPLAINING WHY THERE IS NO Kurdistan requires a long lesson
in geopolitical history, but one major factor has been the Kurds'
penchant for fighting one another. The Kurds have never carried the
weight in the region that their numbers imply, because they have
never exercised their power as a single people. Rather, they have
been divided by geographical and clan feuds, and their response to

external threats has been piecemeal and often self-defeating: the Kurds who fight the Turks fight the Kurds who fight the Iraqis who fight the Kurds who fight inside Iran. This communal fractiousness is most evident in the Protected Zone, split between the Kurdish Democratic Party and the Patriotic Union of Kurdistan, with one occasionally shooting at the other. For all its good intentions, the Protected Zone is unable to protect the Kurds from themselves.

The most recent fighting between the Kurdish factions took place in Erbil in September 1996. Six months later, Erbil still feels like the frontlines. The road into the KDP-controlled city is dotted with *peshmerga* machine-gun nests. A high-ranking KDP official was killed in a car-bomb explosion not long after my arrival, and many Kurds, so that they can leave on a moment's notice, are selling their furniture, clothes, and jewelry in the bazaar two blocks from the Erbil Tower Hotel.

The Erbil Tower is an eight-story modern concrete pillar visible from all the rooftops of this ancient city. The house rules there require machine guns to be checked at the desk, so there is a constantly evolving stack of Kalashnikovs behind the clerk. The hotel boasts modern elevators, but everyone uses the stairs because the Patriotic Union of Kurdistan still controls the city's power plant and frequently interrupts the electricity. The PUK also controls the reservoir, so the rooms only have running water for brief, widely separated intervals. In the restaurant, the interruption of commerce is evident, even in the peculiar syntax of our Kurdish waiter. When I ask for jam, the waiter answers, "There is jam" (meaning that, indeed, jam still exists somewhere in the universe) "but there is no jam" (meaning that in the immediate moment, the hotel is without it). Yogurt? "There is yogurt," the waiter affirms, "but"—he shrugs—"I am afraid there is no yogurt, either."

After lunch, I sit in the Erbil Tower's lobby, talking with an old Kurdish man. We discuss how much longer the enmity between the parties can last. The old man advises me not to forget how stubborn Kurds are. To illustrate his point, he tells a Kurd joke: "There was a man trying to pound a nail into a wall, but he couldn't make it go in, no matter how hard he struck it. Finally, he threw down his hammer in disgust, went around the wall, and found a Kurd leaning his head against the other side." The old Kurd almost falls off the couch laughing at the punchline, and he is still chuckling when I leave a few minutes later.

SAFE FROM IRAQ, AT LEAST until U.S. interest wanes, the Protected Zone has no protection from Turkey. The Turks are the Americans' longest-standing ally in the region, and the U.S. has never publicly criticized the Turks' treatment of the Kurds, even when it has been as brutal as the Iraqis'. Since the inception of the Protected Zone, the Turks have regularly crossed the border into Iraq to attack Turkey's own Kurdish rebels, led by the Kurdistan Workers' Party, known as the PKK. For years, the PKK has called for turning southeast Turkey, where some ten million Kurds live, into a separate Kurdish nation. (It has, however, recently shown signs that it is willing to accept a negotiated settlement that maintains Kurdish rights.) The PKK guerrillas use the Iraqi border in the Zagros as a staging area for their assaults inside Turkey, and the Turkish army pursues the PKK at will.

One of the Turks' Iraqi battlegrounds has been Kani Masi village, a settlement close to the Turkish border that is marked by one hundred huts built around an Assyrian Christian church. We are shown around by Zayiad Michel, the master of the local school, which until recently taught children up to the third grade. "When the Turks were here last," Zayiad says, "every night was lit up by muzzle flashes and tracer bullets from their fighting with the PKK. Our school is now closed because the classrooms are full of people from the villages that the Turks attacked. We have Kurds from Tranish who were attacked by helicopters, Kurds from Beduha, where cannons killed seven children and eight mules, and Kurds from Betkar, where the Turks burned the almond orchards."

"What do the Kurds of Kani Masi want?" I ask.

"Peace," Zayiad says.

The schoolmaster's wish stands no chance of coming true. Instead, in early May, two months after our visit, the Turks crossed the border at Zachoe, with 350 tanks and 50,000 motorized troops, and struck east into the Iraqi Protected Zone. The Turks claim to have killed some 960 PKK guerrillas during the first month of their occupation; Kani Masi was one of the Kurdish villages that disappeared behind Turkish lines.

There is no loose talk about Kurdistan inside Turkey. Simply using the word is a violation of Turkish law, as is flying the traditional Kurdish flag or referring to people by their Kurdish names. Since 1984, the PKK has fielded Kurdish guerrillas against this suppression, and it has grown to some 15,000 troops, which operate largely from mountain redoubts in southeastern Turkey. The Turks deploy an army of around 350,000 against them, along with a corps of about 60,000 dragooned Kurdish irregulars. These irregulars are recruited from the rural Kurdish villages in the war zone. The men of each village are offered the opportunity to join the Turks' force and fight the PKK. The Turks then destroy those villages that refuse. According to Human Rights Watch, at least 2,685 Kurdish villages inside Turkey have been completely or partially depopulated since fighting with the PKK began, and most of the destruction has occurred in the past five years.

I first encounter the Turks' war in Atroosh Camp, a haven for some 12,000 Kurdish refugees from Turkey who fled across the border into the Iraqi Protected Zone and now live in a sea of tents spread across a valley below the road from Duhok to Erbil. The U.N. is now closing the camp in response to Turkish complaints about PKK recruitment there. Trucks have arrived to haul the worldly possessions of the Kurds who are leaving today. The vehicles are piled high with mattresses, bedding, cooking pots, and live chickens strung up by their feet so that they can't fly off. Nearby, a group of Turkish Kurds sit barefoot around the perimeter of a white canvas tent. They serve chai and recount what happened when the Turkish army visited their village, Hellal, in 1993.

The Turks gathered all the men and asked who wanted to join the Village Guards and help the Turkish army protect Hellal from the Kurdistan Workers' Party. When no one volunteered, one villager was thrown under the tracks of a tank and run over, and two others were shot in the doorway of their houses. Next, the Turkish artillery started random bombardments. When the soldiers returned again, they killed five brothers from one family, tied their bodies to the bumper of a truck, and dragged them back and forth in front of their family's house. One mother had a son kidnapped, and when his corpse was returned the next day, a hand had been cut off. Two of her remaining sons were shot to death in front of her.

Eventually, the villagers fled for Iraq. The journey took seven days, and they were bombed and strafed by Turkish aircraft all the way to the border. I ask one woman if she will ever go back to Turkey. She is fifty-five, with henna stains on her fingertips, and she makes no attempt to hide her fury. "Turkey?" she wails. "I would bury my husband and children before I would ever go back there. Never. I would set fire to myself first."

PERSECUTED AT HOME, KURDS flee to Baghdad, Istanbul, Tehran, and Damascus. They flee to Beirut and to Athens and to Nashville, Tennessee. At least five million Kurds live outside their native countries. The preferred destinations are Germany and Sweden. There are some six hundred thousand expatriate Kurds in Germany, most of whom arrived during the West German boom, thirty years ago, when the Germans were eager to import labor. There is no such importation going on now, and migration to Germany is arduous. Only those with resources can try. Even then, some make it and some don't.

Forty-six Kurds who did not are being held by the Republic of Lithuania in the Pabradė Foreigners Registration Centre, among the flat conifer forests an hour outside Vilnius. These people are officially stateless, since all of them were traveling on forged documents, and they remain in legal limbo. The Pabradė FRC is a former Soviet tank base that was reclaimed as an immigration prison last January. I visit two days before the Kurdish holiday of Nowruz, which celebrates a mythic Kurdish liberation.

Kamal Hussein Maloud, 35, acts as the Kurds' spokesman. He fled, in June 1996 from Duhok, in the Protected Zone. He had been a *peshmerga* and a rising young officer in the Kurdish Democratic Party. Fluent in English, he acted as a KDP press liaison for foreign journalists, but, finally, he decided to flee the war and set out for Germany. His twenty-six-year-old brother-in-law insisted on coming with him, so they sold their possessions and bought stolen Iraqi passports. Leaving his wife and children with his father-in-law, Kamal and his brother-in-law crossed into Turkey on ten-day visas, issued at a border crossing, then rode the bus from the border all the way to Istanbul, where they made contact with a Kurdish middleman who sold them visas for Ukraine, the only country between the Bosporus strait and Berlin that would accept their Iraqi papers. The plane ride to Kiev, Ukraine, was Kamal's first ever.

In Ukraine, Kamal contacted a Kurdish smuggler named Salah, who agreed to include them in a group of ten people he planned to transport to Germany, for $3,500 a piece. The plan was to cross into neighboring Belarus by van, then continue across Poland to Germany, shepherded on the journey by a Russian on Salah's payroll. At the Polish border, the Russian took them on foot through the woods, where, in a matter of minutes, the Polish border police tracked them down with dogs, arrested them, and turned them over to the Belarus authorities. The Belarus border patrol locked them in a windowless cell for ten days, then put them on a train to Moscow.

In Moscow, Kamal says, the group was taken in by a fellow Kurd, who contacted Salah in Minsk, Belarus. Salah sent them money to travel back to Belarus to try again, since the Russia-Belarus border required no papers to cross. This time, Salah had a new plan. There would be forty-six Kurds making the next attempt, including five women and nine children. Salah hired a new Russian, and he led the Kurds on a five-hour march through the forest and across the Lithuanian border. Next, they were carried by bus to the Polish border. They planned to cross into Poland at night, so they waited, in a shed previously occupied by pigs, for dark to fall. But suddenly, in an explosion of searchlights, the door crashed in, a dozen armed men stormed into the shed, and someone shouted, "You're under arrest!" in Lithuanian, a language none of the Kurds understood.

At the Pabradė Foreigners Registration Centre, where the Kurds have been held for almost a year, the men share the second floor of a shabby brick barracks with a group of Afghan prisoners. They sleep on bunks in a single large room heated by steam pipes, and they have cleared one corner for a mosque, where prayers are conducted five times a day. The bathroom includes a dozen sinks and squat toilets, half of which are stopped up. The Kurds smoke whatever cigarettes they can afford. Relatives occasionally wire money to the local Western Union, but otherwise the prisoners are all broke. The women and children live in a separate building, where they sleep in double beds. All of them had to leave their husbands and either all or some of their children behind when they fled. Three of the women are close to catatonic. Another, Nadia Tahir, is nearly hysterical. She breaks down sobbing as she talks about her flight from Baghdad, where her Kurdish husband had been an Iraqi military officer and was discovered spying for the Kurds. He fled and told her to follow, so she left her children behind with in-laws and went. Nadia never found him. While looking at her children's picture, she wails, once so hard that she falls from her chair. "We have jumped from the oven into the lime kiln," she says. "What are we to do?"

This, of course, is the Kurdish question without an answer. Still, it is Nowruz, and when the holiday begins, even the Kurds in the Pabradė Centre celebrate. The Nowruz myth tells of the overthrow of an evil tyrant who once ruled the Kurds. The blacksmith who finally slew the tyrant king passed the news of the regicide to the rest of Kurdistan by lighting signal fires at night. So, to mark the first night of Nowruz, Kurds light bonfires. When informed of this, the center's administration grants permission for the Kurds here to do likewise, in the yard where the Lithuanian guards normally train. Their blaze is a few discarded beams and a truck tire, stacked and ignited with gasoline. As the fire gains hold, the Kurds huddle near it in the frigid dark, absorbing its warmth, until finally they form lines and begin to clap and dance a Kurd step: right forward, right back, right across left, side step, and repeat. The lines shift and scissor to the music of the claps—left forward, left back, left across right, side step, and repeat. Black smoke swarms off the flaming tire, snow falls in large white clots, and the Kurds dance until midnight, trying their best not to worry about what happens next.

[*Rolling Stone*, October 16, 1997]

My Redwood Confession

[ME AND MY TREE]

I am seventy-one years old, a fourth-generation Californian. As my life winds down, one of the companions I am most grateful to have had happens to be a tree, odd as that may seem.

It is not just any old tree but a very particular species, to be exact: *Sequoia sempervirens*, the coastal redwood, the tallest of all, found only within forty miles of the Pacific Ocean along the California coast, from south of Monterey Bay all the way north across the Oregon border, colonizing damp creases in the landscape, feeding off the winter rain that falls in sheets and the slabs of summer fog that make landfall every afternoon. It crowds the riverbanks of the Eel, the Navarro, the Russian, the Mattole, the Mad, and the Smith Rivers, as well as all the lesser watercourses that drain into them. If left uncut and to its own devices, this tree will grow as tall as 370 feet, longer than a football field, and almost thirty feet thick. And with a natural life span well beyond a thousand years, a *Sequoia sempervirens* is not even considered an adult until it reaches the age of four hundred.

That said, the only redwoods that remain unlogged and able to pursue adulthood these days are crowded inside one of some ninety Northern California parks devoted to the old-growth redwood's fragmentary preservation. These refuges collectively cover only a fraction of the coastal redwood's native range, but on all sides of those enclaves, where once their trunks grew, every logged redwood stump sprouts a new tree—hence the name *sempervirens*, "always living."

In Humboldt, Mendocino, and Del Norte Counties, where the forest is its thickest and much of it is controlled by the lumber industry, second-, third-, and fourth-cut redwoods still swarm up and over ridges as far as you can see, the last diminished fragment of a sixty-million-year-old primeval forest that dominated much of North America, Europe, and Asia. As the logging of *Sequoia sempervirens* has played out over the last one hundred and fifty years, each successive cut has been of a tree even smaller than the one before, some impatiently logged off when not yet a foot thick, mere newborns in light of their species' genetic blueprint—the result a once ancient forest now trapped in perpetual infancy.

Sempervirens are by design, of course, far grander than that. When mature and well stocked with four-hundred-year-olds, redwood groves are typically canopied, casting the forest floor in perpetual shade and capturing an airy, cathedral emptiness between the bottom and the top. That enormous space—with patches of light filtering through its ceiling and drifting earthward like leaves on a stream—explains why a visit to an old-growth redwood grove, even in a park, is often considered a spiritual experience of the first order.

And I take no exception to that description. Indeed, I have come to love this tree. I have bonded with it, we have been through much together, and it has cast an inspirational shadow on the last half of my life. Our relationship turned into something far more profound than the usual human-to-plant interaction, with us eventually connecting, I believe, as just one being to another, without intermediation. My confessed communion with this tree seems anthropomorphic, I suppose, but it is no less real to me for seeming so. It is a story I have never revealed previously, intimidated by the potential disbelief of others and my own embarrassment, but I will tell this tale now: Speaking without saying a word, *Sequoia sempervirens* reached out to me, saw me through much difficulty, and has hovered over my life like a totem right up to this day, often guiding me when I needed it most and teaching me much about myself that I might never have learned otherwise.

But it did not start out that way. Far from it.

I first met *Sequoia sempervirens* not as a fellow being or even as a tree but as lumber sold by the board foot. Our introduction to each other took place behind my maternal grandparents' house on Fresno's McKenzie Avenue, in my Grandpa Jensen's rundown shop on the second floor over the storage room next to the garage that backed up on the alley. The fifties had just begun, my dad had just finished law school on the G.I. Bill, and I was on the verge of kindergarten. The workshop was lit by a single overhead bulb and was full of shadows, sawdust, and the smell of lubricating oil. Grandpa Jensen was a master woodworker at the Fresno Planing Mill and was missing part of a forefinger from an accident with a band saw when he was a young man. Over the years, he had accumulated pieces of wood he found "interesting," storing them in the rafters above his table saw and lathe. The redwood plank Grandpa revealed to me that first time was an inch thick, two feet wide, and eight feet long. Dust billowed throughout the shop as he fetched the plank and brushed it off. He made it very clear that this was no ordinary board he was showing me. He pointed out the grain and how tight and straight it was, how the growth rings pressed together, which meant it had been sawed from a very, very, very old tree. In my memory, the plank is scarlet and massive and I am small and awestruck by the scene. Grandpa claimed that he could leave that red board outside for the next twenty years and it would never rot. There was no wood like redwood, he told me. Orange light was leaking in the shop window, dust was still swirling. He also told me that there wouldn't be any boards left like that one when I got to be his age, and he turned out to be right.

I as yet, however, had no clue that *Sequoia sempervirens* would ever be more to me than just a special grade of lumber, much less that it would end up lodged so close to my heart.

[WOOD GETS PERSONAL]

Like all Northern Californians, redwood has been white noise in my life, always present in the background—so much so that it goes unaccounted for, just Muzak in our collective elevator.

Without us having to pay much if any attention to it, there is redwood everywhere here, even when there are no trees: we can buy a bag of Redwood Burgers from the Redwood Drive-In's drive-through window; fix our exhaust pipe at Redwood Muffler; acquire a second mortgage from the Redwood Credit Union; get down and dirty over cocktails at the Redwood Lounge; break the speed limit along the Redwood Highway; watch movies at the Redwood Theatre; graduate from Redwood High School or Redwood Middle School or Redwood Elementary School or Redwood Preschool, or even Redwood Daycare, not to mention College of the Redwoods; we can order linguini at the Redwood Café; mess around in the afternoon on the day rate at the Redwood Motel; buy potting soil from the Redwood Garden Center and Nursery; wash our cars at Redwood In-And-Out Car Wash; get our timepieces fixed at the Redwood Jewelry Emporium; fill our prescriptions at the Redwood Pharmacy; clean our drains with Redwood Roto-Rooter; and of course buy our redwood at Redwood Lumber.

The permutations have become endless: Redwood Dairy, Redwood Partners, Redwood Nursing Home, Redwood Construction, Redwood Used Cars, Redwood Cemetery, Redwood Veterinary Hospital, Redwood Answering Service, Redwood Roofing, Redwood Bicycle Shop, Redwood Video Rentals, Redwood Hair Salon, Redwood Steam Cleaning, and Redwood Etc., etc.

I moved from Fresno to the Bay Area, where redwoods are native, to attend a university whose mascot is a tree and whose logo is the profile of a *Sequoia sempervirens*, though it took me years to pay the silhouette of that tree much due. My daughter went to a high school that had a *sempervirens* on its logo as well. And we were just two of millions of Californians whose lives pass under a forest of such redwood shapes to this day.

By the time I was born, in 1946, the coastal redwood had already provided an underpinning to the entire region. Literally. It was felled so San Francisco, Alameda, San Mateo, Santa Clara, Contra Costa, Marin, Sonoma, and Solano Counties could build and expand. Indeed, from the redwood's perspective, the Bay Area amounts to a massive *sempervirens* graveyard. I have been personally involved in remodeling three Bay Area houses over my lifetime, and each had been originally framed in studs cut from the same magnificent tight-grained ancient scarlet wood that my grandfather had treasured for me in his workshop, those boards nailed in place back in the days when such spectacular redwood seemed plentiful enough to be profligate within even the most common constructions, including forms for pouring concrete. This urban growth brought a Timber Rush to the Bay Area, fed at first by the nearby primeval forests and then, once all the easily available virgin first forest had been felled, reaching all the way to the Oregon border, where proximity to ancient dead redwood has become almost universal along the western slope of the Coast Range. Millions of Northern Californians are exposed to long-since-cut *Sequoia sempervirens* every day, and even if they don't know it, they are absorbing the species' energy—and even its perspective—through physical immersion, its chopped and sawed heartwood radiating behind our sheetrock and providing a seemingly everlasting presence.

Even so, few of us Californians notice, much less pursue, our connection to this tree any further than that. But I did. I took it a lot further. The truth is, out of the blue, it got personal for me, very personal, and things between myself and this species took on an intimate character that I would never have thought possible.

The precipitating event was my purchase of Number 841, the house I have lived in for the last thirty-four years. Stepping down a Marin County slope, just fifteen minutes by automobile from San Francisco, it is three miles as the crow flies from the Muir Woods National Monument and right next door to the Golden Gate National Recreation Area. Two of my new house's public rooms were lined with old-growth redwood, long since painted over, and most of its old walls were framed with the same. And just a foot away from the right front corner of its roof stood the trunk of the redwood that was about to become my companion in a sudden moment of epiphany, awakening me to the Presence of *sempervirens*, being to being, from then on out.

I named that redwood in front of my new home "Tree."

Judging by its size, I guess Tree had been growing for some thirty years when the original ranch house that became Number

841 was constructed on the slopes of Mount Tamalpais in 1932. By the time I bought 841 in 1984, Tree's trunk, now some 150 feet tall and 7 feet thick at its base, was almost rubbing the front lip of the roof, a spacing no modern building department would ever have permitted, but now happily grandfathered in. Tree's branches hovered over three-quarters of the top floor, and the wired glass ceiling in the dining room allowed me to look right up its shaft to where the tip foreshortened into emptiness and swayed in the gusts blowing off the Pacific onto the foot of Coyote Ridge.

I was led to my connection with Tree by trust as well as proximity. You see, to live in Number 841, right next to this considerable redwood, was to be at Tree's mercy. Should for any reason Tree come down, even at such an immature size—from the redwood perspective—the house and most everything in it would be crushed. Nothing short of solid granite can deflect a *sempervirens* in the grip of gravity. Once I accepted that reality, it was only a small step further to make Tree seem a benign presence just for continuing to stand up straight. I took that approach with Tree immediately. It and I obviously had to be on the same side for both of our sakes.

I introduced myself to my new redwood while the movers were unloading their tractor trailer in the driveway. I had been packing boxes at our old house down the Peninsula for the last week, often twelve hours a day, and was already fried—I had put a dent in my new minivan, and my back felt like leftover trench warfare—and our moving day was only half done. Looking for a momentary respite, I ducked behind Tree, out of view. My wife Lacey and I had just mortgaged ourselves up to our eyebrows even though Number 841 was considered an "old white elephant": vacant for two years, with squirrels living in the dining room and a septic tank that leaked onto the hillside, not to mention the immense tree towering over it like a guillotine. The real estate agent didn't even want to show it to us, and the bank that owned it acted as if they were doing us a favor by even considering our bid. So by the time we completed four weeks of negotiations and reached moving day, I was feeling overrun and looking for an ally.

And in that moment I leaned on Tree, leading with the crown of my head.

And right then I must have slipped through some spiritual portal into this redwood's force field, because I immediately felt a flow between us that carried my mind on the run straight into epiphany. I suppose it was a vision of sorts. This *sempervirens* was so big, with such incredible purchase on the earth, that it spoke to me and my need in a primal language of place. And, to my stunned surprise, I listened. The sensation resembled a hum, only it was silent, a three-dimensional vibration unlike anything I had ever experienced. It was accompanied by an abiding sense of safety. In that moment, Tree made me feel like I was connected all the way to the middle of the planet. Then I went into some kind of trance state in which my fatigue evaporated and I lost track of time. I felt reassured all over.

After perhaps three minutes, I stepped away from the redwood and receded back into the world of words, somewhat dazed but smiling like a crocodile. I felt like I had been welcomed, though I had no idea how what had just happened between myself and the tree had actually happened.

"Hey, Tree," I said.

Tree, however, made no more response, at least for the moment.

But that was the beginning between us.

From here on, I would search out Tree's hum at critical moments when I needed redwood mojo to help me cope, or understand, or both, and sometimes Tree would answer.

Which is why I'm so grateful still.

[THE THEORY OF PRESENCE]

While I obviously mean to make much of the extraordinary link that joined Tree and me, I don't mean to present my *sempervirens* as simply a large paranormal stick transmitting on an altogether different wavelength. Tree also played a rich and full role as a major participant in the ordinary daily life of our front yard: A rope swing was anchored to Tree's lowest branch, some twenty feet off the ground, and my children and their friends spent hours swinging back and forth, sometimes drifting sideways and fending off Tree's trunk with their feet, launching themselves into a spin. Two of our friends got married under Tree. Three times a year, I clipped off the four-foot bush of suckers that sprouted over and over out of a large knot at Tree's base, intent on intervening before any of those suckers could *sempervirens* their way into being a Tree themselves. That same cluster of fledgling would-be-tree redwood served as one of our favorite locations to hide Easter eggs. I hired a climber to thin out Tree's limbs to avoid the sail effect in high winds and regularly walked around Tree during rainy season looking for cracks in the earth that might indicate instability, but I never found any. In the autumn, my redwood shed copious amounts of brown needles, in several waves, and I gathered them with my rake year after year, swearing amazement that any plant could produce so much for me to rake, which led to me imploring Tree to "lighten the fuck up." One year, I had to rebuild a chunk of the poured concrete front porch that Tree had knuckled with one of its roots. During a half dozen different winters, at least one of Tree's enormous limbs broke loose in the high wind and came tumbling, twice clipping the front corner of the roof and doing damage, and twice splintering the handrail on the stairs leading down to the garage. Falling limbs also took out a small stretch of fence running along the driveway.

Among Tree's lower branches, a host of nuthatches nests every year, sweeping down on our bird feeder in squadrons. There, they hang upside down and stuff themselves. Tree's higher branches also provide a roost for the juvenile red-tailed hawk that inevitably appears for a month in the late summer, making its first stop after being kicked out of its parental nest and forced to forage for itself. And Tree serves as a freeway for the gray and red squirrels accessing the roof. Raccoons have been spotted about halfway up on several occasions. Once a hive of wasps constructed a mud nest at the very tip of one of Tree's longest low limbs, terrorizing the front yard, and I had to hire a guy to drive up from Monterey to take down the nest. He walked out on Tree's limb until he got within range with a long stick, then dislodged the nest so it plunged through the air into a garbage can on the ground, held by his assistant, who immediately clapped a lid on the can so none of the furious wasps could escape.

Tree would have been a member of my family had there been nothing but these homespun encounters between us. But, of course, there was much more, and it was out of the ordinary, to say the least.

Looking back on my accumulated years of fragmentary communion with Tree—a moment here and a moment there, me always wondering what was going on while the incidents transpired, looking for the redwood to elevate me over the hurdle I was facing—I have developed a theory about what made our relationship possible: It seems to me that Presence, the energy pattern that living things displace in the way they occupy their space, is itself a language capable of communication with another Presence, despite existing in, in effect, a separate dimension in which words themselves had no immediate traction. Such an interchange is conditional on both Presences being awake to the moment and occupying the same present tense, witness to both themselves and the other—all internal energy channeled to their respective corporeal postures and their mutual intersection, Thought turned off, Being to the max. My exhaustion had put me in just such an available posture when Tree and I first engaged, and over the years that followed, I learned by trial and error that my distress seemed to trigger the flow of vibration between me and my tree. In such a state, I was often hurt and lost to the point that I was more present than ever, events having crowded me into a closet of pain or despair, contracting my focus to only the most immediate sensations, excluding past or future through total immersion in the Now, by force of circumstance if not spiritual mastery. As I observed it, Tree seemed to have little interest in the small shit of my life and ignored such situations wholesale. But when big and trying times arrived on my doorstep and I brought them to it, Tree was ready to engage them, and me. Afterward, I would search out words into which to translate the hum for memory's sake.

In those encounters with Tree, I usually stood close by Tree's trunk, closing my eyes and locating its Presence in the air that drifted across my shoulders. When I finally sensed that the redwood was There with a capital T, I touched the trunk and, if it was to be, the hum of *sempervirens* energy would jump down my arm and into my heart, shaped and targeted to the dilemma plaguing me, a message to be experienced rather than described or evoked.

When my dog Fat Albert died, old and sick, my first loss since moving to Number 841, Tree's hum carried me back to Albert's younger days, when he had ruled our block down the Peninsula. Then Tree revealed a mental path to an Albert who still lived on inside me and would never disappear until I did. The encounter lasted only a minute but seemed timeless. And I felt whole and full of Albert after it was over.

When my health collapsed following a six-month run of working sixteen-hour days, seven days a week in order to meet a publisher's deadline, then instantly followed by three more grueling months starting up another project and commuting back and forth to New York, I finally threw myself at the foot of Tree. Some days, I barely had the strength to stand, but the doctors I consulted could find no obvious physical reason for my weakness. When I curled up against the redwood, my eyes closed, I felt as though I was being cradled and rocked as soon as I touched its bark, and my weakness immediately devolved into of a wave of complete helplessness. Then the hum amplified and I could no longer distinguish myself from Tree's mighty purchase on the earth beneath me, and a current of strength flowed out of the ground, carried on the hum, and into my belly. My body absorbed it like a dry sponge. And while that was going on, I was reminded of my own resourcefulness. I found myself in the dirt under Tree fifteen minutes after I had started. Two weeks later, I had recouped the physical wherewithal to return to work.

Tree was also there for the worst moment of my professional career. After traveling back and forth to New York over three years, working as the authorized biographer of a Manhattan media tycoon and almost burning myself out in the process, the whole arrangement came a cropper when the tycoon's lawyers killed my project. I was devastated at having been used as shabbily as I had, and for weeks I refused to be consoled, to the point of being a genuine pain in the ass to everyone who came in contact with me, myself included. I spent weeks hunkered down in my office, feeling very sorry for myself and grinding my teeth. When I finally turned to Tree, the *sempervirens* hummed open my clenched hands and allowed me to exhale. I stood for almost an hour at its base, my eyes closed, slowly realizing that if I didn't separate myself from my anger and dial back my self-pity, I would blow up my life and my family out of sheer petulance. With that, I felt myself tumbling head over heels until Tree's hum snatched me out of the air. From there on, the *sempervirens* just soothed me over and over, like a hand petting a cat. And at the end of the hour, I felt released from my hurt. Tree's hum seemed to have suctioned all the bile out of me.

A year later, I was back to Tree as I tried to quit smoking after twenty-five years as a three-pack-a-day tobacco addict. For two weeks running, as my system struggled to detoxify, I started each day by taking to the *sempervirens* in the front yard the morning tremors that made me rattle like an old truck on a bad road. I would touch with my open palms, trying to remain still, sensing calm flowing my way against much resistance, and feeling the urge to suck smoke into my lungs dissipate sufficiently to proceed with the rest of my day. I have never lit up a cigarette since.

My special connection to Tree was confirmed forever three years after that, in the immediate aftermath of the greatest loss of my life. I spent the last two of those years nursing my wife Lacey through a painful struggle with breast cancer that ended with her in Intensive Care, on a breathing machine, and me petitioning to have her removed so she could die on her own terms. As prescribed for Buddhists, her body was laid out in our front room, some ten yards from Tree, and then cremated. The day after, I walked out to Tree. For the previous two years, I had never allowed myself to face up to my helplessness in the situation, a way of clinging to the notion that I was supposed to save her and could somehow find a way to do so by trying even harder than I already had. I dropped into an emotional free fall now that no such rescue was possible. I felt more empty and spent than I had ever felt. But I could never bring myself to cry. Then, at last, I pressed my body against Tree, chest to bark, and grabbed it with my arms spread in a hug. And it was as if a door had blown open in a stiff breeze. Tears gushed where before none would. Sobs engulfed me and I was sure Tree must have been crying too.

[SEVEN REDWOOD VIRTUES]

I have to admit that my strange companionship with Tree not only opened my heart and transformed my perspective of the species *Sequoia sempervirens,* but it also changed how I viewed my own *Homo sapiens* species as well. Indeed, I have come to realize that this very, very large plant—depicted on postcards, embossed on ashtrays, and commonly used by humans to construct patio decks and garden planters—is in truth a repository of virtues not only essential to *sempervirens* but necessary to the rejuvenation and eventual survival of modern humanity as well. There is much we need to know that *sempervirens* might teach us. That is a lot to lay off on a tree, even one so very large, but consider the species as a role model:

Redwoods take very good care of themselves. Indeed, self-reliance is embedded in the *sempervirens* gene pool. Its red flesh is resistant to insects, fungal infections, and rot. Its outer bark, sometimes more than a foot thick, is a fire inhibitor. It has adapted to the resource of drippy coastal fog by growing water receptors in its foliage, enabling it to nourish itself not just through its roots but through its crown as well. It controls its birth rate by generating a toxicity in the ground around it that limits the fertility of the seeds it spews out in tiny cones. Left alone, *Sequoia sempervirens* is a very efficient, self-contained organism for propagating life as it has known it. In contrast, *Homo sapiens,* rather than self-nurturing, are instead dependent on a steadily expanding social and commercial infrastructure to survive; we are often emotionally helpless when stripped of our technological exoskeletons, and our sustainability without the intervention of elaborate external apparatuses is suspect at best. This, of course, bids serious ill for *Homo sapiens* as our complex systems begin to crumble under the weight of our accumulated carbon exhaust. We always need something else to give us a leg up and cover our blind spots lest we unravel. That may be unavoidable, at least to a degree, but such dependency on Stuff is also debilitating and stands out as the proverbial canary in the mineshaft of human existence. And it offers us a good reason to act more like a tree, odd as that may seem.

Redwood is quiet. Human life is increasingly framed in clatter and cacophony at every turn, generating disorientation, delusion, and discord. Our noise never ceases. It amps up the speed of everything it touches and contributes mightily to our failure to listen to each other or to ourselves, thereby diminishing both our intellectual understanding and our spiritual grasp. It ensures that we are, in effect, never alone and never still. And without the experience of being alone and still, we short ourselves of insight, self-knowledge, and, ultimately, wisdom. A grove of *sempervirens*, however, is still and soundless, Quiet writ large, so silent that it amounts to its own kind of loud. Standing motionless under a redwood canopy, I found the quiet tangible, as though I could reach out and shake its hand. The virtue in that experience is apparent to those who have had it. Such quiet throws us back on our own inner workings, the first step toward learning who we are or who we need to be, or both.

Redwood is long-term. As a species, modern *Homo sapiens* have trouble thinking beyond the remainder of the day, much less into the next week; we are short-term. Our attention spans are shorter still, ruled by the immediate gratification of text messages, instant mashed potatoes, and galvanic response that leave us living in the Now in the most narrow and debilitating version of such a posture. The thought of planning or acting over the horizon in the interest of generations yet to come is largely political and social anathema. And that contortion may very well prove our undoing. Not surprisingly, the result of such truncated vision is a legacy of Shortsightedness, Thoughtless Consumption, and Institutionalized Selfishness, eventually to be overrun by Bills Come Due and Chickens Come Home to Roost. *Sempervirens*, however, operates in cycles hundreds of years long. Its today is derived from centuries of yesterdays and projected into centuries of tomorrows. Typically, the coastal redwood acts in pursuit of outcomes in the next millennia as a matter of course. Its clock has no second hand, or minute hand either. It flows with time rather than conquering, consuming, and then disposing of it hour by hour. There are no transients in a redwood grove; every tree is in it for the long haul. Yet among *Homo sapiens*, everyone seems to be just passing through, with allegiance to the immediate moment and only the immediate moment.

Redwood is a community. From a human-design standpoint, questions are sometimes raised about the *sempervirens*'s root system because it lacks a deep taproot to support its enormous height. Indeed, its roots are shallow and widespread, a "deficiency" for which it compensates with mutual assistance. Its shallow roots reach out to wrap around and join with those of the surrounding trees, creating a network of shared strength and stability to empower each and all to resist the leverage of winds that might otherwise pose a mortal threat. We *sapiens*, on the other hand, have pursued an obsession with singularity and individualism to a point that our obsession often denies us access to the mutuality that is a critical, if often ignored or defiled, ingredient in the human possibility. Without such community, we suffer through loneliness, abandonment, hopelessness, and anomie, for which the only antidote is access to each other. We also separate our fates and eliminate our pooling of resources so that we are always afflicted with haves and have-nots, as well as with the nightmare of scarcity. There are circumstances in which togetherness and sharing are required above all else and, having nurtured privatization to the exclusion of tenancy in common, we find ourselves ill equipped to realize that aspect of our humanity when we need it most. Compassion is our highest human calling, but we cannot pursue it without membership in a larger circle, and so, by default, we end up trapped in our lesser selves.

Redwood is patient. Sometimes positive outcomes require us to simply wait. Yet tolerance of such waiting has become a casualty in the pace of modern civilization and *sapiens*' growing insistence on forcing the issue rather than allowing it to ripen into the opportune. We are in a constant hurry, anxious to get on to whatever is supposed to be next, occupying a mental space only a half step short of panic when faced with inaction or stymied in our pursuit of seemingly forward motion, epitomized by our road rage at the traffic jam, always inclined to drop what we are doing and try a different approach on the promise of immediate resolution, no matter how flimsy. *Sempervirens*, on the other hand, waits. In a redwood grove, where among the cluster of trees each struggles to find a patch of sunlight under the canopy, a young tree may spend decades the size of a seedling until an old tree nearby dies and topples, at last leaving a sunny open space overhead for the patient seedling to fill, the potential of growth now available to it in the nurturing light, its time having finally arrived. It often seems to me that a strong dose of such patience would cure half our modern ills.

Redwood knows where it came from. Under a *Sequoia sempervirens* canopy, the air is heavy with the time that preceded, and I feel the years in that air on my skin like I feel the weather, our planetary timeline present at every turn. Not only are many of the trees ancient in their own right but the species itself provides a long genetic pathway back through centuries to a common memory of which we can partake in its company. Under *sempervirens*'s shadow, I feel membership in the accumulation of time and experience that is the underpinning of wisdom, digesting what brought us so far and identifying the dead ends and shortfalls discarded along the way. Meanwhile, our human history, subject to the limits of our own consciousness, is increasingly obscured by our disinterest, narcissism, ignorance, and shriveled attention span. Indeed, most modernized *sapiens* have lost track of events more than a decade behind us, effectively orphaned from themselves and their ancestry. We cannot learn because we are so busy forgetting. Who we are is not just a manufacture of the moment, it is an inheritance that needs to be embraced or lost. And it seems we have chosen to lose it, having convinced ourselves that we somehow started with a blank slate. Like all species, however, we start where those before us left off, even if we pretend otherwise.

Redwood is calm. This is the redwood's companion virtue to Quiet. Under the *sempervirens* canopy there is none of the seething energy and incessant activity associated with tropical rainforests, full of birds and monkeys and rodents of every description in perpetual motion. Redwood groves, on the other hand, are flat water. A few sea birds leave the canopy in the morning and return as the sun sets, but otherwise the old-growth redwood forest feels unoccupied, undisturbed, and largely devoid of internal pressure. To those experiencing it, it seems a world at rest. This, again, stands in marked contrast to the world of *Homo sapiens*, where hysteria and modernity quite often go hand in hand. In our human world, anxiety has become a constant, along with obsession, fixation, tension, and the delusion that accompanies all things hyper. Everything and everyone is unsettled and becoming more so. Worry is ubiquitous, and we're all hooked on the internal uneasiness that threatens everything with disturbance and disruption. In the human world, calm is ordinarily noticeable only in its absence—except under the redwood canopy, where frantic is forever out of place and equanimity is broadcast from tree to tree to tree. Without it, we are working overtime and driving ourselves crazy at every opportunity.

[THE REDWOOD MASSACRE]

In addition to experiencing *Sequoia sempervirens* as a spiritual and emotional resource, I have also come to identify it as a victim that endured an incalculable loss at the hands of *Homo sapiens*— indeed, a holocaust from the redwood perspective—in which the entire species was targeted in a one-sided war and forced to run a gauntlet of misery over the course of a century and a half in which its historic identity was culled almost to its vanishing point. In 1850, just before the assault on the ancient redwood forest began in earnest, California was host to more than two million acres of full-fledged old-growth primeval *sempervirens* forest, groves dotted with hundred-year-old juveniles, four-hundred-year-old adults, and thousand-year-old-elders grouped around an inner cathedral catacomb, direct descendants in a line of trees that had never been cut or sawed or felled in sixty million years, their woodland floor instead littered with gigantic fallen trunks, dead of old age, who had sprouted around the time the New Testament was being written, or even earlier. Then commenced some hundred and fifty years of cutting, sawing, and felling old-growth coastal redwood following the discovery of gold in the Sacramento watershed and California's almost immediate induction as the thirty-first state in the union. And after those hundred and fifty years, a little more than a hundred thousand acres of virgin forest remained, divided among scattered patches around the North Coast, under the protection of the state and federal governments, and sheltered by the insistent concern of generations of Good Samaritans intent on saving the species from extinction.

Looking over Tree's proverbial shoulder at those hundred and fifty years, it now appears to have been a massacre of epic proportions, despite the efforts to stop it.

Typically, this scourge's arrival in an old-growth *Sequoia sempervirens* grove took form as a crew of a dozen or so men, invading early in the new year to set up camp nearby and begin assessing where to start dealing out the premature death and dismemberment that was, from the redwood perspective, the *Homo sapiens'* calling card. The initial crew would be followed by three or four dozen more *sapiens* as their attack progressed into the spring and summer. Redwood had to be felled one by one, and felling was a challenging technique. If a falling *sempervirens* crashed to the ground with the wrong distribution of weight, the corpse would shatter and instantly lose most of its monetary value, so a landing bed was prepared along an unobstructed avenue to soften the impact. It was the job of the "choppers" to make sure the doomed tree fell where it was supposed to, with its worth intact. Working with razor-sharp double-headed axes mounted on handles almost four feet long, the choppers first constructed a platform that allowed them to cut into the redwood about six feet above ground level. They then carved out a wedge-shaped "undercut," a slice whose mouth was tall enough for an adult to stand up in. The undercut extended to the tree's central core and would eventually control the direction of the *sempervirens's* dying collapse. That accomplished, the "sawyers" went to work slightly higher on the opposite side of the wounded redwood's trunk, using a twelve-foot saw pushed and pulled by *sapiens* at each end. As their cut advanced, steel wedges were driven into the breach in the redwood's trunk. Those wedges eventually provided the leverage necessary to topple the mortally wounded tree along the trajectory laid out by the undercut. That toppling into redwood death could be heard all over the surrounding hillside: a "whoosh" as it fell, displacing so much air that it sucked the crew's breath right out of their lungs, followed by a thunderous concussion and shock wave that shook the earth under their feet.

Once that fresh *sempervirens* corpse was brought to ground, the "peelers" set to work stripping off its bark and limbs using saws and long pointed bars. Then the sawyers went back at it, this time wielding a one-man eight-foot saw to divide the twenty-foot-thick dead trunk into logs somewhere between twelve and twenty feet long. In the meantime, the *sapiens* attackers had constructed a skid road, composed of foot-thick logs corduroyed into the earth. Each enormous dismembered segment of the dead redwood would be dragged out of the grove on that skid road by a team of eight to twelve oxen, driven by the "bull puncher" with the assistance of a "water packer" and a "chain tender." If the enormous section of dead redwood moved too slowly, it would hang up and require a crew to leverage it back into motion using hand tools and a winch. If it moved too fast, it would run over the oxen towing it, and their bull puncher. The skid road ended at a landing next to a spur railroad, where the remains of the once two-hundred-foot-tall *sempervirens* were leveraged onto railroad cars, one log per car. The spur line brought those remains to a mill pond where they were floated, waiting for their turn to be run through the massive saws that were the final step necessary to turn an ancient living tree into a very tall stack of dead boards, laid out in a drying yard before shipment to construction projects all over the state, each board some fifteen or twenty times older than California itself.

Back at the grove where the massacre had started, the ground was awash in sun for the first time in millennia. Ferns and sorrel were shriveling in the hot light. Fragments of dead trees were strewn across the landscape—a limb here, a strip of bark there. The inner cathedral had vanished into thin air. The only trees left standing were those too small to be worth killing. And stumps? Everywhere, and soon to be covered in sprouts as the decapitated roots of thousand-year-old giants began patiently trying to regenerate what they had once been.

This pattern of extermination was repeated tens of thousands of times over the holocaust years, up and down the Coast Range, along the watersheds of the Eel, the Navarro, the Russian, the Mattole, the Mad, and the Smith Rivers, the region relentlessly updated with steam engines, tractors, and chain saws along the way. Thanks to the citizen advocacy led by Save the Redwoods League, in the 1920s the first parks were created to give refuge to surviving old-growth *Sequoia sempervirens*, but the process was slow and arduous and terribly incomplete.

And then the old-growth redwood holocaust was over. The meager 5 percent of old-growth *sempervirens* that was going to be saved had been; all 95 percent of old-growth *sempervirens* that was going to be executed and dismembered had been as well. And we are left—lining up at Muir Woods, Redwood Creek, Rockefeller Forest, and the Avenue of the Giants—to try to recognize and account for that which is now irretrievably diminished or lost to us, to our children, to their children, and to all the children from here on, or for at least a thousand years, if *Homo sapiens* make it that far. We inherited an astonishing artifact, unique and delicately crafted by the life force that turned this planet into our home, and we proceeded to trash it in the name of building materials.

Shame on us.

[THE LAST STAND]

I witnessed the final episode in that *Homo sapien* assault on the coastal redwood's original forest. And driven by the fruits of my own professional investigation and my eventual reporter's indignation at how this final showdown had come to pass, I ended up outraged by this last chapter as well—not just because of my relationship with Tree but particularly by how much the end was dominated by *sapiens*'s lesser self. And when it was over, I was also overrun with a new reverence for that which remained.

By 1989, the only significant concentration of old-growth *sempervirens* whose fate still hung in the balance between parkland and lumber was some 7,500 contiguous acres owned by the Pacific Lumber Company in Humboldt County at the headwaters of Salmon Creek and the Elk River, four miles northwest of the town of Fortuna and eight miles south of the city of Eureka, on the western slope that sweeps down to Humboldt Bay and the mouth of the Eel. When the spotlight eventually fell on this last stand, it would be referred to as the Headwaters Forest, and for several years it would become the most notorious and newsworthy forest in the state. Its fate started getting personal for me after I emerged from the haze following my collapsed project with the media tycoon—assisted out of my funk by Tree, as you will recall—and I convinced my publisher to underwrite a book about the struggle that broke out on the North Coast when the Pacific Lumber Company and its last old-growth *sempervirens* came into play. I eventually spent the next six years—including a two-year break to nurse Lacey—driving back and forth to Humboldt County, staying in a $25-a-night motel on Highway 101, interviewing some fifty participants and reviewing reams of court documents and depositions in order to portray "the struggle between Wall Street and Main Street over California's ancient redwoods." I told my publisher that the book would chronicle how *Homo sapiens* decided what to do with the last virgin outpost of California's signature species. And the book did so, in spades.

The Pacific Lumber Company—known around Humboldt as PL—had old growth remaining when none of the other timber companies in California did because PL had husbanded its ancient forest while the other corporations massacred theirs in the interest of short-term profits. Indeed, by the 1980s, PL's Mill B, in the company town of Scotia, upstream from the Eel delta, housed the one remaining saw rig in the state big enough to handle elder virgin *sempervirens* logs. PL's foresters calculated how many board feet had to be harvested each year to match the forest's estimated annual growth and never let the former exceed the latter, showing singular restraint in an industry notorious for cutting with abandon at breakneck pace. By PL's calculations, its maverick rate of harvest left it with enough old growth to allow PL's choppers and sawyers to assault virgin *sempervirens* forest at that same rate until 2045. That "slow" cut, however, cast the company as an "underperformer" on Wall Street, and by 1985, the Street's financial sharks, armed with junk bonds, were on the hunt for companies like PL, which not only had cornered the market in a valuable resource but also had no debt to speak of.

That caught the attention of one Charles Hurwitz, a Texas-based "corporate takeover artist," who secretly purchased control of PL using money borrowed with the assistance of junk-bond king Michael Milken, before Milken was convicted of securities fraud and sent to prison. At Hurwitz's first appearance in Humboldt County after his purchase, he addressed the company's workforce and reassured them that despite all the scary rumors they might have heard about him, he believed in the Golden Rule as it is apparently practiced in the state of Texas: "Those who have the gold rule." His audience laughed nervously. Hurwitz then began remaking Pacific Lumber according to his own financial imperatives. He liquidated the employee retirement fund, sold off PL's ancillary companies, and "upstreamed" all the proceeds to his Texas parent corporation. In the forest, he tripled PL's rate of cut, finishing off isolated stands of old growth and clear-cutting the company's sizeable inventory of very large second growth as though there were not a minute to lose, again upstreaming the considerable proceeds back to Texas. Then he turned his corporate gaze on the Headwaters Forest, and the final battle over primeval California was joined.

Hurwitz had faced opposition since his raid on PL stock first became known; dissent included lawsuits from PL stockholders, complaints from local residents, suits over the erosion resulting from the company's logging practices, and political and media campaigns by environmental activists. That opposition became statewide when he dispatched cutters and sawyers into the Headwaters. There, Hurwitz's plans were challenged under California's belated forestry statutes and timbering permit process, and he was eventually held at bay when the courts invoked the Endangered Species Act to delay most of his Headwaters logging plans. That stalemate lasted until 1999, when California's senior United States senator cut a deal with the Texas raider. According to its terms, the state and federal governments purchased the entire Headwaters Forest for some $460 million—all quickly upstreamed—and those old-growth groves at the origin of Salmon Creek and the Elk River joined *Sequoia sempervirens*'s surviving 5 percent. Hurwitz also agreed to cut none of the remaining tiny pockets of old growth on PL's other lands and, shortly thereafter, the gargantuan Mill B and its old-growth saws were dismantled, now too big to be of any practical use.

In 2007, the Pacific Lumber Company—out of old growth, having used up much of its second- and third-growth forest in Charles Hurwitz's logging frenzy, and then spun off into a separate free-standing corporate entity—filed for bankruptcy relief from its bondholders. The company that had once been debt free now had more than $1 billion in unpayable liabilities, and bankruptcy court would soon auction off its remaining assets, including the company town of Scotia and whatever additional items of worth had not yet been forwarded on to Texas. According to court documents, Charles Hurwitz walked away with more than $3 billion of the company's value, all of which had long since been parked beyond the reach of PL's creditors.

Shame on him.

[SNEAKING INTO THE PRIMEVAL]

Before the Headwaters Forest had been rescued from Charles Hurwitz, I visited it on the sly. And that visit pretty much closed the circle on the devotion to *Sequoia sempervirens* that had first been kindled in me by Tree and has since become such a significant, if heretofore hidden, feature in my personal cosmology.

The Headwaters Forest was still private property, trespassing forbidden, and I had already been denied official permission to enter it by PL's local manager. But as a reporter, I felt I needed to at least eyeball this grove in order to really understand the story

I was collecting. So I contacted Greg, one of the environmental activists leading the fight to stop PL, and took him up on his offer to smuggle me in. Greg was under a court injunction to stay off PL's lands, but he was game to guide me nonetheless. I also brought along my then twenty-five-year-old son, Gabe, and Cheri, the woman I would eventually marry. There was active logging going on right next to our old-growth destination, so the plan was to wait for Friday night after the PL crew had left the site and the sun was down, then hike in on the logging road, hide in the old growth until Sunday evening, and then sneak back out under the cover of darkness, leaving no one the wiser when PL's crew returned Monday morning.

Cheri and I rendezvoused with Greg and Gabe around 9 p.m. at the home of another environmental activist in Fortuna, where we left our cars. Our host then dropped the four of us at the locked gate to the logging road. We hopped over it and took off, each carrying about twenty-five pounds in our backpacks. The hike was some twelve miles with a gain of eighteen hundred feet in elevation, passing through the dark shadows of the second-growth forest as we climbed, pushing the pace like a pack of burglars, which, technically, we were. Everyone was gassed by 2 a.m., when we reached an open spot off the road and Greg announced we had arrived. For secrecy's sake, no one turned on a flashlight as we laid out in our sleeping bags. After dozing fitfully, we would enter the Headwaters at the first light of day.

It was only then that I realized we had been sleeping in a clear-cut. The area was dotted with fresh redwood stumps, and slash from the logging was all over the otherwise bald ground. The sap was pungent, laced with the smell of chain saws. Insects swarmed the debris. The scene was as ugly as ugly could be, complete with a couple of discarded Coca-Cola cans. We got moving again right away and crossed the cut, took a hard left downhill, where the ugliest ugly ended, and plunged into the Headwaters Forest. Within ten more steps we had entered another dimension, one of perpetual shade and half-light, green and more green, and the softest air I have ever breathed.

Though I hadn't anticipated it, my entry was a step through another spiritual portal, like that first time with Tree, only now the silent hum was at an order of magnitude beyond what I had ever experienced before, the envelopment total and immediate, with more Presence going down than you could shake a stick at, even if it wasn't much of a picture-postcard place. The Headwaters Forest did not look like the more famous redwood refuges down on the rich alluvial flats; much of the Headwaters was sloped and scruffy, littered with its own discards. But I was transported by it anyway. A working-man's cathedral lived on under the canopy. Dead wood cluttered the view upward, with many trees wedged against each other; it was not much in the way of majestic, but it was long on earnestness and tenacity as it somehow managed to feel holy from the inside out.

At first, we pushed through a thicket of four-foot-tall salal bushes, with their leathery leaves and occasional bunches of inedible red berries. Then we entered a stretch of fallen *sempervirens* elders. Twelve- and twenty-foot-thick redwood trunks had toppled in profusion over centuries and were layered one atop another atop another, in a waffle pattern, the lowest layer the most deteriorated. The only way through was to climb to the top and walk along the highest trunk, which looked to have been seeded about the time the Normans invaded England. The one underneath it may very well have dated from when Mohammad conquered Mecca. When the one beneath that was still a seedling, Carthage was a world power. And standing on top of them all, absorbing Presence from each, I felt like I was elevated on the tip of time itself, going back as far as back goes. I lingered there for a while, drawing power from what had once been, feeling the hum rising through my feet.

Eventually we left the waffle and found our way to a flat where the canopy was a little thinner and sunlight flickered like confetti. Two-foot-high sorrel covered the ground, and every seat on it was soft. We made that clearing our base camp. It was marked by a young tree, perhaps a hundred feet tall. This *sempervirens* had spent its life chasing light, growing upward in a corkscrew, and was an easy landmark to locate. From there, we explored, following a creek bed for a while, heading downslope, then circling around and returning to the corkscrew tree as the light began to fade and the silence was broken by a flock of marbled murrelets returning to their nests in the canopy, having spent their day chasing fish in the Pacific Ocean.

That night I dreamt I was lying in sorrel three times as deep as the cover I was actually in. I seemed to be hiding, with great trepidation, yoked with the weight of grief I had woken to every morning since Lacey's death. Then, in full dream mode, I suddenly sprang to my feet and lifted up in the air, sailing along underneath the canopy. The weight I had been carrying was replaced with a lightness of being that powered my flying about through the treetops, though I had no idea how it did so. I looked down and I saw myself balanced on the waffle, then again sprawled in the sorrel, feeling a hum that was wound to its top-end r.p.m. and that lifted off both scenes like heat off a griddle. Then, as I swooped around, I woke halfway and found myself on the real ground. I looked up and could barely discern the corkscrew against a more-than-charcoal sky. I was momentarily convinced the twisted tree was watching me. Then I tumbled back into sleep, woke the next morning without that weight for the first time in months, and spent the day exploring some more.

The most impressive trait the Headwaters Forest brought to the table was its wildness. From every angle, it was savage and untamed. There were no tracks to follow through this old growth besides the ones we had made ourselves. Indeed, these 7,500 acres had been the last to be scheduled for cutting because they were an out-of-the-way, cluttered tangle, all uphill and downhill that would be a challenge to scalp. Even so, the vigor of this final survivor defied its unprepossessing veneer. It was truly uncontrolled and untrammeled, a place where every time we touched something, it seemed to be the first touch of it ever. When Sunday night arrived, I felt renewed and enlarged by this forest's stubborn grip on life and grateful that such a place might be saved, even if no one ever visited it. The hum it generated followed me into the clear-cut for a bit on our hike out.

We were met at the locked gate just before midnight on Sunday and taken to fetch our cars. When I got home to Number 841 the next day, I went straight to Tree, still inspired and lightened and thinking I could somehow share what I had been through and the boost it had given me. But Tree showed no sign of recognition, not saying anything one way or another.

[SAVE THE REDWOOD, SAVE THE HUMAN]

This is not to say that there was any breakdown between Tree and me. We continue as boon, if occasional, companions to this day. Cheri and I got married next to Tree. Tree provided solace when my mother died and comfort through my dog Pancho's end, and then my dog Tyrone's. It gave me something to hold on to while under fire from some serious PTSD. There were also several best friends whose deaths Tree bolstered me through, as well as the approaching deaths of several more, not to mention the withering of my career. And these days I spend a lot of time leaning against its trunk considering my own death as well.

Choosing to confess what has gone on between the coastal redwood and myself was a big decision, but Tree wasn't involved in making it. Tree only came to me in my misery, and this story has made me anything but miserable. Tree taught me to see at least a few things through another species' eyes, and that turns out to have been a liberation and an empowerment. I confess and explain my feelings now because I am an old man and want to make myself clear while I still can.

Homo sapiens have done serious, potentially fatal, damage to the planet's capacity to sustain life as we have known it. And now we have reached a moment when we must drastically change our behavior or collapse. For the first time in ten thousand years, and thanks to our own actions, *Homo sapiens* are about to be in as much danger as all the rest of the species around us have previously been at our hands. And the path to our own species' rescue and redemption going forward has already been marked by the Good Samaritans who saved what they could among these surrounding species in years past. Now all of us must do likewise: nurturing, husbanding, and protecting all those other beings—animal, vegetable, mineral—who have managed to make it this far. We save ourselves by saving them; we prosper when they prosper; their ongoing diminishment diminishes us; their elevation is our uplift; and we can only make ourselves whole by insisting that they be included in our reconstruction.

The time has come for all forms of life to make common cause.

So *sempervirens* and I went ahead and did just that.

[from *The Once and Future Forest: California's Iconic Redwoods*, 2019]

ABOUT THE AUTHOR

After ten years as a leader in the movement to stop the Vietnam War, including almost two years in federal prison for civil disobedience against military conscription, David Harris pursued a forty-seven-year career as a national and international journalist. A former contributing editor at *Rolling Stone* and the *New York Times Magazine*, he is the author of eleven books. He lives in Marin County, California.

NOTE ON TYPE

CORMORANT GARAMOND, an open-source type family, was developed by the Swiss type designer Christian Thalmann of Catharsis Fonts. Named in homage to Claude Garamond, this type family takes loose inspiration from the sixteenth-century designer's work without drawing heavily on any particular font. The result is classic in feel without being overly indebted to a traditional design sensibility.